Poets' Choice

An Anthology of English Poetry
from Spenser to the present day

compiled by Patric Dickinson and Sheila Shannon

 Evans Brothers Limited London

Published by Evans Brothers Limited
Montague House, Russell Square,
London WC1

© Patric Dickinson and Sheila Shannon 1967
First published 1967

Set in 10 on 13 point Garamond and printed in Great Britain
by C. Tinling and Co. Ltd., Liverpool, London and Prescot
7/5495   PR/3674

Poets' Choice

An Anthology of English Poetry
from Spenser to the present day

Contents

Introduction

We have called this book *Poets' Choice* for a variety of reasons. You will certainly find poems in it, but we also hope the poets who wrote them. We ourselves are poets and the poems are, of course, our choice, but we would like to think the poets we have chosen would approve of our choices, not for reasons of sentiment but because each poem is a true poem, whether its author is famous or obscure, and a poem—were the dead to come back to life—any poet would be glad to have written and to see published for other people to share.

The very first poem is a love poem, written by Edmund Spenser in the reign of Elizabeth I to celebrate his marriage to Elizabeth Boyle, on June 11th, 1594. It is a romantic, tender poem and reveals the poet to you at a moment of intense happiness. The very last poem in the book, written by Alan Brownjohn is a sardonic poem describing the predicament in which the last surviving rabbit in England finds itself in this age of motorways and over-population. In both poems, the poet gives away something of himself and if, as you read his poem, you are able to enter his mood and share his feelings, you have found a new person as well as a new poem.

We chose the poems firstly, of course, because we think they are good poems, and secondly because they seem to reveal something of the men and women who wrote them, something of the age they lived or live in, something of their personal attitude to things—to pain and pleasure, love and death, tyranny and injustice.

We have arranged the poems more or less in chronological order and have divided the book into five sections, each with an introduction which attempts to analyse very simply the individual character of the period; a character which derives in part from historical and political events, in part from new scientific discoveries which upset accepted beliefs and values. For poets are usually far more aware of what is going on in the world around them than they are generally supposed to be. They belong essentially to their own age and record it for us in their poems sometimes more truthfully than the historians. But this is no history book, the poems can be read in any order, although they have in fact been arranged in a particular order. Poets' lives may be long or short, they may write when they are young or old. So, in any age, there is another kind of progression, a chronology of the spirit-of-the-age, a chronology of poems which does not always relate exactly to birthdays and death-days. The poems of any period arrange themselves in an order of their own which may differ from the actual span of the writers' lives. To take just one example, Thomas Hardy was born in 1840 but he did not begin to publish poetry until he was 58, and he went on writing until he was over 80. His poetry belongs in the period it was written and not to his youthtime in the 1860s.

So we have made our own arrangement of the poets we have chosen, keeping this idea in mind. We have a particular sequence of poems in each section so that the reader may enjoy echoes and contrasts of thought and style and even of words. Naturally there is no need whatsoever to read these poems consecutively, only we hope you will have an added pleasure if you recognise and approve (or disapprove) of the pattern. Sometimes you will find we refer you from one poem to another—often far apart in time—because it may be interesting to compare or contrast them.

For some of the poems, but not all, we have written a brief note; not to give you facts you can easily find for yourselves, but as if we were talking with you and thought of some point which might add to your pleasure in the poem or your interest in the poet.

P.D.

S.S.

I

circa 1575–1660

During the period covered by this section, Drake sailed round the world for the first time and eight years later defeated the Armada; Raleigh founded Virginia, explored much of Central and South America, became Elizabeth's favourite, fell from grace, was imprisoned in the Tower and finally executed by James I; the Gunpowder plot misfired; Shakespeare's plays were acted for the first time, and first printed. Milton was eight years old when Shakespeare died and twelve when the Pilgrim Fathers sailed for North America in the 'Mayflower'. In the first half of the seventeenth century, explorations of the mind and discoveries in the world of Science were as strange and exciting as the geographical discoveries of the last half of the sixteenth century, and culminated in the founding of the Royal Society in 1660. The Civil War was fought and kings and favourites fell. Here, Cavaliers are represented by Herrick and Suckling, Roundheads by Milton and Marvell. Great houses were centres of the Arts; where music, masque and poetry were both written and enjoyed.

Yet life was never more uncertain—threatened by illness, for which there was no remedy; by childbirth, in which both mother and child so often died; and by political events, which divided father from son and brought threat of treason, imprisonment and death. But if life was uncertain it was lived with intensity. It was an age of brilliant achievement; of daring and experiment; of courage and fatalism.

The love poems in this section range from the triumphant celebration of Spenser's *Epithalamion,* through the conventional poem that follows it, through Shakespeare's sonnets, through Donne, Marvell, and Herrick to the gay mockery of George Wither and Sir John Suckling; different aspects of love and loving which together present us with a picture of love in the sixteenth and seventeenth centuries not much different from our own.

Here, too, are poets facing death, each in his own way—Raleigh, Nashe, Ben Jonson and Henry King among them; poets celebrating good living; poets describing the life of their times, as Ben Jonson in his long poem *Penshurst,* Wither in his *Christmas Carroll,* Strode in the *Devonshire Countryman,* and William Basse in his *Angler's Song.* Taken all together, the poems in this section can give you a vivid insight into the age in which these poets lived.

Edmund Spenser (1552-1599)

Verses from EPITHALAMION

Epithalamion, which means in Greek 'a marriage song', was written to celebrate the poet's marriage. It is written in the full intensity of happy and successful love—rare among poets, who are more often mourning their rejection (see Heywood, p. 8), or courting (see Herrick, p. 69; MacNeice, p. 412), or hitting back and saying they don't care anyway, like Wither (p. 55) and Suckling (p. 70).

Bid her awake

Early, before the world's light-giving lampe
His golden beame upon the hills doth spred,
Having disperst the night's unchearefull dampe,
Doe ye awake, and with fresh lusty hed,
Go to the bowre of my beloved love,
My truest turtle dove:
Bid her awake; for Hymen is awake,
And long since ready forth his maske to move,
With his bright tead[1] that flames with many a flake,
And many a bachelor to waite on him,
In theyr fresh garments trim.
Bid her awake therefore and soone her dight,[2]
For lo the wished day is come at last,
That shall for al the paynes and sorrowes past,
Pay to her usury of long delight:
And whylest she doth her dight,
Doe ye to her of joy and solace sing,
That all the woods may answer and your echo ring.

My love is now awake

Wake, now, my love, awake! for it is time:
The rosy Morne long since left Tithones bed,
All ready to her silver coche to clyme,
And Phœbus gins to shew his glorious hed.

---

[1] torch.
[2] dress.

Hark how the cheerefull birds do chaunt theyr laies,
And carroll of loves praise!
The merry larke hir mattins sings aloft,
The thrush replyes, the mavis descant playes,
The ouzell shrills, the ruddock warbles soft,
So goodly all agree, with sweet consent,
To this dayes merriment.
Ah! my deere love, why doe ye sleepe thus long,
When meeter were that ye should now awake,
T'awayt the coming of your joyous make,[1]
And hearken to the birds love-learnèd song,
The deawy leaves among?
For they of joy and pleasance to you sing,
That all the woods them answer, and theyr echo ring.
My love is now awake out of her dreame,
And her fayre eyes like stars that dimmèd were
With darksome cloud, now shew theyr goodly beams
More bright then Hesperus his head doth rere.
Come now, ye damzels, daughters of delight,
Helpe quickly her to dight.
But first come ye, fayre Houres, which were begot,
In Jove's sweet paradice, of Day and Night,
Which doe the seasons of the year allot,
And all that ever in this world is fayre
Doe make and still repayre.
And ye three handmayds of the Cyprian Queene,
The which doe still adorne her beauties pride,
Helpe to adorne my beautifullest bride:
And as ye her array, still throw betweene
Some graces to be seene:
And as ye use to Venus, to her sing,
The whiles the woods shall answer, and your echo ring.

---

[1] mate.

Harke how the Minstrels gin to shrill aloud
Their merry Musick that resounds from far,
The pipe, the tabor, and the trembling croud,[1]
That well agree withouten breach or jar.
But most of all the Damzels doe delite,
When they their tymbrels smyte,
And thereunto doe daunce and carrol sweet,
That all the sences they doe ravish quite,
The whyles the boyes run up and downe the street,
Crying aloud with strong confused noyce,
As if it were one voyce.
'Hymen, Io Hymen, Hymen,' they doe shout,
That even to the heavens theyr shouting shrill
Doth reach, and all the firmament doth fill;
To which the people standing all about,
As in approvance doe thereto applaud,
And loud advaunce her laud,[2]
And evermore they 'Hymen, Hymen' sing,
That all the woods them answer, and theyr echo ring.

Loe! where she comes along with portly pace,
Lyke Phœbe from her chamber of the East,
Arysing forth to run her mighty race,
Clad all in white, that seemes[3] a virgin best.
So well it her beseemes that ye would weene
Some angell she had beene.
Her long loose yellow locks lyke golden wyre,
Sprinckled with perle, and perling flowres atweene,
Doe lyke a golden mantle her attyre,
And being crownèd with a girland greene,
Seeme lyke some mayden Queene.
Her modest eyes, abashèd to behold
So many gazers as on her do stare,
Upon the lowly ground affixèd are;

---

[1] fiddle.
[2] praise.
[3] beseems, suits.

Ne dare lift up her countenance too bold,
But blush to heare her prayses sung so loud,
So farre from being proud.
Nathlesse doe ye still loud her prayses sing,
That all the woods may answer, and your echo ring.

The sacred ceremonies

Open the temple gates unto my love,
Open them wide that she may enter in,
And all the postes adorne as doth behove,
And all the pillours deck with girlands trim,
For to receyve this Saynt with honour dew,
That commeth in to you.
With trembling steps and humble reverence,
She commeth in before th'Almightie's view:
Of her, ye virgins, learne obedience,
When so ye come into those holy places,
To humble your proud faces.
Bring her up to th'high altar, that she may
The sacred ceremonies there partake,
The which do endlesse matrimony make;
And let the roring organs loudly play
The praises of the Lord in lively notes,
The whiles with hollow throates
The choristers the joyous Antheme sing,
That all the woods may answere, and their echo ring.

Now day is doen

Now ceasse, ye damsels, your delights forepast;
Enough is it that all the day was youres:
Now day is doen, and night is nighing fast:
Now bring the Bryde into the brydall boures.
Now night is come, now soone her disaray,
And in her bed her lay;
Lay her in lillies and in violets,
And silken courteins over her display,
And odourd sheetes, and Arras coverlets.

Behold how goodly my faire love does ly
In proud humility!
Like unto Maia, when as Jove her tooke
In Tempe, lying on the flowry grass,
Twixt sleepe and wake, after she weary was
With bathing in the Acidalian brooke.
Now it is night, ye damsels may be gon,
And leave my love alone,
And leave likewise your former lay to sing:
The woods no more shall answere, nor your echo ring.

Now welcome, night! thou night so long expected,
That long daies labour doest at last defray,
And all my cares, which cruell Love collected,
Hast sumd in one, and cancellèd for aye:
Spread thy broad wing over my love and me,
That no man may us see,
And in thy sable mantle us enwrap,
From feare of perrill and foule horror free.
Let no false treason seeke us to entrap,
Nor any dread disquiet once annoy
The safety of our joy:
But let the night be calme and quietsome,
Without tempestuous storms or sad afray:
Lyke as when Jove with fayre Alcmena lay,
When he begot the great Tirynthian groome:
Or lyke as when he with thy selfe did lie,
And begot Majesty.
And let the mayds and yongmen cease to sing:
Ne let the woods them answer, nor theyr echo ring.

John Heywood (c. 1497-1580)

'ALL A GREEN WILLOW IS MY GARLAND'

Alas! by what mean may I make ye to know
The unkindness for kindness that to me doth grow?
That one who most kind love on me should bestow,
Most unkind unkindness to me she doth show,
    For all a green willow is my garland.

To have love and hold love, where love is so sped,
Oh, delicate food to the lover so fed!
From love won to love lost, where lovers be led,
Oh, desperate dolour, the lover is dead!
    For all a green willow is his garland.

She said she did love me, and would love me still,
She sware above all men I had her good will;
She said and she sware she would my will fulfil:
The promise all good, the performance all ill;
    For all a green willow is my garland.

Could I forget thee, as thou canst forget me,
That were my sound fault, which cannot nor shall be;
Though thou, like the soaring hawk, every way flee,
I will be the turtle most steadfast to thee,
    And patiently wear this green willow garland.

All ye that have had love, and have my like wrong,
My like truth and patience plant you among;
When feminine fancies for new love do long,
Old love cannot hold them, new love is so strong,
    For all a green willow is your garland.

Thomas Nashe (1567-1601)

From SUMMER'S LAST WILL AND TESTAMENT

Song

> In an age of uncertain fortune, life itself was uncertain. When plague
> was abroad, no doctor could save and death was a haunter of every
> man's home (see Jonson's sorrow for his little son, p. 35). Without
> the hope of an after-life, such tragedies would have been almost
> unbearable. Compare Hood, p. 243.

Adieu, farewell earth's blisse,
This world uncertaine is;
Fond are life's lustful joyes,
Death proves them all but toyes;
None from his darts can flye;
I am sick, I must dye:
    Lord, have mercy on us.

Rich men, trust not in wealth!
God cannot buy you health;
Phisick[1] himselfe must fade;
All things to end are made;
The plague full swift goes bye;
I am sick, I must dye:
    Lord, have mercy on us.

Beauty is but a flowre,
Which wrinckles will devoure;
Brightnesse falls from the ayre;
Queenes have died yong and faire;
Dust hath closde Helen's eye;
I am sick, I must dye:
    Lord, have mercy on us.

---

[1] the doctor.

Strength stoopes unto the grave:
Wormes feed on Hector brave;
Swords may not fight with fate;
Earth still holds ope her gate.
Come! come! the bells do crye.
I am sick, I must dye:
    Lord, have mercy on us.

Wit with his wantonesse
Tasteth death's bitternesse:
Hell's executioner
Hath no eares for to heare
What vaine art can reply.
I am sick, I must dye:
    Lord, have mercy on us.

Haste, therefore, eche degree
To welcome destiny:
Heaven is our heritage,
Earth but a player's stage;
Mount wee unto the sky.
I am sick, I must dye:
    Lord, have mercy on us.

William Shakespeare (1564-1616)

SONNETS

A tremendous lot of argument still goes on about the person to whom Shakespeare addressed his love sonnets. It is still a mystery which really has nothing to do with the quality of the poems. They say so much about love in all its aspects—romantic, realistic, tender, brutal, ironic—that these few can give only a taste of what is to be found by reading them all.

XVIII

Shall I compare thee to a summer's day?
Thou art more lovely and more temperate.
Rough winds do shake the darling buds of May,
And summer's lease hath all too short a date:
Sometime too hot the eye of heaven shines,
And often is his gold complexion dimm'd;
And every fair from fair sometime declines,
By chance or nature's changing course untrimm'd;
But thy eternal summer shall not fade,
Nor lose possession of that fair thou ow'st;
Nor shall Death brag thou wander'st in his shade,
When in eternal lines to time thou grow'st:
    So long as men can breathe, or eyes can see,
    So long lives this, and this gives life to thee.

XXIX

When, in disgrace with fortune and men's eyes,
I all alone beweep my outcast state,
And trouble deaf heaven with my bootless cries,
And look upon myself, and curse my fate,
Wishing me like to one more rich in hope,
Featured like him, like him with friends possess'd,
Desiring this man's art and that man's scope,
With what I most enjoy contented least;
Yet in these thoughts myself almost despising,
Haply I think on thee,—and then my state,
Like to the lark at break of day arising
From sullen earth, sings hymns at heaven's gate;
    For thy sweet love remember'd such wealth brings
    That then I scorn to change my state with kings.

LXXI

No longer mourn for me when I am dead
Than you shall hear the surly sullen bell
Give warning to the world that I am fled
From this vile world, with vilest worms to dwell:
Nay, if you read this line, remember not
The hand that writ it; for I love you so,
That I in your sweet thoughts would be forgot,
If thinking on me then should make you woe.
O, if, I say, you look upon this verse
When I perhaps compounded am with clay,
Do not so much as my poor name rehearse,
But let your love even with my life decay;
    Lest the wise world should look into your moan,
    And mock you with me after I am gone.

XCI

Some glory in their birth, some in their skill,
Some in their wealth, some in their body's force;
Some in their garments, though new-fangled ill;
Some in their hawks and hounds, some in their horse;
And every humour hath his adjunct pleasure,
Wherein it finds a joy above the rest:
But these particulars are not my measure;
All these I better in one general best.
Thy love is better than high birth to me,
Richer than wealth, prouder than garments' cost,
Of more delight than hawks or horses be;
And having thee, of all men's pride I boast:
    Wretched in this alone, that thou mayst take
    All this away, and me most wretched make.

CVI

When in the chronicle of wasted[1] time
I see descriptions of the fairest wights,
And beauty making beautiful old rhyme
In praise of ladies dead and lovely knights,
Then, in the blazon of sweet beauty's best,
Of hand, of foot, of lip, of eye, of brow,
I see their antique pen would have express'd
Even such a beauty as you master now.
So all their praises are but prophecies
Of this our time, all you prefiguring;
And, for they look'd but with divining eyes,
They had not skill enough your worth to sing:
    For we, which now behold these present days,
    Have eyes to wonder, but lack tongues to praise.

CXVI

Let me not to the marriage of true minds
Admit impediments. Love is not love
Which alters when it alteration finds,
Or bends with the remover to remove:
O, no! it is an ever-fixèd mark,
That looks on tempests and is never shaken;
It is the star to every wandering bark,[2]
Whose worth's unknown, although his height be taken.
Love's not Time's fool, though rosy lips and cheeks
Within his bending sickle's compass come;
Love alters not with his brief hours and weeks,
But bears it out even to the edge of doom.
    If this be error, and upon me proved,
    I never writ, nor no man ever loved.

---

[1] past.
[2] boat.

Then, as now, there were fashions as to what women should look like. The Elizabethans disliked dark women—maybe because the Queen was ginger. Some people have even thought this woman— 'black wires grow on her head'—was a negress. What is certain is that this is no make-believe; but nobody knows who 'the dark lady of the sonnets' actually was.

CXXX

My mistress' eyes are nothing like the sun;
Coral is far more red than her lips' red:
If snow be white, why then her breasts are dun;
If hairs be wires, black wires grow on her head.
I have seen roses damask'd, red and white,
But no such roses see I in her cheeks;
And in some perfumes is there more delight
Than in the breath that from my mistress reeks.
I love to hear her speak, yet well I know
That music hath a far more pleasing sound:
I grant I never saw a goddess go,—
My mistress, when she walks, treads on the ground:
    And yet, by heaven, I think my love as rare
    As any she, belied with false compare.

Robert Greene (c. 1560-1592)

A MOTHER'S SONG TO HER CHILDE

This song from an Elizabethan play makes one look ahead to Blake's *Songs of Innocence*.

Weepe not, my wanton, smile upon my knee;
When thou art olde ther's griefe enough for thee.
    Mother's wag, prettie boy,
    Father's sorrow, father's joy.

When thy father first did see
Such a boy by him and mee,
He was glad, I was woe;
Fortune changde made him so,
When he left his prettie boy,
Last his sorowe, first his joy.

Weepe not, my wanton, smile upon my knee;
When thou art olde ther's griefe enough for thee.
Streaming teares that never stint,
Like pearle drops from a flint,
Fell by course from his eyes,
That one another's place supplies:
Thus he grievd in everie part,
Teares of bloud fell from his hart,
When he left his prettie boy,
Father's sorrow, father's joy.

Weepe not, my wanton, smile upon my knee;
When thou art olde ther's griefe enough for thee.
The wanton smiled, father wept;
Mother cried, babie lept:
More he crowed, more we cried;
Nature could not sorowe hide.
He must goe, he must kisse
Childe and mother, babie blisse:
For he left his prettie boy,
Father's sorowe, father's joy.

Weepe not, my wanton, smile upon my knee;
When thou art olde ther's griefe enough for thee.

WEEPE YOU NO MORE, SAD FOUNTAINES

It was part of any well-brought-up and well-bred Elizabethan's education to be able to read a part in a song. There was a great vogue for rounds and catches, madrigals and so on. Words and music were very closely allied and this poem is really 'words for music'.

Weepe you no more, sad fountaines;
    What need you flowe so fast:
Looke how the snowie mountaines,
    Heav'ns sunne doth gently waste.
But my sunne's heav'nly eyes
    View not your weeping,
    That nowe lies sleeping
Softly, now softly lies
      Sleeping.

Sleepe is a reconciling,
    A rest that peace begets:
Doth not the sunne rise smiling,
    When faire at ev'n he sets?
Rest you, then, rest sad eyes
    Melt not in weeping,
    While she lies sleeping
Softly, now softly lies
      Sleeping.

John Davies of Hereford (c. 1565-1618)

IF THERE WERE, OH! AN HELLESPONT OF CREAM

Most poets enjoy good living and there are many splendid poems which celebrate the pleasures of eating and drinking (see, for example, pages 36 and 42).

The Author loving these homely meats specially, viz.: Cream, Pancakes, Buttered Pippin-pies and Tobacco; writ to that worthy and virtuous gentle-woman, whom he calleth Mistress, as followeth:

If there were, oh! an Hellespont of cream
Between us, milk-white mistress, I would swim
To you, to show to both my love's extreme,
Leander-like,—yea! dive from brim to brim.
But met I with a buttered pippin-pie
Floating upon 't, that would I make my boat
To waft me to you without jeopardy,
Though sea-sick I might be while it did float.
Yet if a storm should rise, by night or day,
Of sugar-snows and hail of caraways,
Then, if I found a pancake in my way,
It like a plank should bring me to your kays;[1]
    Which having found, if they tobacco kept,
    The smoke should dry me well before I slept.

[1] quays.

Michael Drayton (1563-1631)

AGINCOURT

An heroic ballad in the old tradition. This celebration of heroism is no contradiction to the almost universal condemnation of war by poets of all ages. Individual heroism is seen against the background of general suffering (compare Byron, p. 204; Housman, p. 339; Owen, p. 373).

Fair stood the wind for France
When we our sails advance,
Nor now to prove our chance
 Longer will tarry;
But putting to the main,
At Caux, the mouth of Seine,
With all his martial train
 Landed King Harry.

And taking many a fort
Furnished in warlike sort,
Marcheth towards Agincourt
 In happy hour;
Skirmishing day by day
With those that stopped his way,
Where the French general lay
 With all his power;

Which, in his height of pride,
King Henry to deride,
His ransom to provide
 To the king sending;
Which he neglects the while
As from a nation vile,
Yet with an angry smile
 Their fall portending.

And turning to his men,
Quoth our brave Henry then,
'Though they to one be ten,
    Be not amazèd;
Yet have we well begun,
Battles so bravely won
Have ever to the sun
    By fame been raisèd.

'And for myself,' quoth he,
'This my full rest shall be:
England ne'er mourn for me,
    Nor more esteem me;
Victor I will remain
Or on this earth lie slain,
Never shall she sustain
    Loss to redeem me.

'Poitiers and Cressy tell,
When most their pride did swell,
Under our swords they fell;
    No less our skill is
Than when our grandsire great,
Claiming the regal seat,
By many a warlike feat
    Lopped the French lilies.'

The Duke of York so dread
The eager vaward[1] led;
With the main Henry sped,
    Amongst his henchmen.
Exeter had the rear,
A braver man not there;
O Lord, how hot they were
    On the false Frenchmen!

---

[1] vanguard.

They now to fight are gone,
Armour on armour shone,
Drum now to drum did groan,
    To hear was wonder:
That with the cries they make
The very earth did shake;
Trumpet to trumpet spake,
    Thunder to thunder.

Well it thine age became,
O noble Erpingham,
Which didst the signal aim
    To our hid forces!
When, from a meadow by,
Like a storm suddenly
The English archery
    Struck the French horses:

With Spanish yew so strong,
Arrows a cloth-yard long,
That like to serpents stung,
    Piercing the weather;
None from his fellow starts,
But, playing manly parts,
And like true English hearts,
    Stuck close together.

When down their bows they threw,
And forth their bilbos[1] drew,
And on the French they flew,
    Not one was tardy;
Arms were from shoulders sent,
Scalps to the teeth were rent,
Down the French peasants went:
    Our men were hardy.

---

[1] swords.

This while our noble King,
His broad sword brandishing,
Down the French host did ding
    As to o'erwhelm it;
And many a deep wound lent,
His arms with blood besprent,
And many a cruel dent
    Bruisèd his helmet.

Gloucester, that duke so good,
Next of the royal blood,
For famous England stood
    With his brave brother:
Clarence, in steel so bright,
Though but a maiden knight,
Yet in that furious fight
    Scarce such another.

Warwick in blood did wade,
Oxford the foe invade,
And cruel slaughter made
    Still as they ran up;
Suffolk his axe did ply,
Beaumont and Willoughby
Bare them right doughtily,
    Ferrers and Fanhope.

Upon Saint Crispin's day
Fought was this noble fray,
Which fame did not delay
    To England to carry;
Oh, when shall English men
With such acts fill a pen?
Or England breed again
    Such a King Harry?

Michael Drayton

SONNET: SINCE THERE'S NO HELP, COME LET US KISS AND PART

An Elizabethan craze was the writing of sonnets and sonnet sequences, like Sidney's *Astrophel and Stella*. Quite often these were entirely 'made-up'. There wasn't a lovely girl, nor was the poet heart-broken; they were as much a make-believe as the lyrics of pop songs. Only sometimes real sincerity seems to break through the convention, as it does in Shakespeare and—do you agree?—in this sonnet of Drayton's.

Since there's no help, come let us kiss and part—
Nay, I have done, you get no more of me;
And I am glad, yea, glad with all my heart,
That thus so cleanly I myself can free.
Shake hands for ever, cancel all our vows,
And when we meet at any time again,
Be it not seen in either of our brows
That we one jot of former love retain.
Now at the last gasp of love's latest breath,
When, his pulse failing, passion speechless lies,
When faith is kneeling by his bed of death,
And innocence is closing up his eyes,—
    Now, if thou would'st, when all have given him over,
    From death to life thou might'st him yet recover!

Samuel Rowlands (c. 1570-1630)

THE POETASTER

Rapier, lie there! and there, my hat and feather!
    Draw my silk curtain to obscure the light,
Goose-quill and I must join awhile together:
    Lady, forbear, I pray! keep out of sight!
Call Pearl away, let one remove him hence!
Your shrieking parrot will distract my sense.

Would I were near the rogue that crieth, 'Black!'
  'Buy a new almanac!' doth vex me too:
Forbid the maid she wind not up the jack![1]
    Take hence my watch, it makes too much ado!
Let none come at me, dearest friend or kin,
Whoe'er it be I am not now within.

Sir Walter Raleigh (c. 1552-1618)

THE PASSIONATE MAN'S PILGRIMAGE

A man faced with death is set apart from other men. Such was Sir Walter Raleigh's fate—and he was, in addition, a great man. Fallen from Elizabeth's favour, he was imprisoned in the Tower and finally condemned to be executed by James I. He had time to write and he was free at last to expose the corruption of the age in some of the bitterest indictments ever written. The courage and wit, especially in the last verse, are typical of the times as well as the man. In the game of promotion, the stakes were high; to lose favour was often to lose liberty and even life. Life was held cheaper then and enjoyed more intensely.

Give me my scallop-shell of Quiet,
My staff of Faith to walk upon,
My scrip of Joy, immortall diet,
My bottle of Salvation,
My gowne of Glory, hope's true gage;
And thus I'll take my pilgrimage.

Blood must be my bodie's balmer—
No other balme will there be given—
Whilst my soule, like a white Palmer,
Travels to the land of Heaven,
Over the silver mountaines,
Where spring the nectar fountaines:
And there I'll kiss
The Bowle of Blisse,

[1] the spit for roasting meat.

And drinke my eternall fill
On every milken hill.
My soule will be a-dry before,
But after it will ne'er thirst more.

And by the happie blisfull way
More peacefull Pilgrims I shall see,
That have shook off their gownes of clay,
And goe appareld fresh like mee.
I'll bring them first
To slake their thirst,
And then to taste those nectar suckets
At the cleare wells
Where sweetnes dwells,
Drawne up by Saints in christall buckets.

And when our bottles and all we,
Are filled with immortalitie:
Then the holy paths we'll travell,
Strewde with rubies thicke as gravell,
Ceilings of diamonds, saphire floores,
High walles of corall and pearl bowres.

From thence to Heaven's bribeless Hall
Where no corrupted voyces brawl,
No Conscience molten into gold,
Nor forg'd Accusers bought and sold;
No cause deferred; nor vaine-spent Jorney;
For there Christ is the King's Attorney,
Who pleades for all without degrees,
And he hath Angells, but no fees.

When the grand twelve million Jury
Of our sinnes and sinfull fury,
'Gainst our soules blacke verdicts give,
Christ pleades his death, and then we live.
Be thou my speaker, taintless Pleader,
Unblotted Lawyer, true Proceeder.

Thou movest salvation even for almes;
Not with a bribèd Lawyer's palmes.

And this is my eternall plea,
To him that made Heaven, Earth and Sea:
Seeing my flesh must die so soone
And want a head to dine next noone—
Just at the stroke, when my vaines start and spred,
Set on my soul an everlasting head:
Then am I readie like a palmer fit,
To tread those blest paths which before I writ.

THE LIE

Goe soule the bodie's guest
    upon a thankelesse arrant,[1]
Fear not to touch the best
    the truth shall be thy warrant:
Goe since I needs must die,
    and give the world the lie.

Say to the Court it glowes
    and shines like rotten wood;
Say to the Church it showes
    what's good, and doth no good.
If Church and Court reply,
    then give them both the lie.

Tell Potentates they live
    acting by other's action,
Not loved unlesse they give,
    not strong but by affection.
If Potentates reply,
    give Potentates the lie.

---

[1] errand.

Tell men of high condition,
    that mannage the estate,
Their purpose is ambition,
    their practise onely hate:
And if they once reply,
    then give them all the lie.

Tell them that brave it most,
    they beg for more by spending,
Who in their greatest cost
    like nothing but commending.
And if they make replie,
    then give them all the lie.

Tell zeale it wants devotion
    tell love it is but lust,
Tell time it meets but motion,
    tell flesh it is but dust.
And wish them not replie
    for thou must give the lie.

Tell age it daily wasteth,
    tell honour how it alters.
Tell beauty how she blasteth
    tell favour how it falters
And as they shall reply,
    give every one the lie.

Tell wit how much it wrangles
    in tickle points of nycenesse,
Tell wisedome she entangles
    her selfe in over-wisenesse.
And when they doe reply
    straight give them both the lie.

Tell phisicke of her boldnes,
    tell skill it is prevention:
Tell charity of coldnes,
    tell law it is contention,
And as they doe reply
    so give them still the lie.

Tell fortune of her blindnesse,
    tell nature of decay,
Tell friendship of unkindnesse,
    tell justice of delay.
And if they will reply,
    then give them all the lie.

Tell Arts they have no soundnesse,
    but vary by esteeming,
Tell schooles they want profoundnesse
    and stand so much on seeming.
If Arts and Schooles reply,
    give arts and schooles the lie.

Tell Faith its fled the Citie,
    tell how the country erreth,
Tell, manhood shakes off pittie,
    tell, vertue least preferrèd.
And if they doe reply,
    spare not to give the lie.

So when thou hast as I
    commanded thee, done blabbing,
Because to give the lie,
    deserves no lesse than stabbing,
Stab at thee he that will,
    no stab thy soule can kill.

AS YOU CAME FROM THE HOLY LAND

Pilgrimages were still very much a part of life. There is, even today, a shrine at Walsingham and people still visit it.

As you came from the holy land
    Of Walsingham,
Met you not with my true Love
    By the way as you came?

'How shall I know your true Love,
    That have met many one
As I went to the holy land,
    That have come, that have gone?'

She is neither white, nor brown,
    But as the heavens fair;
There is none hath a form so divine
    In the earth, or the air.

'Such a one did I meet, good sir!
    Such an angelic face,
Who like a queen, like a nymph, did appear
    By her gait, by her grace.'

She hath left me here all alone,
    All alone, as unknown,
Who sometimes did me lead with herself,
    And me loved as her own.

'What's the cause that she leaves you alone,
    And a new way doth take,
Who loved you once as her own,
    And her joy did you make?'

I have loved her all my youth;
 But now old, as you see,
Love likes not the falling fruit
 From the withered tree.

Know that Love is a careless child,
 And forgets promise past;
He is blind, he is deaf when he list,
 And in faith never fast.[1]

His desire is a dureless content,
 And a trustless joy:
He is won with a world of despair,
 And is lost with a toy.

Of womenkind such indeed is the love,
 Or the word love abused,
Under which many childish desires
 And conceits are excused.

But true love is a durable fire,
 In the mind ever burning,
Never sick, never old, never dead,
 From itself never turning.

---

[1] steadfast

Anon.

EPITAPH: ON SIR WALTER RALEIGH AT HIS EXECUTION

Great heart, who taught thee so to dye?
Death yielding thee the victory?
Where took'st thou leave of life? if there,
How couldst thou be so freed from feare?
But sure thou dy'st and quit'st the state
Of flesh and blood before thy fate.
Else what a miracle were wrought,
To triumph both in flesh and thought?
I saw in every stander by,
Pale death, life onely in thine eye:
Th'example that thou left'st was then,
We look for when thou dy'st agen.
    Farewell, truth shall thy story say,
We dy'd, thou onely liv'dst that day.

Anon.

EPIGRAM: ON SIR FRANCIS DRAKE

Isn't it strange how words can alter their meanings? To us, a 'fellow
traveller' has a political meaning of being a near-Communist. To the
author of this poem it simply meant Drake going round the world—
and the poet obviously thought that the sun did so, too, instead of
vice versa. It took Drake three years to sail round the world in his ship,
the *Golden Hind*, the voyage lasting from 1577 to 1580.

Sir Drake, whom well the world's end knew,
    Which thou didst compasse round,
And whom both Poles of Heaven once saw,
    Which North and South do bound,
The Stars above would make thee known,
    If men here silent were;
The Sun himselfe cannot forget
    His fellow Traveller.

Anon. (pub. 1611)

THE BELLMAN'S SONG

> Maids to bed and cover coal;
> Let the mouse out of her hole;
> Crickets in the chimney sing
> Whilst the little bell doth ring:
> If fast asleep, who can tell
> When the clapper hits the bell?

Anon. (pub. 1619)

SWEET SUFFOLK OWL

It seems, sometimes, as if people think no-one wrote about nature before Wordsworth. This, of course, is nonsense. There have always been poets who loved the country and wrote about it: Shakespeare superbly—and many before and after him (compare Basse, p. 43; Cotton, p. 84; Gray, p. 112).

> Sweet Suffolk owl, so trimly dight[1]
> With feathers, like a lady bright,
> Thou sing'st alone, sitting by night,
> *Te whit, te whoo! Te whit, te whoo!*
>
> Thy note, that forth so freely rolls,
> With shrill command the mouse controls;
> And sings a dirge for dying souls,
> *Te whit, te whoo! Te whit, te whoo!*

[1] dressed.

John Donne (c. 1571-1631)

Donne writes poetry with a violence and intensity which makes most other poets seem cautious by comparison. He is of the new age—the seventeenth century—the age of discovery in the world of science and mathematics. Donne is what we now call a metaphysical poet: that is, he relates his vision of the physical world to the world of thoughts and feelings.

THE SUNNE RISING

Busie old foole, unruly Sunne,
    Why dost thou thus,
Through windowes, and through curtaines call on us?
Must to thy motions lovers' seasons run?
        Sawcy pedantique wretch, goe chide
        Late schoole boyes and sowre prentices,
    Goe tell Court-huntsmen, that the King will ride,
    Call countrey ants to harvest offices;
Love, all alike, no season knowes, nor clyme,
Nor hours, days, months, which are the rags of time.

        Thy beames, so reverend, and strong
        Why shouldst thou thinke?
I could eclipse and cloud them with a winke,
But that I would not lose her sight so long:
        If her eyes have not blinded thine,
        Looke, and to morrow late, tell mee,
    Whether both the Indias of spice and myne
    Be where thou leftst them, or lie here with mee.
Aske for those Kings whom thou saw'st yesterday,
And thou shalt heare, All here in one bed lay.

        She is all States, and all Princes, I,
        Nothing else is.
Princes doe but play us; compared to this,
All honor's mimique; all wealth alchimie.
        Thou Sunne art halfe as happy as wee,
        In that the world's contracted thus;

Thine age askes ease, and since thy duties bee
To warme the world, that's done in warming us.
Shine here to us, and thou art every where;
This bed thy centre is, these walls, thy spheare.

PHRYNE

In Donne's day, nearly all literary allusions were to past classical times; so here, he attacks some woman under the name of 'Phryne'. Phryne was a professional model in fourth century B.C. Athens. She was mistress of the great sculptor Praxiteles and sat for the first famous painter of the west, Apelles, none of whose pictures has survived. (For other epigrams see Blake and Belloe pp. 137, 354).

Thy flattering picture, Phryne, is like thee
    Onely in this, that you both painted be.

SONNETS

Donne entered the Church in 1615 (becoming Dean of St Paul's in 1621) and turned away from the world of soldiering, politics and court intrigue which is reflected in the early poems. He now wrote some of the finest religious poems in the English language, among which are the sonnets which follow.

SONNET: AT THE ROUND EARTH'S IMAGIN'D CORNERS

At the round earth's imagin'd corners, blow
Your trumpets, Angells, and arise, arise
From death, you numberlesse infinities
Of soules, and to your scattred bodies goe;
All whom the flood did, and fire shall o'erthrow,
All whom warre, dearth, age, agues, tyrannies,

Despaire, law, chance, hath slaine, and you whose eyes,
Shall behold God, and never tast death's woe.
But let them sleepe, Lord, and mee mourne a space;
For, if above all these, my sinnes abound,
'Tis late to aske abundance of thy grace,
When wee are there; here on this lowly ground,
Teach mee how to repent; for that's as good
As if thou hadst seal'd my pardon with thy blood.

SONNET: DEATH BE NOT PROUD

Death be not proud, though some have callèd thee
Mighty and dreadfull, for thou art not soe,
For those whom thou think'st thou dost overthrow,
Die not, poore death, nor yet canst thou kill mee.
From rest and sleepe, which but thy pictures bee,
Much pleasure; then from thee much more must flow,
And soonest our best men with thee doe goe,
Rest of their bones, and soules' deliverie.
Thou art slave to fate, chance, kings, and desperate men,
And dost with poyson, warre, and sicknesse dwell,
And poppie, or charmes can make us sleepe as well
And better than thy stroake; why swell'st thou then?
One short sleepe past, wee wake eternally,
And death shall be no more; death, thou shalt die.

SONNET: BATTER MY HEART, THREE PERSON'D GOD

Batter my heart, three person'd God; for you
As yet but knocke, breathe, shine, and seeke to mend;
That I may rise and stand, o'erthrow mee and bend
Your force to breake, blowe, burn, and make me new.
I, like an usurpt towne, to another due,
Labour to admit you, but Oh, to no end;

Reason your viceroy in mee, mee should defend,
But is captived, and proves weake or untrue.
Yet dearely I love you, and would be lovèd faine,
But am betrothed unto your enemie:
Divorce mee, untie or breake that knot againe,
Take mee to you, imprison mee, for I
Except you enthrall[1] mee, never shall be free,
Nor ever chast, except you ravish mee.

Ben Jonson (c. 1572-1637)

ON MY FIRST SON[2]

Farewell, thou child of my right hand, and joy;
    My sin was too much hope of thee, loved boy,
Seven years thou wert lent to me, and I thee pay,
    Exacted by thy fate, on the just day.
O, could I lose all father, now. For why
    Will man lament the state he should envie?[3]
To have so soon 'scaped world's and flesh's rage,
    And, if no other miserie, yet age?
Rest in soft peace, and, asked, say here doth lye
    Ben Jonson his best piece of Poetrie.
For whose sake, hence-forth, all his vows be such,
    As what he loves may never like too much.

[1] enslave.
[2] Compare Nashe and King, pp. 9 and 46.
[3] to rhyme with 'why'.

Ben Jonson

HYMN TO COMUS[1]

Room! room! make room for the bouncing belly,
First father of sauce and deviser of jelly;
Prime master of arts, and the giver of wit,
That found out the excellent engine the spit,
The plough and the flail, the mill and the hopper,
The hutch and the bolter, the furnace and copper,
The oven, the bavin,[2] the mawkin,[3] the peel,[4]
The hearth and the range, the dog and the wheel:
He, he first invented the hogshead and tun,
The gimlet and vice too, and taught 'em to run;
And since with the funnel and hippocras bag
He has made of himself, that he now cries swag!
Which shows, though the pleasure be but of four inches,
Yet he is a weasel, the gullet that pinches
Of any delight, and not spares from his back
Whatever to make of the belly a sack!
Hail, hail, plump paunch! O the founder of taste,
For fresh meats, or powdered,[5] or pickle, or paste;
Devourer of broiled, baked, roasted, or sod,[6]
And emptier of cups be they even or odd:
All which have now made thee so wide i' the waist,
As scarce with no pudding thou art to be laced;
But eating and drinking until thou dost nod,
Thou break'st all thy girdles, and break'st forth a god.

---

[1] Compare Davies of Hereford, p. 17.
[2] bundle of brushwood as fuel for oven.
[3] oven mop.
[4] baker's shovel.
[5] salted.
[6] boiled.

Ben Jonson

TO PENSHURST

Penshurst, home of the great Sidney family, was an Elizabethan
manor house tacked on to a fourteenth century building which, with
its settled family life, its music, masques and poetry, its mixture of
politics and culture, its flower gardens etc., was something new, a
pattern of civilised life in a great country family home. (Compare
Tennyson, p. 263.)

Thou art not, Penshurst, built to envious show,
    Of touch, or marble; nor canst boast a row
Of polished pillars, or a roof of gold:
    Thou hast no lantherne, whereof tales are told;
Or staire, or courts; but stand'st an ancient pile,
    And these grudged at, art reverenced the while.
Thou joy'st in better marks, of soil, of air,
    Of wood, of water: therein thou art fair.
Thou hast thy walks for health, as well as sport:
    Thy Mount, to which the Dryads doe resort,
Where Pan, and Baccus their high feasts have made,
    Beneath the broad beech, and the chest-nut shade;
That taller tree, which of a nut was set,
    At his great birth, where all the Muses met.
There, in the writhèd bark, are cut the names
    Of many a Sylvane, taken with his flames.
And thence, the ruddy Satyres oft provoke
    The lighter Faunes to reach thy Ladies oak.
Thy copse, too, named of Gamage, thou hast there,
    That never fails to serve thee seasoned deer,
When thou would'st feast, or exercise thy friends.
    The lower land, that to the river bends,
Thy sheep, thy bullocks, kine, and calves do feed:
    The middle grounds thy mares, and horses breed.
Each bank doth yeild thee coneyes; and the tops
    Fertile of Wood, Ashore, and Sydney's copse
To crown thy open table, doth provide
    The purpled pheasant, with the speckled side:

The painted partridge lies in every field,
    And, for thy messe,[1] is willing to be killed.
And if the high-swolne Medway fail thy dish,
    Thou hast thy ponds, that pay thee tribute fish,
Fat, agèd carps, that run into thy net.
    And pikes, now weary their owne kind to eat,
As loth the second draught or cast to stay,
    Officiously, at first, themselves betray.
Bright eels, that emulate them, and leap on land
    Before the fisher, or into his hand.
Then hath thy orchard, fruit; thy garden, flowers;
    Fresh as the ayre, and new as are the houres.
The early cherry, with the later plum,
    Fig, grape, and quince, each in his time doth come:
The blushing apricot, and woolly peach
    Hang on thy walls, that every child may reach.
And though thy walls be of the country stone,
    They'are reared with no man's ruin, no man's groan,
There's none that dwell about them, wish them down;
    But all come in, the farmer and the clowne:
And no one empty-handed, to salute
    Thy lord and lady, though they have no suit.[2]
Some bring a capon, some a rural cake,
    Some nuts, some apples; some that think they make
The better cheeses, bring 'hem; or else send
    By their ripe daughters, whom they would commend
This way to husbands; and whose baskets beare
    An emblem of themselves, in plum or peare.
But what can this (more then express their love)
    Add to thy free provisions, far above
The need of such? whose liberal board doth flow
    With all that hospitalitie doth know!
Where comes no guest, but is allowed to eat,
    Without his fear, and of thy lord's own meat:

---

[1] stew.
[2] plea.

Where the same beer, and bread, and self-same wine,
    That is his Lordships, shall be also mine.
And I not fain to sit (as some, this day,
    At great men's tables) and yet dine away.
Here no man tells[1] my cups; nor, standing by,
    A waiter, doth my gluttony envy,
But gives me what I call and lets me eate;
    He knowes, below, he shall find plentie of meat,
Thy tables hoard not up for the next day;
    Nor, when I take my lodging, need I pray
For fire, or lights, or livorie: all is there;
    As if thou, then, wert mine, or I reign'd here:
There's nothing I can wish, for which I stay.
    That found King James, when hunting late this way;
With his brave son, the Prince, they saw thy fires
    Shine bright on every hearth as the desires
Of thy Penatès[2] had been set on flame
    To entertain them; for the country came,
With all their zeal, to warm their welcome here.
    What (great, I will not say, but) sudden cheer
Did'st thou, then, make 'hem! and what praise was heaped
    On thy good lady, then! who, therein reaped
The just reward of her high huswifery;
    To have her linen, plate, and all things nigh,
When she was far: and not a room, but drest,
    As if it had expected such a guest!
These, Penshurst, are thy praise, and yet not all.
    Thy lady's noble, fruitful, chaste withal.
His children thy great lord may call his own:
    A fortune, in this age, but rarely known.
They are, and have been taught religion: thence
    Their gentler spirits have sucked innocence.
Each morn, and even, they are taught to pray,
    With the whole household, and may, every day,
Read, in their vertuous parents noble parts,
    The mysteries of manners, arms, and arts.

---

[1] counts.

[2] household gods.

> Now, Penshurst, they that will proportion thee
> 　　With other edifices, when they see
> Those proud, ambitious heaps, and nothing else,
> 　　May say, their lords have built, but thy lord dwells.

Song from A CELEBRATION OF CHARIS

See the Chariot at hand

In all ages poets and readers of poetry have delighted in the craft of verse, in the actual way in which the verses and lines and rhymes and rhythms are made. Apart from its meaning, this poem is a superb example of craftsmanship.

> See the Chariot at hand here of Love,
> 　　Wherein my Lady rideth!
> Each that drawes, is a Swan, or a Dove,
> 　　And well the carre Love guideth.
> As she goes, all hearts doe duty
> 　　　　Unto her beauty;
> And enamoured, doe wish, so they might
> 　　　　But enjoy such a sight,
> 　　That they still were to run by her side,
> Thorough swords, thorough seas, wither she would ride.
>
> Doe but looke on her eyes, they doe light
> 　　All that Love's world compriseth!
> Doe but looke on her haire, it is bright
> 　　As Love's starre when it riseth!
> Doe but marke, her forehead's smoother
> 　　　　Than words that soothe her!
> And from her arched browes, such a grace
> 　　　　Sheds it selfe through the face,
> 　　As alone there triumphs to the life
> All the gaine, all the good, of the Elements' strife.

Have you seene but a bright Lillie grow,
  Before rude hands have touched it?
Ha' you marked but the fall o' the Snow
  Before the soyle hath smutched it?
Ha' you felt the wool o' the Bever?
        Or Swan's downe ever?
Or have smelt o' the bud o' the Brier?
        Or the nard, i' the fire?
Or have tasted the bag o' the Bee?
O so white, O so soft, O so sweet is she!

John Webster (c. 1580-1625)

Song from **THE WHITE DEVIL**

Call for the robin-redbreast

> Webster was a playwright in the reign of James I, famous as the
> author of the *Duchess of Malfi* and *The White Devil*, from which this
> song comes. Few people read the Jacobean playwrights in the
> eighteenth and nineteenth centuries. But Charles Lamb in the
> nineteenth and T. S. Eliot in the twentieth century re-discovered
> them. Eliot is continually quoting Webster; in *The Wasteland*, for
> example, he deliberately writes:
>> Oh keep the Dog far hence, that's friend to men
>> Or with his nails he'll dig it up again!
> so that in his poem you may be aware of Webster, too.

Call for the robin-redbreast and the wren,
Since oe'r shadie groves they hover,
And with leaves and flowres doe cover
The friendless bodies of unburied men.
Call unto his funerall dole
The ant, the field-mouse, and the mole
To rear him hillocks that shall keep him warm,
And (when gay tombs are robbed) sustain no harm,
But keep the wolf far thence, that's foe to men,
For with his nails he'll dig them up agen.

T. Bonham (d. 1629?)

IN PRAISE OF ALE [1]

Whenas the chill Sirocco blowes,
    And Winter tells a heavy tale;
When Pyes[2] and Dawes and Rookes and Crows,
    Sit cursing of the frosts and snowes;
        Then give me Ale.

Ale in a Saxon Rumkin then,
    Such as will make grim Malkin prate;
Rouseth up valour in all men,
    Quickens the Poet's wit and pen,
        Despiseth Fate.

Ale that the absent battle fights,
    And scorns the march of Swedish drums;
Disputes the Prince's lawes and rights,
    And what is past and what's to come,
        Tells mortal wights.

Ale that the Plowman's heart upkeeps,
    And equals it to Tyrant's thrones;
That wipes the eye that over weepes,
    And lulls in dainty and secure sleepes,
        His wearied bones.

Grandchild of Ceres, Barley's Daughter,
    Wines emulous neighbour, if but stale;
Ennobling all the Nymphs of water,
    And filling each man's heart with laughter;
        Ha, ha, give me ale.

---

[1] Compare other poems in praise of good living, especially pp. 17, 36 and 381
[2] magpies.

William Basse (d. 1653?)

THE ANGLERS SONG

Walton's *Compleat Angler,* one of the earliest text-books on fishing, was published in 1653 and included this poem. Compare other country poems, pages 154, 370-2 and 439.

As inward love breeds outward talk,
The hound some praise, and some the hawk,
Some better pleased with private sport
Use tennis; some a mistris court:
    But these delights I neither wish,
    Nor envy, while I freely fish.

Who hunts, doth oft in danger ride;
Who hawks, lures oft both far and wide;
Who uses games, may often prove
A loser; but who falls in love,
    Is fettered in fond Cupid's snare:
    My Angle[1] breeds me no such care.

Of recreation there is none
So free as fishing is alone;
All other pastimes do no less
Than mind and body both possess;
    My hand alone my work can do,
    So I can fish and study too.

I care not, I, to fish in seas,
Fresh rivers best my mind do please,
Whose sweet calm course I contemplate,
And seek in life to imitate;
    In civil bounds I fain would keep,
    And for my past offences weep.

---

[1] rod.

And when the timorous Trout I wait
To take, and he devours my bait,
How poor a thing, sometimes I find,
Will captivate a greedy mind;
    And when none bite, I praise the wise,
    Whom vain allurements ne'er surprise.

But yet though while I fish I fast,
I make good fortune my repast,
And thereunto my friend invite,
In whom I more than that delight:
    Who is more welcome to my dish,
    Than to my Angle is my fish.

As well content no prize to take
As use of taken prize to make;
For so our Lord was pleasèd when
He Fishers made Fishers of men;
    Where (which is in no other game)
    A man may fish and praise his name.

The first men that our Saviour dear
Did chuse to wait upon him here,
Blest Fishers were; and fish the last
Food was, that he on earth did taste:
    I therefore strive to follow those
    Whom he to follow him hath chose.

Aurelian Townshend (c. 1583-1643)

UPON KINDE AND TRUE LOVE

'Tis not how witty, nor how free,
Nor yet how beautifull she be,
But how much kinde and true to me.
Freedom and Wit none can confine,
And Beauty like the Sun doth shine,
But kinde and true are only mine.

Let others with attention sit,
To listen, and admire her wit,
That is a rock where I'll not split.
Let others dote upon her eyes,
And burn their hearts for sacrifice,
Beauty's a calm where danger lyes.

But Kinde and True have been long tried
A harbour where we may confide,
And safely there at anchor ride.
From change of winds there we are free,
And need not feare Storme's tyrannie,
Nor Pirate, though a Prince he be.

Henry King (1592-1669)

From THE EXEQUY

Lines to his dead wife

Donne was better known to his contemporaries, and to those who
came soon after him, than is usually supposed and *The Exequy* is very
much in Donne's style. This was a period of exploration, particularly
to the Americas; many were seeking the north-west passage. There
are many geographical puns in Donne, like 'By these straits I die',
where a sea-strait is used to make a pun on being in straits, in diffi-
culties. So, when King speaks of being 'neerer my West', he means
discovery, he means everlasting life found through the straits of
death. Compare also with Nashe, p. 9 and Jonson, p. 36.

Sleep on my Love in thy cold bed
Never to be disquieted!
My last good night! Thou wilt not wake
Till I thy fate shall overtake:
Till age, or grief, or sickness must
Marry my body to that dust
It so much loves; and fill the room
My heart keeps empty in thy Tomb.
Stay for me there; I will not faile
To meet thee in that hollow Vale.
And think not much of my delay;
I am already on the way,
And follow thee with all the speed
Desire can make, or sorrows breed.
Each minute is a short degree,
And ev'ry houre a step towards thee.
At night when I betake to rest,
Next morn I rise neerer my West
Of life, almost by eight houres saile,
Than when sleep breathed his drowsie gale.

Thus from the Sun my Bottom[1] stears,
And my dayes Compass downward bears:
Nor labour I to stemme the tide
Through which to Thee I swiftly glide.

---

[1] ship.

'Tis true, with shame and grief I yield,
Thou like the Van first took'st the field,
And gotten hast the victory
In thus adventuring to die
Before me, whose more years might crave
A just precèdence in the grave.
But heark! My pulse like a soft drum
Beats my approach, tells Thee I come;
And slow howe'er my marches be,
I shall at last sit down by Thee.

The thought of this bids me go on,
And wait my dissolution
With hope and comfort. Dear (forgive
The crime) I am content to live
Divided, with but half a heart,
Till we shall meet and never part.

SIC VITA

Riddles have often pleased poets; and there was a great fashion for
them in the sixteenth and seventeenth centuries. This one is attributed
to various other poets, including Francis Beaumont. The reason is
that admirers often copied down poems they liked and got the
names wrong.

Like to the falling of a Starre;
Or as the flights of Eagles are;
Or like the fresh springs gawdy hew;
Or silver drops of morning dew;
Or like a wind that chafes the flood;
Or bubbles which on water stood;
Even such is man, whose borrowed light
Is straight called in, and paid to night.

The Wind blowes out; the Bubble dies;
The Spring entombed in Autumn lies;
The Dew dries up; the Starre is shot;
The Flight is past; and Man forgot.

James Shirley (1596-1666)

From THE CONTENTION OF AJAX AND ULYSSES

Dirge

It is often the fate of a minor poet to be remembered for a single
poem; it is certainly Shirley's. He wrote a great deal but this song,
from one of his plays, is all we now remember of him.

The glories of our blood and state,
    Are shadows, not substantial things,
There is no armour against fate,
    Death lays his icy hand on Kings,
        Scepter and Crown,
        Must tumble down,
And in the dust be equal made,
With the poor crooked scythe and spade.

Some men with swords may reap the field,
    And plant fresh laurels where they kill,
But their strong nerves at last must yield,
    They tame but one another still;
        Early or late,
        They stoop to fate,
And must give up their murmuring breath,
When they, pale Captives, creep to death.

The Garlands wither on your brow,
    Then boast no more your mighty deeds,
Upon Death's purple Altar now,
    See where the Victor-victim bleeds,
        Your heads must come,
        To the cold Tomb;
Onely the actions of the just
Smell sweet, and blossom in their dust.

George Wither (1588-1667)

A LOVE SONNET

In the fifteenth, sixteenth and seventeenth centuries, the term 'sonnet' did not always mean a poem of fourteen lines in a certain form, like the familiar Petrarchan and Shakespearean sonnets. A sonnet, to Wyatt and many poets after him (as Wither here), meant simply a 'song'. Donne called his poems *Songs and Sonnets* when they were in all sorts of metres.

I loved a lass, a fair one,
    As fair as e'er was seen;
She was indeed a rare one,
    Another Sheba queen.
But fool as then I was,
    I thought she loved me too,
But now alas she's left me,
    Falero, lero, loo.

Her hair like gold did glister,
    Each eye was like a starre;
She did surpass her sister,
    Which passed all others farre.
She would me honie call,
    She'd, O she'd kiss me too;
But now alas she's left me,
    Falero, lero, loo.

In summer time to Medley
    My love and I would goe;
The boatmen there stood ready,
    My love and I to rowe.
For Cream there would we call,
    For Cakes, and for Prunes too
But now alas she's left me,
    Falero, lero, loo.

Many a merry meeting
    My love and I have had;
She was my only sweeting,
    She made my heart full glad,
The tears stood in her eies,
    Like to the morning dew,
But now alas she's left me,
    Falero, lero, loo.

And as abroad we walkèd,
    As Lovers' fashion is,
Oft as we sweetly talkèd
    The Sun should steal a kisse:
The winde upon her lips
    Likewise most sweetly blew;
But now alas she's left me,
    Falero, lero, loo.

Her cheeks were like the cherrie,
    Her skin as white as snow,
When she was blithe and merrie,
    She Angel-like did show.
Her waist exceeding small,
    The fives did fit her shoe;
But now alas she's left me,
    Falero, lero, loo.

In Summer time or winter
    She had her heart's desire;
I still did scorne to stint her
    From sugar, sacke,[1] or fire:
The world went round about,
    No cares we ever knew,
But now alas she's left me,
    Falero, lero, loo.

---

[1] wine.

As we walked home together
    At midnight through the towne,
To keep away the weather
    O'er her I'd cast my gowne.
No cold my Love should feel,
    Whate'er the heavens could do;
But now alas she's left me,
    Falero, lero, loo.

Like Doves we would be billing,
    And clip and kiss so fast;
Yet she would be unwilling
    That I should kiss the last;
They're Judas kisses now,
    Since that they proved untrue.
For now alas she's left me,
    Falero, lero, loo.

To Maidens vows and swearing
    Henceforth no credit give,
You may give them the hearing,
    But never them beleeve.
They are as false as faire,
    Unconstant, fraile, untrue;
For mine alas has left me,
    Falero, lero, loo.

'Twas I that paid for all things,
    'Twas others dranke the wine,
I cannot now recall things,
    Live but a foole to pine.
'Twas I that beat the bush,
    The bird to others flew,
For she alas hath left me,
    Falero, lero, loo.

If ever that Dame Nature,
    For this false lover's sake,
Another pleasing creature
    Like unto her would make,
Let her remember this,
    To make the other true;
For this alas hath left me,
    Falero, lero, loo.

No riches now can raise me,
    No want make me despair,
No misery amaze me,
    Nor yet for want I care:
I have lost a world it selfe,
    My earthly heaven, adieu,
Since she alas hath left me,
    Falero, lero, loo.

A CHRISTMAS CARROLL

Compare this with Jonson's picture of the great country house of Penshurst, p. 37.

So, now is come our joyfulst Feast;
Let ever man be jolly.
Each Roome, with Ivie leaves is drest,
And every Post, with Holly.
    Though some Churles at our mirth repine,
    Round your foreheads Garlands twine,
    Drowne sorrow in a Cup of Wine.
And let us all be merry.

Now, all our Neighbours' Chimneys smoke,
And Christmas blocks are burning;
Their Ovens, they with bakt-meats choke,
And all their Spits are turning.
    Without the doore, let sorrow lie:
    And, if for cold, it hap to die,
    We'll bury 't in a Christmas Pie.
And evermore be merry.

Now, every Lad is wondrous trim,
And no man minds his Labour.
Our Lasses have provided them,
A Bag-pipe, and a Tabor.
    Young men, and Mayds, and Girles and Boyes,
    Give life, to one anothers Joyes:
    And you, anon, shall by their noyse,
Perceive that they are merry.

Ranke Misers now, doe sparing shun:
Their Hall of Musicke soundeth:
And, Dogs, thence with whole shoulders run,
So, all things there aboundeth.
    The Countrey-folke, themselves advance;
    For Crowdy-Mutton's come out of France:
    And Jack shall pipe, and Jill shall dance,
And all the Towne be merry.

Ned Swash hath fetcht his Bands from pawne,
And all his best Apparell.
Brisk Nell hath brought a Ruffe of Lawne,
With droppings of the Barrell.
    And those that hardly all the yeare
    Had Bread to eat, or Raggs to weare,
    Will have both Clothes, and daintie fare:
And all the day be merry.

Now poore men to the Justices,
With Capons make their arrants,
And if they hap to faile of these,
They plague them with their Warrants.

But now they feed them with good cheere,
And what they want, they take in Beere:
For, Christmas comes but once a yeare :
And then they shall be merry.

Good Farmers, in the Country, nurse
The poore, that else were undone,
Some Land-lords spend their money worse
On Lust and Pride at London.
  There, the Roysters they doe play;
  Drabb and Dice their Lands away,
  Which may be ours, another day:
And therefore let's be merry.

The Client now his suit forbeares,
The Prisoner's heart is eased,
The Debtor drinks away his cares,
And, for the time is pleased.
  Though others purses be more fat,
  Why should we pine or grieve at that?
  Hang sorrow, care will kill a Cat.
And therefore let's be merry.

Harke, how the Wagges, abroad doe call
Each other foorth to rambling.
Anon, you'll see them in the Hall,
For Nuts and Apples scambling.
  Harke, how the Roofes with laughter's sound
  Anon they'll thinke the house goes round:
  For, they the Cellar's depth have found.
And there they will be merry.

The Wenches with their Wassell-Bowles,
About the Streets are singing:
The Boyes are come to catch the Owles,
The Wild-mare, in is bringing.

Our Kitchin-Boy hath broke his Boxe,
And, to the dealing of the Oxe,
Our honest neighbours come by flocks,
And here they will be merry.

Now Kings and Queenes, poore Sheep-cotes have,
And mate with every body:
The honest, now, may play the knave,
And wise men play at Noddy.
Some Youths will now a Mumming goe;
Some others play at Rowland-hoe,
And twenty other Gameboyes moe:
Because they will be merry.

When wherefore in these merry daies,
Should we, I pray, be duller?
No; let us sing some Roundelayes,
To make our mirth the fuller.
And, whilest thus inspired we sing,
Let all the Streets with echoes ring:
Woods, and Hills, and every thing,
Beare witnesse we are merry.

SHALL I WASTING IN DISPAIRE

Shall I wasting in Dispaire,
Dye because a Woman's faire?
Or make pale my cheeks with care,
Cause another's Rosie are?
Be shee fairer than the Day,
Or the Flowry Meads in May;
If She be not so to me,
What care I how faire shee be.

Should my heart be grieved or pined,
Cause I see a Woman kind?
Or a well disposèd Nature,
Joynèd with a lovely Feature?
Be shee meeker, kinder, than
Turtle-Dove, or Pelican:
    If shee be not so to me,
    What care I, how kind she be.

Shall a Woman's Virtues move
Me, to perish for her love?
Or, her well-deserving knowne,
Make me quite forget mine owne?
Be shee with that Goodnesse blest,
Which may gaine her, name of Best:
    If she be not such to me,
    What care I, how good she be.

Cause her Fortune seemes too high,
Shall I play the foole, and dye?
Those that beare a Noble minde,
Where they want of Riches find,
Thinke, what with them they would doe,
That without them, dare to wooe.
    And, unlesse that mind I see,
    What care I, though great she be.

Great, or *Good*, or *Kind*, or *Faire*,
I will ne'er the more dispaire,
If She love me, this beleeve;
I will die, ere she shall grieve.
If she slight me, when I wooe;
I can scorne, and let her goe.
    For, if shee be not for me,
    What care I, for whom she be.

William Strode (1602-1645)

A DEVONSHIRE SONG

Strode's West Country dialect poem is not really difficult to under-
stand if read aloud. Remember that:
     ee = ĭ; that is, leeke = like, skee-a = sky
     z = s;   zea = sea
     v = f;   vrom = from
An amusing picture of the seventeenth century bumpkin who had
never seen the sea or imagined ships upon it is given in verse 5.

'Thou ne're wutt riddle, neighbour Jan
    Where ich a late ha been-a?
Why ich ha been at Plymoth, Man,
    The leeke was yet ne're zeen-a.
Zutch streetes, zutch men, zutch hugeous zeas,
    Zutch things with guns there tumbling,
Thy zelfe leeke me thou'dst blesse to see,
    Zutch overmonstrous grumbling.

'The towne orelaid with shindle stone
    Doth glissen like the skee-a:
Brave shopps stand ope, and all yeare long
    I thinke a Vaire there bee-a:
A many gallant man there goth
    In gold that zaw the King-a;
The King zome zweare himzelfe was there,
    A man or zome zutch thing-a.

'Voole thou that hast no water past,
    But thicka in the Moore-a,
To zee the zea would be agast,
    It doth zoe rage and roar-a:
Zoe zalt it tasts thy tongue will thinke
    The vier is in the water;
It is zoe wide noe lande is spide,
    Looke ne're zoe long thereafter.

'The Water vrom the Element
    None can dezeave cha vore-a,
It semmeth low, yet all consent
    Tis higher than the Moore-a.
Tis strang how looking down the Cliffe
    Men looke mere upward rather;
If these same Eene had it not zeen
    Chud scarce beleeve my Vather.

'Amid the water woodden birds,
    And vlying houses zwimme-a,
All vull of goods as ich have heard
    And men up to the brimm-a:
They venter to another world
    Desiring to conquier-a,
Vow which their guns, vowle develish ons,
    Doe dunder and spitt vier-a.'

'Good neighbour Tom, how varre is that?
    This meazell towne chill leave-a;
Chill mope noe longer here, that's vlatt
    To watch a Sheepe or Sheare-a:
Though it as varre as London be,
    Which ten mile ich imagin,
Chill thither hie for this place I
    Doe take in greate indulgin.'

George Herbert (1593-1633)

THE COLLAR

I struck the board, and cry'd, No more.
　　　I will abroad.
　　What? shall I ever sigh and pine?
My lines and life are free; free as the road,
　　Loose as the winde, as large as store.
　　　Shall I be still in suit?
　　Have I no harvest but a thorn
　　To let me bloud, and not restore
What I have lost with cordiall fruit?
　　　Sure there was wine
Before my sighs did drie it: there was corn
　　Before my tears did drown it.
　　Is the yeare onely lost to me?
　　Have I no bayes to crown it?
No flowers, no garlands gay? all blasted?
　　　All wasted?
　　Not so, my heart: but there is fruit,
　　　And thou hast hands.
　　Recover all thy sigh-blown age
On double pleasures: leave thy cold dispute
Of what is fit, and not; forsake thy cage,
　　　Thy rope of sands,
Which pettie thoughts have made, and made to thee
　　Good cable, to enforce and draw,
　　　And be thy law,
While thou didst wink and wouldst not see.
　　　Away; take heed:
　　　I will abroad.
Call in thy death's head there: tie up thy fears.
　　　He that forbears
　　To suit and serve his need,
　　　Deserves his load.
But as I raved and grew more fierce and wilde
　　　At every word,
　　Me thought I heard one calling, *Childe*
　　And I reply'd *My Lord.*

George Herbert

THE SACRIFICE

The story of George Herbert's life is a strange one. Like Donne, who was a friend of his mother, he wanted a career and a position in the world but he had no success. In 1625, when he was 32, James I died and this put an end to his hopes. He turned his mind to the Church; he was ordained in 1630 and three years later he was dead and lay buried under the altar of his church at Bemerton in Wiltshire. In that short time he wrote poems which have established him as one of the great religious poets of our language. (Compare, from our own time, Gascoyne's *Ecce Homo*, p. 418.)

Oh all ye, who passe by, whose eyes and minde
To worldly things are sharp, but to me blinde;
To me, who took eyes that I might you finde:
   Was ever grief like mine?

The Princes of my people make a head
Against their Maker: they do wish me dead,
Who cannot wish, except I give them bread:
   Was ever grief like mine?

Without me each one, who doth now me brave,
Had to this day been an Egyptian slave.
They use that power against me, which I gave:
   Was ever grief like mine?

Mine own Apostle, who the bag did beare,
Though he had all I had, did not forbeare
To sell me also, and to put me there:
   Was ever grief like mine?

For thirtie pence he did my death devise,
Who at three hundred did the ointment prize,
Not half so sweet as my sweet sacrifice:
   Was ever grief like mine?

Therefore my soul melts, and my heart's deare treasure
Drops bloud (the onely beads) my words to measure:
O let this cup passe, if it be Thy pleasure:
        Was ever grief like mine?

These drops being tempered with a sinner's tears
A Balsome are for both the Hemispheres:
Curing all wounds, but mine; all, but my fears:
        Was ever grief like mine?

Yet my Disciples sleep: I cannot gain
One houre of watching; but their drowsie brain
Comforts not me, and doth my doctrine stain:
        Was ever grief like mine?

Arise, arise, they come. Look how they runne!
Alas! what haste they make to be undone!
How with their lanterns do they seek the sunne!
        Was ever grief like mine?

With clubs and staves they seek me, as a thief,
Who am the Way and Truth, the true relief;
Most true to those, who are my greatest grief:
        Was ever grief like mine?

Judas, dost thou betray me with a kisse?
Canst thou finde hell about my lips? and misse
Of life, just at the gates of life and blisse?
        Was ever grief like mine?

See, they lay hold on me, not with the hands
Of faith, but furie: yet at their commands
I suffer binding, who have loosed their bands:
        Was ever grief like mine?

All my Disciples flie; fear puts a barre
Betwixt my friends and me. They leave the starre,
That brought the wise men of the East from farre.
        Was ever grief like mine?

Then from one ruler to another bound
They leade me; urging, that it was not sound
What I taught: Comments would the text confound.
                Was ever grief like mine?

The Priest and rulers all false witness seek
'Gainst him, who seeks not life, but is the meek
And readie Paschal Lambe of this great week:
                Was ever grief like mine?

Then they accuse me of great blasphemie,
That I did thrust into the Deitie,
Who never thought that any robberie:
                Was ever grief like mine?

Some said, that I the Temple to the floore
In three dayes razed, and raisèd as before.
Why, he that built the world can do much more:
                Was ever grief like mine?

Then they condemmne me all with that same breath,
Which I do give them daily, unto death.
Thus Adam my first breathing rendereth:
                Was ever grief like mine?

They binde, and leade me unto Herod: he
Sends me to Pilate. This makes them agree;
But yet their friendship is my enmitie:
                Was ever grief like mine?

Herod and all his bands do set me light,
Who teach all hands to warre, fingers to fight,
And onely am the Lord of Hosts and might:
                Was ever grief like mine?

Herod in judgement sits, while I do stand;
Examines me with a censorious hand:
I him obey, who all things else command:
        Was ever grief like mine?

The Jews accuse me with despitefulnesse;
And vying malice with my gentlenesse,
Pick quarrels with their only happinesse:
        Was ever grief like mine?

I answer nothing, but with patience prove
If stonie hearts will melt with gentle love.
But who does hawk at eagles with a dove:
        Was ever grief like mine?

My silence rather doth augment their crie;
My dove doth back into my bosome flie,
Because the raging waters still are high:
        Was ever grief like mine?

Heark how they crie aloud still, *Crucifie*:
It is not fit he live a day, they crie,
Who cannot live lesse than eternally:
        Was ever grief like mine?

Pilate, a stranger, holdeth off; but they,
Mine owne deare people, cry *Away, Away,*
With noises confused frighting the day:
        Was ever grief like mine?

Yet still they shout, and crie, and stop their eares,
Putting my life among their sinnes and fears,
And therefore wish *my bloud on them and theirs*:
        Was ever grief like mine?

See how spite cankers things. These words aright
Used, and wished, are the whole world's light:
But honey is their gall, brightnesse their night:
      Was ever grief like mine?

They choose a murderer, and all agree
In him to do themselves a courtesie:
For it was their own case who killèd me:
      Was ever grief like mine?

And a seditious murderer he was:
But I the Prince of peace; peace that doth passe
All understanding, more then heav'n doth glasse:
      Was ever grief like mine?

Why, Caesar is their onely King, not I:
He clave the stonie rock, when they were drie;
But surely not their hearts, as I well trie:
      Was ever grief like mine.

Ah! how they scourge me! yet my tendernesse
Doubles each lash: and yet their bitternesse
Windes up my grief to a mysteriousnesse:
      Was ever grief like mine?

They buffet him, and box him as they list,
Who grasps the earth and heaven with his fist,
And never yet, whom he would punish, missed:
      Was ever grief like mine?

Behold, they spit on me in scornfull wise,
Who by my spittle gave the blinde man eies,
Leaving his blindnesse to my enemies:
      Was ever grief like mine?

My face they cover, though it be divine.
As Moses face was vailèd, so is mine,
Lest on their double-dark souls either shine:
        Was ever grief like mine?

Servants and abjects flout me; they are wittie:
Now prophesie who strikes thee, is their dittie.
So they in me denie themselves all pitie:
        Was ever grief like mine?

And now I am delivered unto death,
Which each one calls for so with utmost breath,
That he before me well nigh suffereth:
        Was ever grief like mine?

Weep not, deare friends, since I for both have wept
When all my tears were bloud, the while you slept:
Your tears for your own fortunes should be kept:
        Was ever grief like mine?

The souldiers lead me to the Common Hall;
There they deride me, they abuse me all:
Yet for twelve heav'nly legions I could call:
        Was ever grief like mine?

Then with a scarlet robe they me aray;
Which shews my bloud to be the onely way
And cordiall left to repair man's decay:
        Was ever grief like mine?

Then on my head a crown of thorns I wear:
For these are all the grapes Sion doth bear,
Though I my vine planted and watered there:
        Was ever grief like mine?

So sits the earth's great curse in Adam's fall
Upon my head: so I remove it all
From th'earth unto my brows, and bear the thrall:
      Was ever grief like mine?

Then with the reed they gave to me before,
They strike my head, the rock from whence all store
Of heav'nly blessings issue evermore:
      Was ever grief like mine?

They bow their knees to me, and cry, *Hail King*:
What ever scoffes and scornfulnesse can bring,
I am the floore, the sink, where they it fling:
      Was ever grief like mine?

Yet since man's scepters are as frail as reeds,
And thorny all their crowns, bloudie their weeds;
I, who am Truth, turn into truth their deeds:
      Was ever grief like mine?

The souldiers also spit upon that face,
Which Angels did desire to have the grace,
And Prophets, once to see, but found no place:
      Was ever grief like mine?

Thus trimmèd, forth they bring me to the rout,
Who *Crucifie Him*, crie with one strong shout.
God holds his peace at man, and man cries out:
      Was ever grief like mine?

They leade me in once more, and putting then
Mine own clothes on, they leade me out agen.
Whom devils flie, thus is he tossed of men:
      Was ever grief like mine.

And now wearie of sport, glad to ingrosse
And spite in one, counting my life their losse,
They carrie me to my most bitter crosse:
   Was ever grief like mine.

My crosse I bear my self, untill I faint:
Then Simon bears it for me by constraint,
The decreed burden of each mortall Saint:
   Was ever grief like mine?

O all ye who passe by, behold and see;
Man stole the fruit, but I must clime the tree;
The tree of life to all, but only me:
   Was ever grief like mine?

Lo, here I hang, charged with a world of sinne,
The greater world o' th' two; for that came in
By words, but this by sorrow I must win:
   Was ever grief like mine?

Such sorrow as, if sinfull man could feel,
Or feel his part, he would not cease to kneel,
Till all were melted, though he were all steel:
   Was ever grief like mine?

But, O *my God, my God*! why leav'st thou me,
The sonne, in whom thou dost delight to be?
My God, my God—
   Never was grief like mine.

Shame tears my soul, my bodie many a wound;
Sharp nails pierce this, but sharper that confound;
Reproches, which are free, while I am bound,
   Was ever grief like mine?

Now heal thy self, Physician; now come down.
Alas! I did so, when I left my crown
And father's smile for you, to feel his frown:
      Was ever grief like mine?

In healing not my self, there doth consist
All that salvation, which ye now resist;
Your safetie in my sicknesse doth subsist:
      Was ever grief like mine?

Betwixt two theeves I spend my utmost breath,
As he that for some robberie suffereth.
Alas! what have I stolen from you? Death.
      Was ever grief like mine?

A king my title is, prefixt on high;
Yet by my subjects am condemned to die
A servile death in servile companie:
      Was ever grief like mine?

They give me vineger mingled with gall,
But more with malice: yet, when they did call,
With Manna, Angel's food, I fed them all:
      Was ever grief like mine?

They part my garments, and by lot dispose
My coat, the type of love, which once cured those
Who sought for help, never malicious foes:
      Was ever grief like mine?

Nay, after death their spite shall further go;
For they will pierce my side, I full well know;
That as sinne came, so Sacraments might flow
      Was ever grief like mine?

But now I die; now all is finishèd.
My woe, man's weal: and now I bow my head.
Onely let others say, when I am dead,
      Never was grief like mine.

Robert Herrick (1591-1674)

TO DIANEME

Donne, Herbert and Herrick all represent a sort of man whom
nowadays we might think of as a hypocrite. They were lively,
worldly, sensual beings who yet 'took to the Church'. The divorce
between faith, good living and science was not yet complete. After
all, Herrick lived from 1591 to 1674—a terrific span of time for those
days. He was by temperament a 'Cavalier' and nobody knows what
he did or how he lived during Cromwell's Protectorate; but so soon
as Charles II was restored, Herrick re-appeared. In spite of all the
girls—real or imagined—that he wrote about, he died a bachelor.
Few cared for his poems until over a hundred years after he was dead.

Sweet, be not proud of those two eyes,
Which Star-like sparkle in their skies:
Nor be you proud, that you can see
All hearts your captives; yours, yet free:
Be you not proud of that rich haire,
Which wantons with the Love-sick aire:
Whenas[1] that Rubie, which you weare,
Sunk from the tip of your soft eare,
Will last to be a precious Stone,
When all your world of Beautie's gone.

---

[1] because

Robert Herrick

TO DAFFADILLS

Faire Daffadills, we weep to see
 You haste away so soone:
As yet the early-rising Sun
 Has not attained his Noone.
  Stay, stay,
 Untill the hasting day
   Has run
 But to the Even-song;
And, having prayed together, we
  Will goe with you along.

We have short time to stay, as you,
 We have as short a Spring;
As quick a growth to meet Decay,
 As you, or any thing.
  We die,
 As your hours doe, and drie
   Away,
 Like to the Summer's raine;
Or as the pearles of Morning's dew
  Ne'r to be found againe.

Sir John Suckling (1609-1642)

SONG: WHY SO PALE AND WAN, FOND LOVER?

Why so pale and wan, fond Lover?
 Prethee why so pale?
Will, when looking well can't move her,
 Looking ill prevail;
 Prethee why so pale?

Why so dull and mute young Sinner?
　　Prethee why so mute?
Will, when speaking well can't win her,
　　Saying nothing do't:
　　Prethee why so mute?

Quit, quit for shame, this will not move,
　　This cannot take her;
If of her selfe she will not love,
　　Nothing can make her:
　　The Devil take her.

OUT UPON IT

Out upon it, I have loved
　　Three whole days together;
And am like to love three more,
　　If it prove fair weather.

Time shall moult away his wings
　　Ere he shall discover
In the whole wide world agen
　　Such a constant Lover.

But the spite on't is, no praise
　　Is due at all to me:
Love with me had made no staies,
　　Had it any been but she.

Had it any been but she,
　　And that very Face,
There had been at least ere this
　　A dozen dozen in her place.

Andrew Marvell (1621-1678)

TO HIS COY MISTRESS

Marvell was perhaps the greatest single influence upon T. S. Eliot
and you will find constant echoes or quotations from him in Eliot's
work; for example, these lines from *The Wasteland*:
> But at my back from time to time I hear
> The sound of horns and motors, which shall bring
> Sweeney to Mrs. Porter in the spring.

Had we but World enough, and Time,
This coyness Lady were no crime.
We would sit down, and think which way
To walk, and pass our long Loves Day.
Thou by the Indian Ganges side
Should'st Rubies find: I by the Tide
Of Humber would complain. I would
Love you ten years before the Flood:
And you should if you please refuse
Till the Conversion of the Jews.
My vegetable Love should grow
Vaster then Empires, and more slow.
An hundred years should go to praise
Thine Eyes, and on thy Forehead gaze.
Two hundred to adore each Breast:
But thirty thousand to the rest.
An Age at least to every part,
And the last Age should show your Heart.
For Lady you deserve this State;
Nor would I love at lower rate.
　　　But at my back I alwaies hear
Times wingèd Charriot hurrying near:
And yonder all before us lye
Deserts of vast Eternity.
Thy Beauty shall no more be found;
Nor, in thy marble Vault, shall sound
My ecchoing Song: then Worms shall try
That long preserved Virginity:
And your quaint Honour turn to dust;
And into ashes all my Lust.

The Grave's a fine and private place,
But none I think do there embrace.
  Now therefore, while the youthful hew
Sits on thy skin like morning dew,
And while thy willing Soul transpires
At every pore with instant Fires,
Now let us sport us while we may;
And now, like am'rous birds of prey,
Rather at once our Time devour,
Than languish in his slow-chapt pow'r.
Let us roll all our Strength, and all
Our sweetness, up into one Ball:
And tear our Pleasures with rough strife,
Thorough the iron gates of Life.
Thus, though we cannot make our Sun
Stand still, yet we will make him run.

John Milton (1608-1674)

From PARADISE LOST

Poets are often the best critics of other poets, and it was Blake who said: 'Milton was of the Devil's party without knowing it.' Certainly in *Paradise Lost*, Milton's Satan—in Heaven the Angel Lucifer, who was defeated in his rebellion against God—is a great and moving figure.

Milton, like Virgil and Chaucer before him, played his part in the political life of his time and many of his comments are political and personal attacks and justifications relating to the events of his own day, and well understood by his contemporaries.

Satan in Hell, after the fall from Heaven

Nine times the Space that measures Day and Night
To mortal men, he with his horrid crew
Lay vanquisht, rowling in the fiery Gulfe
Confounded though immortal: but his doom
Reserved him to more wrath; for now the thought
Both of lost happiness and lasting pain
Torments him; round he throws his baleful eyes
That witnessed huge affliction and dismay
Mixt with obdurate pride and stedfast hate:
At once as far as Angels kenn he views

The dismal situation waste and wilde,
A dungeon horrible, on all sides round
As one great furnace flamed, yet from those flames
No light, but rather darkness visible
Served only to discover sights of woe,
Regions of sorrow, doleful shades, where peace
And rest can never dwell, hope never comes
That comes to all; but torture without end
Still urges, and a fiery Deluge, fed
With ever-burning sulphur unconsumed:
Such place Eternal Justice had prepared
For those rebellious, here their Prison ordained
In utter darkness, and their portion set
As far removed from God and light of Heav'n
As from the Center thrice to th'utmost Pole.

O how unlike the place from whence they fell!
There the companions of his fall, o'erwhelmed
With Floods and Whirlwinds of tempestuous fire,
He soon discerns, and weltring by his side
One next himself in power, and next in crime,
Long after known in Palestine, and named
Bëëlzebub. To whom th'Arch-Enemy,
And thence in Heav'n called Satan, with bold words
Breaking the horrid silence thus began:
    If thou beest he; but O how fall'n! how changed
From him, who in the happy Realms of Light
Clothed with transcendent brightness didst outshine
Myriads though bright: if he whom mutual league,
United thoughts and counsels, equal hope,
And hazard in the glorious enterprize,
Joynd with me once, now misery hath joynd
In equal ruin: into what pit thou seest
From what highth fal'n, so much the stronger proved
He with his thunder: and till then who knew
The force of those dire arms? yet not for those
Nor what the Potent Victor in his rage
Can else inflict do I repent or change,
Though changed in outward lustre; that fixt mind
And high disdain, from sense of injured merit,
That with the mightiest raised me to contend,
And to the fierce contention brought along
Innumerable force of Spirits armed
That durst dislike his reign, and me preferring,
His utmost power with adverse power opposed
In dubious battel on the Plains of Heav'n,
And shook his throne. What though the field be lost?
All is not lost; the unconquerable Will,
And study of revenge, immortal hate,
And courage never to submit or yield:
And what is else not to be overcome?
That Glory never shall his wrath or might
Extort from me, To bow and sue for grace
With suppliant knee, and deifie his power
Who from the terrour of this Arm so late
Doubted his Empire, that were low indeed,

That were an ignominy and shame beneath
This downfall; since by Fate the strength of Gods
And this Empyreal substance cannot fail,
Since through experience of this great event
In Arms not worse, in foresight much advanc't,
We may with more successful hope resolve
To wage by force or guile eternal Warr
Irreconcileable, to our grand Foe,
Who now triumphs, and in th'excess of joy
Sole reigning holds the Tyranny of Heav'n.

Satan's Resolve

Is this the Region, this the Soil, the Clime,
Said then the lost Arch Angel, this the seat
That we must change for Heav'n, this mournful gloom
For that celestial light? Be it so, since hee
Who now is Sovran can dispose and bid
What shall be right: fardest from him is best
Whom reason hath equald, force hath made supream
Above his equals. Farewel happy Fields
Where Joy for ever dwells. Hail horrours, hail
Infernal world, and thou profoundest Hell
Receive thy new Possessor: one who brings
A mind not to be changed by Place or Time.
The mind is its own place, and in it self
Can make a Heav'n of Hell, a Hell of Heav'n.
What matter where, if I be still the same,
And what I should be, all but less than hee
Whom Thunder hath made greater? Here at least
We shall be free; th'Almighty hath not built
Here for his envy, will not drive us hence:
Here we may reign secure, and in my choyce
To reign is worth ambition though in Hell:
Better to reign in Hell, than serve in Heav'n.

O had his powerful Destiny ordained
Me some inferiour Angel, I had stood
Then happie; no unbounded hope had raised
Ambition. Yet why not? some other Power
As great might have aspired, and me though mean
Drawn to his part; but other Powers as great
Fell not, but stand unshak'n, from within
Or from without, to all temptations armed.
Hadst thou the same free Will and Power to stand?
Thou hadst: whom hast thou then or what to accuse,
But Heav'ns free Love dealt equally to all?
Be then his Love accurst, since love or hate,
To me alike, it deals eternal woe.
Nay cursed be thou; since against his thy will
Chose freely what it now so justly rues.
Me miserable! which way shall I flie
Infinite wrauth, and infinite despaire?
Which way I flie is Hell; my self am Hell;
And in the lowest deep a lower deep
Still threatning to devour me opens wide,
To which the Hell I suffer seems a Heav'n.
O then at last relent: is there no place
Left for Repentance, none for Pardon left?
None left but by submission; and that word
Disdain forbids me, and my dread of shame
Among the spirits beneath, whom I seduced
With other promises and other vaunts
Than to submit, boasting I could subdue
Th'Omnipotent. Ay me, they little know
How dearly I abide that boast so vaine,
Under what torments inwardly I groane:
While they adore me on the Throne of Hell,
With Diadem and Scepter high advancd
The lower still I fall, onely Supream
In miserie; such joy Ambition findes,
But say I could repent and could obtaine
By Act of Grace my former state; how soon
Would highth recal high thoughts, how soon unsay

What feigned submission swore: ease would recant
Vows made in pain, as violent and void.
For never can true reconcilement grow
Where wounds of deadly hate have pierced so deep:
Which would but lead me to a worse relapse,
And heavier fall: so should I purchase deare
Short intermission bought with double smart.
This knows my punisher; therefore as farr
From granting hee, as I from begging peace:
All hope excluded thus, behold in stead
Of us out-cast, exiled, his new delight,
Mankind created, and for him this World.
So farwel Hope, and with Hope farwel Fear,
Farwel Remorse: all Good to me is lost;
Evil be thou my Good; by thee at least
Divided Empire with Heav'ns King I hold
By thee, and more than half perhaps will reigne;
As Man ere long, and this new World shall know.

The Sixth Day of Creation

The Sixt, and of Creation last arose
With Eevning Harps and Mattin, when God said,
Let th'Earth bring forth Fowle living in her kinde,
Cattel and Creeping things, and Beast of the Earth,
Each in thir kinde. The Earth obeyed, and strait
Op'ning her fertil Woomb teemed at a Birth
Innumerous living Creatures, perfect formes,
Limbed and full grown: out of the ground up rose
As from his Laire the wilde Beast where he wonns[1]
In Forrest wilde, in Thicket, Brake, or Den;
Among the Trees in Pairs they rose, they walked:
The Cattel in the Fields and Meddowes green:

---

[1] dwells.

Those rare and solitarie, these in flocks
Pasturing at once, and in broad Herds upsprung.
The grassie Clods now Calved, now half appeered
The Tawnie Lion, pawing to get free
His hinder parts, then springs as broke from Bonds,
And Rampant shakes his Brinded main; the Ounce,
The Libbard, and the Tyger, as the Moale
Rising, the crumbled Earth above them threw
In Hillocks; the swift Stag from under ground
Bore up his branching head: scarse from his mould
Behemoth biggest born of Earth upheaved
His vastness: Fleec't the Flocks and bleating rose,
As Plants: ambiguous between Sea and Land
The River Horse and scalie Crocodile.
At once came forth whatever creeps the ground,
Insect or Worme; those waved thir limber fans
For wings, and smallest Lineaments exact
In all the Liveries dect of Summer's pride
With spots of Gold and Purple, azure and green:
These as a line thir long dimension drew,
Streaking the ground with sinuous trace: not all
Minims of Nature; some of Serpent kinde
Wondrous in length and corpulence involved
Thir Snakie foulds, and added wings. First crept
The parsimonious Emmet, provident
Of future, in small room large heart enclosed,
Pattern of just equalitie perhaps
Hereafter, joined in her popular Tribes
Of Commonaltie: swarming next appeered
The Female Bee that feeds her Husband Drone
Deliciously, and builds her waxen Cells
With Honey stored: the rest are numberless,
And thou thir Natures know'st, and gav'st them Names,
Needless to thee repeated; nor unknown
The Serpent suttl'st Beast of all the field,
Of huge extent somtimes, with brazen Eyes
And hairie Main terrific, though to thee
Not noxious, but obedient at thy call.
Now Heav'n in all her Glorie shon, and rowld
Her motions, as the great first-Mover's hand

First wheeld thir course; Earth in her rich attire
Consummate lovly smiled; Aire, Water, Earth,
By Fowl, Fish, Beast, was flown, was swum, was walkt
Frequent; and of the Sixt day yet remained;
There wanted yet the Master work, the end
Of all yet don; a Creature who not prone
And Brute as other Creatures, but endued
With Sanctitie of Reason, might erect
His Stature, and upright with Front serene
Govern the rest, self-knowing, and from thence
Magnanimous to correspond with Heav'n,
But grateful to acknowledge whence his good
Descends, thither with heart and voice and eyes
Directed in Devotion, to adore
And worship God Supream, who made him chief
Of all his works.

From SAMSON AGONISTES

Milton went blind at the age of forty-six. Through the character of
Samson, he expresses his personal anguish.

Samson, now a Slave of the Philistines, laments his Blindness

. . . But chief of all,
O loss of sight, of thee I most complain!
Blind among enemies, O worse then chains,
Dungeon, or beggary, or decrepit age!
Light the prime work of God to me is extinct,
And all her various objects of delight
Annulled, which might in part my grief have eased,
Inferiour to the vilest now become
Of man or worm; the vilest here excel me,
They creep, yet see, I dark in light exposed
To daily fraud, contempt, abuse and wrong,
Within doors, or without, still as a fool,

In power of others, never in my own;
Scarce half I seem to live, dead more then half.
O dark, dark, dark, amid the blaze of noon,
Irrecoverably dark, total Eclipse
Without all hope of day!
O first created Beam, and thou great Word,
Let there be light, and light was over all;
Why am I thus bereaved thy prime decree?
The Sun to me is dark
And silent as the Moon,
When she deserts the night
Hid in her vacant interlunar cave.
Since light so necessary is to life,
And almost life itself, if it be true
That light is in the Soul,
She all in every part; why was the sight
To such a tender ball as th'eye confined?
So obvious and so easie to be quench't,
And not as feeling through all parts diffused,
That she might look at will through every pore?
Then had I not been thus exiled from light;
As in the land of darkness yet in light,
To live a life half dead, a living death,
And buried; but O yet more miserable!
My self, my Sepulcher, a moving Grave,
Buried, yet not exempt
By priviledge of death and burial
From worst of other evils, pains and wrongs,
But made hereby obnoxious more
To all the miseries of life,
Life in captivity
Among inhuman foes.

John Bunyan (1628-1688)

MY LITTLE BIRD

Bunyan is famous as the author of *The Pilgrim's Progress*, written
while he was imprisoned in Bedford Jail, and published in 1678.

My little Bird, how canst thou sit;
And sing amidst so many Thorns!
Let me but hold upon thee get,
My Love with Honour thee adorns.

Thou art at present little worth;
Five farthings none will give for thee.
But prethee little Bird come forth,
Thou of more value art to me.

'Tis true, it is Sun-shine today,
Tomorrow Birds will have a Storm;
My pretty one, come thou away,
My Bosom then shall keep thee warm.

Thou subject art to cold o' nights,
When darkness is thy covering;
At days thy danger's great by Kites,
How canst thou then sit there and sing?

Thy food is scarce and scanty too,
'Tis Worms and Trash which thou dost eat;
Thy present state I pity do,
Come, I'll provide thee better meat.

I'll feed thee with white Bread and Milk,
And Sugar-plums, if them thou crave;
I'll cover thee with finest Silk,
That from the cold I may thee save.

My Father's Palace shall be thine,
Yea, in it thou shalt sit and sing;
My little Bird, if thou'lt be mine,
The whole year round shall be thy Spring.

I'll teach thee all the Notes at Court;
Unthought of Musick thou shalt play;
And all that thither do resort
Shall praise thee for it ev'ry day.

I'll keep thee safe with[1] Cat and Cur,
No manner o' harm shall come to thee;
Yea, I will be thy Succourer,
My Bosom shall thy Cabbin be.

But lo, behold, the Bird is gone:
These Charmings would not make her yield:
The Child's left at the Bush alone,
The Bird flies yonder o'er the Field.

---

[1] from.

EVENING

Gray's *Elegy in a Country Churchyard*, published in 1750, is usually considered a landmark in descriptive country verse, but this poem preceded it by nearly a century! Cotton was known especially for his continuation of Walton's *Compleat Angler* (see note on Basse, p. 43).

The Day's grown old, the fainting Sun
Has but a little way to run,
And yet his Steeds, with all his skill,
Scarce lug the Chariot down the Hill.

With Labour spent, and Thirst opprest,
Whilst they strain hard to gain the West,
From Fetlocks hot drops melted light,
Which turn to Meteors in the Night.

The Shadows now so long do grow,
That Brambles like tall Cedars show,
Mole-hills seem Mountains, and the Ant
Appears a monstrous Elephant.

A very little little Flock
Shades thrice the ground that it would stock;
Whilst the small Stripling following them,
Appears a mighty Polypheme.

These being brought into the Fold,
And by the thrifty Master told,
He thinks his Wages are well paid,
Since none are either lost, or strayed.

Now lowing Herds are each-where heard,
Chains rattle in the Villein's Yard,
The Cart's on Tayl set down to rest,
Bearing on high the Cuckolds Crest.

The hedge is stript, the Clothes brought in,
Nought's left without should be within,
The Bees are hived, and hum their Charm,
Whilst every House does seem a Swarm.

The Cock now to the Roost is prest:
For he must call up all the rest;
The Sow's fast pegged within the Sty,
To still her squeaking Progeny.

Each one has had his Supping Mess,
The Cheese is put into the Press,
The Pans and Bowls clean scalded all,
Reared up against the Milk-house Wall.

And now on Benches all are sat
In the cool Air to sit and chat,
Till Phoebus, dipping in the West,
Shall lead the World the way to Rest.

I I

From Dryden to Burns

The death of Shakespeare and the issue of the Authorised Version of the Bible
mark the end of a period in the development, or change, of the English
language. The seventeenth century was a period of intense political and social
unrest. It saw the end of many old beliefs, such as the Divine Right of Kings;
and Charles I's fanatical determination to exercise this Right, to be above the
Law, led to the Civil War. But the whole age was one of a restless seeking for
new truths. The Royal Society was founded; the cleavage between religious
belief and the scientific attitude to life—what T. S. Eliot calls the 'dissociation
of sensibility' began. This dissociation is strongly reflected in poetry. Whereas
John Donne at the beginning of the century could use scientific metaphors in
his religious poetry, this became less and less possible. Language changed, too.
Dryden thought he could 'improve' the rough language of Shakespeare! In
such an age, when ideas are in a ferment, satire flourishes; and Dryden, Swift
and Pope were all satirical poets. They were almost wholly unable to express
what they felt as opposed to what they thought—nor did they regard the
expression of feeling as the major province of poetry. (This is equally
evident in the poems of the 1960's). Poetry, as Pope wrote, was 'what oft was
thought but ne'er so well expressed'. The key to reading such poetry as Pope's
or Gray's is to take pleasure—as one can—in the way they perfected their
powers of expression. Mostly, their poetry was for the urban intelligentsia
of the day—the wits of London. It was not really concerned with the living
conditions of anyone outside its well-educated, well-off, narrow circle.

But, for contrast, one must not forget that poets such as Goldsmith and
Blake, Cowper and Watts, were deeply concerned in men's beliefs and in the
way life was lived (see Goldsmith's *Deserted Village* or Blake's *London*). The
Age of Reason, then, was also an age of religious revival and re-thinking,
though few people heeded Blake at the time.

Poetry is always changing: moving away from the way men talk to each
other to the more elaborate written word—what was 'ne'er so well expressed'—
and this is followed in nearly every age by a move back. What we must always
remember is that no one in Shakespeare's and Ben Jonson's day went,
consciously, to a 'poetic' drama; for them the language in which the plays
were written was close to how they *talked,* as was the language of the Bible
(which is precisely why in the twentieth century scholars are re-translating the
Bible). But after a period of written, elaborate language comes the swing of
the pendulum back to spoken, natural language. So the poetry of Robert

Burns and William Blake or, indeed, of Christopher Smart is written in the way men *talk* and is totally opposed to the aims of a Jonathan Swift or an Alexander Pope. If you want to see how 'spoken' language turns into 'written' language read Shakespeare's *Antony and Cleopatra* and then Dryden's re-writing of it which he called *All for Love*: and if you want to see how written language turns back into spoken language turn from Pope to Blake and Burns. There are never great guillotines which behead one style in favour of another. Language is on the move all the time; the changes overlap; Blake and Burns foreshadow the romantic revival of Wordsworth, Coleridge, Shelley and Keats; even as Keats leads to the 'written' elaborate language of Tennyson, Arnold and later Victorian poets.

We now are horrified that Dryden 're-wrote' Chaucer and Shakespeare but we are not horrified at swing or pop versions of Shakespeare's songs, or musicals like *Oliver,* based on Dickens' *Oliver Twist*; and it is as well to remember that most of Shakespeare's plays, in whatever period they are set, were played in what was then 'modern dress'—that is, Elizabethan dress.

So when you read these poems consider all the changes of dress, of food, of behaviour which took place between 1660 and 1800. Think then what has taken place between 1800 and 1960; yet Blake's poem about London would not be out of date if it were published today.

John Dryden (1631-1700)

From AMPHITRYON

Mercury's Song to Phaedra

Fashions in pronunciation change. The vowel sounds Shakespeare used were quite different from ours, for instance; if he went to Stratford now, he'd have a job to follow *Hamlet*! In the present poem you'll notice that the last two lines don't rhyme to us; they did to Dryden. Later on, when Pope drank tea, he pronounced it 'tay'. These odd little changes in language are often seen most obviously in poetry.

Fair Iris I love and hourly I die,
But not for a Lip, nor a languishing Eye:
She's fickle and false, and there we agree;
For I am as false, and as fickle as she:
We neither believe what either can say;
And, neither believing, we neither betray.

'Tis civil to swear, and say things of course;
We mean not the taking for better for worse.
When present, we love; when absent, agree:
I think not of Iris, nor Iris of me:
The Legend of Love no Couple can find
So easie to part, or so equally join'd.

Jonathan Swift (1667-1745)

From ON POETRY: A RHAPSODY

Lintot was a famous contemporary printer. In those days there were
no 'publishers' as distinct from printers, and no copyright laws to
protect an author's work. Works are still 'pirated', that is, printed
without the author's permission (as were the Hawker's copies in this
poem) by those countries which do not observe the international
laws, and authors are still defrauded just as Swift was.

How shall a new Attempter learn
Of diff'rent Spirits to discern,
And how distinguish, which is which,
The Poet's Vein, or scribling Itch?
Then hear an old experienc'd Sinner
Instructing thus a young Beginner:
'Consult yourself, and if you find
A powerful Impulse urge your Mind,
Impartial judge within your Breast
What Subject you can manage best;
Whether your Genius most inclines
To Satire, Praise, or hum'rous Lines;
To Elegies in mournful Tone,
Or Prologue sent from Hand unknown.
Then rising with Aurora's Light,
The Muse invok'd, sit down to write;
Blot out, correct, insert, refine,
Enlarge, diminish, interline;
Be mindful, when Invention fails,
To scratch your Head, and bite your Nails.

'Your Poem finish'd, next your Care
Is needful, to transcribe it fair.
In modern Wit all printed Trash, is
Set off with num'rous *Breaks*—and *Dashes*—

'To Statesmen would you give a Wipe,
You print it in *Italik Type*.
When Letters are in vulgar Shapes,
'Tis ten to one the Wit escapes;

But when in *CAPITALS* exprest,
The dullest Reader smoaks[1] the Jest;
Or else perhaps he may invent
A better than the Poet meant,
As learned Commentators view
In Homer more than Homer knew.

'Your Poem in its modish Dress,
Correctly fitted for the Press,
Convey by Penny-Post to Lintot,
But let no Friend alive look into't.
If Lintot thinks 'twill quit the Cost,
You need not fear your Labour lost:
And, how agreeably surpriz'd
Are you to see it advertiz'd!
The Hawker shews you one in Print,
As fresh as Farthings from the Mint:
The Product of your Toil and Sweating;
A Bastard of your own begetting.

Be sure at Will's[2] the following Day,
Lie Snug, and hear what Criticks say.
And if you find the general Vogue
Pronounces you a stupid Rogue;
Damns all your Thoughts as low and little,
Sit still, and swallow down your Spittle.
Be silent as a Politician,
For talking may beget Suspicion:
Or praise the Judgment of the Town,
And help yourself to run it down.
Give up your fond paternal Pride,
Nor argue on the weaker Side;
For Poems read without a Name
We justly praise, or justly blame:
And Criticks have no partial Views,
Except they know whom they abuse.

---

[1] smokes out, discovers.
[2] a famous coffee house.

And since you ne'er provok'd their Spight,
Depend upon't their Judgment's right:
But if you blab, you are undone;
Consider what a Risk you run.
You lose your Credit all at once;
The Town will mark you for a Dunce:
The vilest Doggrel Grubstreet sends,
Will pass for yours with Foes and Friends.
And you must bear the whole Disgrace,
'Till some fresh Blockhead takes your Place.

A SATIRICAL ELEGY ON THE DEATH OF A LATE FAMOUS GENERAL

Most people know Jonathan Swift as the author of *Gulliver's Travels*.
Written as serious and bitter satire, it is read as a children's story—
indeed, 'the success of Swift in scoring a hit on the wrong target is
almost ludicrous.'
What he was, what he was like, would take pages to tell. Like Herbert,
like Herrick, he entered the Church as the only means he had of
betterment. He was, practically speaking, an orphan. 'Stella'—her
real name was Esther Johnson—and 'Vanessa', Hester Vanhomrigh,
were the two women whom he loved. He ended his career as Dean of
St. Patrick's Dublin. Much of his life, against his will, was spent in
Ireland. In fact, his life is something of a mystery: what we have are
his works, and they tell us that he was a great man, passionately
concerned with human ills and the reform of them.

His Grace! impossible! what dead!
Of old age too, and in his bed!
And could that Mighty Warrior fall?
And so inglorious, after all!
Well, since he's gone, no matter how,
The last loud trump must wake him now:
And, trust me, as the noise grows stronger,
He'd wish to sleep a little longer.

And could he be indeed so old
As by the news-papers we're told?
Threescore, I think, is pretty high;
'Twas time, in conscience he should die.
This world he cumber'd long enough;
He burnt his candle to the snuff;
And that's the reason, some folks think,
He left behind *so great a stink.*
Behold his funeral appears,
Nor widow's sighs, nor orphan's tears,
Wont at such times each heart to pierce,
Attend the progress of his herse.
But what of that, his friends may say,
He had those honours in his day.
True to his profit and his pride,
He made them weep before he died.

Come hither, all ye empty things,
Ye bubbles rais'd by breath of Kings;
Who float upon the tide of state,
Come hither, and behold your fate.
Let pride be taught by this rebuke,
How very mean a thing's a Duke;
From all his ill-got honours flung,
Turn'd to that dirt from whence he sprung.

STELLA'S BIRTH-DAY, 1720-1721

All Travellers at first incline
Where-e'er they see the fairest Sign,
And if they find the Chambers neat,
And like the Liquor and the Meat
Will call again and recommend
The Angel-Inn to ev'ry Friend:
And though the Painting grows decay'd
The House will never loose it's Trade;

Nay, though the treach'rous Rascal Thomas
Hangs a new Angel two doors from us
As fine as Dawbers Hands can make it
In hopes that Strangers may mistake it,
They think it both a Shame and Sin
To quit the true old Angel-Inn.
   Now, this is Stella's Case in Fact,
An Angel's Face, a little crack't;
(Could Poets or could Painters fix
How Angels look at thirty six)
This drew us in at first to find
In such a Form an Angel's Mind:
And ev'ry Virtue now supplyes
The fainting Rays of Stella's Eyes:
See, at her Levée crowding Swains
Whom Stella freely entertains
With Breeding, Humor, Wit, and Sense,
And puts them to so small Expence:
Their Minds so plentifully fills,
And makes such reasonable Bills,
So little gets for what she gives
We really wonder how she lives;
And, had her Stock been less, no doubt
She must have long ago run out.
    Then, who can think we'll quit the Place
When Doll hangs out a newer Face
Nail'd to her Window full in Sight
All Christian People to invite;
Or stop and 'light[1] at Cloe's Head
With Scraps and Leavings to be fed.
    Then Cloe, still go on to prate
Of thirty six, and thirty eight;
Pursue thy Trade of Scandall-picking,
Thy Hints that Stella is no Chickin;

---

[1] alight.

Your Innuendo's when you tell us
That Stella loves to talk with Fellows;
But let me warn thee to believe
A Truth for which thy Soul should grieve;
That, should you live to see the Day
When Stella's Locks must all be grey,
When Age must print a furrow'd Trace
On ev'ry Feature of her Face;
Though you and all your senceless Tribe
Could Art or Time or Nature bribe
To make you look like Beauty's Queen
And hold for ever at fifteen;
No Bloom of Youth can ever blind
The Cracks and Wrinckles of your Mind;
All Men of Sense will pass your Dore
And crowd to Stella's at fourscore.

From STELLA'S BIRTH-DAY, 1726-1727

This Day, whate'er the Fates decree,
Shall still be kept with Joy by me:
This Day then, let us not be told,
That you are sick, and I grown old,
Nor think on our approaching Ills,
And talk of Spectacles and Pills;
Tomorrow will be Time enough
To hear such mortifying Stuff.

Jonathan Swift

From VERSES ON THE DEATH OF DR. SWIFT[1]

The Time is not remote

    The Time is not remote, when I
Must by the Course of Nature dye:
When I foresee my special Friends,
Will try to find their private Ends:
Tho' it is hardly understood,
Which way my Death can do them good;
Yet, thus methinks, I hear 'em speak:
'See, how the Dean begins to break:
Poor Gentleman, he droops apace,
You plainly find it in his Face:
That old Vertigo in his Head,
Will never leave him, till he's dead:
Besides, his Memory decays,
He recollects not what he says;
He cannot call his Friends to Mind;
Forgets the Place where last he din'd:
Plyes you with Stories o'er and o'er,
He told them fifty Times before.
How does he fancy we can sit,
To hear his out-of-fashion'd Wit?
But he takes up with younger Fokes,
Who for his Wine will bear his Jokes:
Faith, he must make his Stories shorter,
Or change his Comrades once a Quarter:
In half the Time, he talks them round;
There must another Sett be found.

    'For Poetry, he's past his Prime,
He takes an Hour to find a Rhime:
His Fire is out, his Wit decay'd,
His Fancy sunk, his Muse a Jade.

---

[1] Compare Pope's *Epistle to Dr. Arbuthnot*, p. 105

I'd have him throw away his Pen;
But there's no talking to some Men.'
    And, then their Tenderness appears,
By adding largely to my Years:
'He's older than he would be reckon'd,
And well remembers Charles the Second.
    'He hardly drinks a Pint of Wine;
And that, I doubt, is no good Sign.
His Stomach too begins to fail:
Last Year we thought him strong and hale;
But now, he's quite another Thing;
I wish he may hold out till Spring.'
    Then hug themselves, and reason thus;
'It is not yet so bad with us.'

Suppose me dead

    Suppose me dead; and then suppose
A Club assembled at the *Rose*;
Where from Discourse of this and that,
I grow the Subject of their Chat:
And, while they toss my Name about,
With Favour some, and some without;
One quite indiff'rent in the Cause,
My Character impartial draws:
    'The Dean, if we believe Report,
Was never ill-receiv'd at Court:
As for his Works in Verse and Prose,
I own my self no Judge of those:
Nor, can I tell what Criticks thought 'em;
But, this I know, all People bought 'em;
As with a moral View design'd
To cure the Vices of Mankind:
His Vein, ironically grave,
Expos'd the Fool, and lash'd the Knave:
To steal a Hint was never known,
But what he writ, was all his own.
    'He never thought an Honour done him,
Because a Duke was proud to own him:
Would rather slip aside, and chuse
To talk with Wits in dirty Shoes:

Despis'd the Fools with Stars and Garters,
So often seen caressing Chartres:[1]
He never courted Men in Station,
Nor Persons had in Admiration;
Of no Man's Greatness was afraid,
Because he sought for no Man's Aid.
Though trusted long in great Affairs,
He gave himself no haughty Airs:
Without regarding private Ends,
Spent all his Credit for his Friends:
And only chose the Wise and Good;
No Flatt'rers; no Allies in Blood;
But succour'd Virtue in Distress,
And seldom fail'd of good Success;
As Numbers in their Hearts must own,
Who, but for him, had been unknown.

---

[1] a successful careerist and scoundrel.

Alexander Pope (1688-1744

From THE RAPE OF THE LOCK

Pope is the master of the 'heroic' couplet, which he uses in all the following poems. These couplets are almost invariably complete in themselves. Critics got so used to this form that when Keats in his first published poem, *Endymion* (p. 184), used a couplet form in which the sense ran on for several lines at a time, he was said to be unintelligible!

The 'heroic' couplet, as you will see, uses a line the same length as a blank verse line—that is, five stresses in a line of roughly ten syllables, the stresses falling on the even beats.

Close by those Meads forever crown'd with Flow'rs,
Where *Thames* with Pride surveys his rising Tow'rs,
There stands a Structure of Majestic Frame,
Which from the neighb'ring *Hampton* takes its Name.
Here *Britain's* Statesmen oft the Fall foredoom
Of Foreign Tyrants and of Nymphs at home;
Here thou, great *Anna*![1] whom three realms *obey,*
Dost sometimes Counsel take—and sometimes Tea.
 Hither the Heroes and the Nymphs resort,
To taste awhile the Pleasures of a Court;
In various talk th' instructive hours they past,
Who gave the *Ball,* or paid the Visit last:
One speaks the *Glory* of the *British Queen,*
And one describes a charming *Indian Screen*;
A third interprets Motions, Looks, and Eyes;
At ev'ry Word a Reputation dies.
Snuff, or the *Fan,* supply each pause of Chat,
With singing, laughing, ogling, *and all that.*
Mean while declining from the Noon of Day,
The Sun obliquely shoots his burning Ray;
The hungry Judges soon the Sentence sign,
And Wretches hang that Jury-men may Dine.

---

[1] Queen Anne.

Alexander Pope

From AN ESSAY ON CRITICISM

The eighteenth century judged a poet by the smoothness and regularity of his verse; irregularities were not tolerated. That is why nobody then liked Donne, for instance.

A little learning

Of all the Causes which conspire to blind
Man's erring judgment, and misguide the mind,
What the weak head with strongest bias rules,
Is *Pride*, the never-failing vice of fools.
Whatever Nature has in worth deny'd,
She gives in large recruits of needful Pride;
For as in bodies, thus in souls, we find
What wants[1] in blood and spirits, swell'd with wind:
Pride, where Wit fails, steps in to our defence,
And fills up all the mighty Void of sense.
If once right reason drives that cloud away,
Truth breaks upon us with resistless day.
Trust not yourself; but you defects to know,
Make use of ev'ry friend—and ev'ry foe.
A *little learning* is a dang'rous thing;
Drink deep, or taste not the Pierian spring;
There shallow draughts intoxicate the brain,
And drinking largely, sobers us again.
Fir'd at first sight with what the Muse imparts,
In fearless youth we tempt the heights of Arts,
While from the bounded level of our mind
Short views we take, nor see the lengths behind;
But more advanc'd, behold with strange surprize
New distant scenes of endless science rise!
So pleas'd at first the tow'ring Alps we try,
Mount o'er the vales, and seem to tread the sky,
Th' eternal snows appear already past,
And the first clouds and mountains seem the last:
But, those attain'd, we tremble to survey
The growing labours of the lengthen'd way,

---

[1] lacks.

Th' increasing prospect tires our wand'ring eyes,
Hills peep o'er Hills, and Alps on Alps arise!

The Poet's Art

But most by *Numbers*[1] judge a Poet's song;
And smooth or rough, with them, is right or wrong:
In the bright Muse tho' thousand charms conspire,
Her Voice is all these tuneful fools admire;
Who haunt Parnassus but to please their ear,
Not mend their minds; as some to Church repair,
Not for the doctrine, but the music there.
These, equal syllables alone require,
Tho' oft the ear the open vowels tire;
While èxpletives their feeble aid do join;
And ten low words oft creep in one dull line:
While they ring round the same unvary'd chimes,
With sure returns of still expected rhymes.
Where-e'er you find 'the cooling western breeze,'
In the next line, it 'whispers thro' the trees';
If crystal streams 'with pleasing murmurs creep,'
The reader's threatened (not in vain) with 'sleep.'
Then, at the last and only couplet fraught
With some unmeaning thing they call a thought,
A needless Alexandrine ends the song,
That, like a wounded snake, drags its slow length along.
Leave such to tune their own dull rhymes, and know
What's roundly smooth, or languishingly slow;
And praise the easy vigour of a line,
Where Denham's strength, and Waller's sweetness join.
True ease in writing comes from art, not chance,
As those move easiest who have learned to dance.
'Tis not enough no harshness gives offence,
The sound must seem an Echo to the sense:
Soft is the strain when Zephyr gently blows,
And the smooth stream in smoother numbers flows;
But when loud surges lash the sounding shore,
The hoarse, rough verse should like the torrent roar:

---

[1] metre.

When Ajax strives some rock's vast weight to throw
The line too labours, and the words move slow;
Not so, when swift Camilla scours the plain,
Flies o'er th' unbending corn, and skims along the main.

From AN ESSAY ON MAN

The eighteenth century is called 'the Age of Reason'. It was the first time in which the word 'science' really began to be used in the sense that we understand it now. Before, science had simply meant learning. Pope's attack on science, or rather upon its limitations, has a very modern ring.

What would this Man?

What would this Man? Now upward will he soar,
And little less than Angel, would be more;
Now looking downwards, just as grieved appears
To want the strength of bulls, the fur of bears.
Made for his use all creatures if he call,
Say what their use, had he the pow'rs of all?
Nature to these, without profusion, kind,
The proper organs, proper pow'rs assigned;
Each seeming want compensated of course,
Here with degrees of swiftness, there of force;
All in exact proportion to the state;
Nothing to add, and nothing to abate.
Each beast, each insect, happy in its own:
Is Heav'n unkind to Man, and Man alone?
Shall he alone, whom rational we call,
Be pleased with nothing, if not blessed with all?
The bliss of Man (could Pride that blessing find)
Is not to act or think beyond mankind;
No pow'rs of body or of soul to share,
But what his nature and his state can bear.
Why has not Man a microscopic eye?
For this plain reason, Man is not a Fly.

Say what the use, were finer optics giv'n,
T' inspect a mite, not comprehend the heav'n?
Or touch, if tremblingly alive all o'er,
To smart and agonize at ev'ry pore?
Or quick effluvia darting thro' the brain,
Die of a rose in aromatic pain?
If Nature thundered in his op'ning ears,
And stunned him with the music of the spheres,
How would he wish that Heav'n had left him still
The whisp'ring Zephyr, and the purling rill?
Who finds not Providence all good and wise,
Alike in what it gives, and what denies?

    Far as Creation's ample range extends,
The scale of sensual, mental pow'rs ascends:
Mark how it mounts, to Man's imperial race,
From the green myriads in the peopled grass:
What modes of sight betwixt each wide extreme,
The mole's dim curtain, and the lynx's beam:
Of smell, the headlong lioness between,
And hound sagacious on the tainted green:
Of hearing, from the life that fills the flood,
To that which warbles thro' the vernal wood:
The spider's touch, how exquisitely fine!
Feels at each thread, and lives along the line:
In the nice bee, what sense so subtly true
From pois'nous herbs extracts the healing dew:
How Instinct varies in the grov'ling swine,
Compared, half-reas'ning elephant, with thine!
'Twixt that, and Reason, what a nice barrier;[1]
Forever sep'rate, yet forever near!
Remembrance and Reflection how ally'd;
What thin partitions Sense from Thought divide:
And Middle natures, how they long to join,
Yet never pass th'insuperable line!
Without this just gradation, could they be
Subjected, these to those, or all to thee?

The pow'rs of all subdued by thee alone,
Is not thy Reason all these pow'rs in one?

---

[1] to rhyme with near.

The proper study of mankind

Know then thyself, presume not God to scan;
The proper study of Mankind is Man.
Placed on this isthmus of a middle state,
A Being darkly wise, and rudely great:
With too much knowledge for the Sceptic side,
With too much weakness for the Stoic's pride,
He hangs between; in doubt to act, or rest,
In doubt to deem himself a God, or Beast;
In doubt his Mind or Body to prefer;
Born but to die, and reas'ning but to err;
Alike in ignorance, his reason such,
Whether he thinks too little, or too much:
Chaos of Thought and Passion, all confused;
Still by himself abused, or disabused;
Created half to rise, and half to fall;
Great lord of all things, yet a prey to all;
Sole judge of Truth, in endless Error hurled:
The glory, jest, and riddle of the world!

Go, wondrous creature! mount where Science guides,
Go measure earth, weigh air, and state the tides;
Instruct the planets in what orbs to run,
Correct old Time, and regulate the Sun;
Go, soar with Plato to th'empyreal sphere,
To the first good, first perfect, and first fair;
Or tread the mazy round his follow'rs trod,
And quitting sense call imitating God;
As Eastern priests in giddy circles run,
And turn their heads to imitate the Sun.
Go, teach Eternal Wisdom how to rule—
Then drop into thyself, and be a fool!

Superior beings, when of late they saw
A mortal Man unfold all Nature's law,
Admired such wisdom in an earthly shape,
And showed a Newton as we show an Ape.

Could he, whose rules the rapid Comet bind,
Describe or fix one movement of his Mind?

Who saw its fires here rise, and there descend,
Explain his own beginning, or his end?
Alas what wonder! Man's superior part
Unchecked may rise, and climb from art to art;
But when his own great work is but begun,
What Reason weaves, by Passion is undone.

Trace Science then, with Modesty thy guide;
First strip off all her equipage of Pride,
Deduct what is but Vanity, or Dress,
Or Learning's Luxury, or Idleness;
Or tricks to shew the stretch of human brain,
Mere curious pleasure, or ingenious pain;
Expunge the whole, or lop th'excrescent parts
Of all our Vices have created Arts;
Then see how little the remaining sum,
Which served the past, and must the times to come!

Alexander Pope

From EPISTLE TO DR. ARBUTHNOT[1]

Pope speaks:

'Shut, shut the door, good John!' fatigued, I said,
'Tie up the knocker! say I'm sick, I'm dead.
The Dog-star rages! nay, 'tis past a doubt,
All Bedlam, or Parnassus, is let out:
Fire in each eye, and papers in each hand,
They rave, recite, and madden round the land.

What walls can guard me, or what shades can hide?
They pierce my thickets, thro' my Grot they glide,
By land, by water, they renew the charge,
They stop the chariot, and they board the Barge.
No place is sacred, not the Church is free,
Ev'n Sunday shines no Sabbath-day to me:
Then from the Mint walks forth the man of rhyme,
Happy to catch me just at Dinner-time.

Is there a Parson much be-mused in beer,
A maudlin Poetess, a rhyming Peer,

---

[1] Compare with Swift, p. 96.

A Clerk, foredoomed his father's soul to cross,
Who pens a Stanza, when he should engross?
Is there, who, locked from ink and paper, scrawls
With desp'rate charcoal round his darkened walls?
All fly to Twit'nam,[1] and in humble strain
Apply to me, to keep them mad or vain.
Arthur, whose giddy son neglects the Laws,
Imputes to me and my damned works the cause:
Poor Cornus sees his frantic wife elope,
And curses Wit, and Poetry, and Pope.

I lisp'd in numbers

    'Why did I write? What sin to me unknown
Dipt me in ink: my parents', or my own?
As yet a child, nor yet a fool to fame,
I lisped in numbers,[2] for the numbers came.
I left no calling for this idle trade,
No duty broke, no Father disobeyed.
The Muse but served to ease some friend, not Wife,
To help me thro' this long disease, my Life,

Poor guiltless

    'Oh, let me live my own! and die so too!
(To live and die is all I have to do:)
Maintain a Poet's dignity and ease,
And see what friends, and read what books I please:
Above a Patron, tho' I condescend
Sometimes to call a Minister my friend.
I was not born for Courts or great affairs;
I pay my debts, believe, and say my pray'rs;
Can sleep without a Poem in my head,
Nor know, if Dennis be alive or dead.
    Why am I asked what next shall see the light?
Heav'ns! was I born for nothing but to write?
Has Life no joys for me? or (to be grave)
Have I no friend to serve, no soul to save?

---

[1] Twickenham: where Pope had a villa.
[2] metre.

"I found him close with Swift"—"Indeed? no doubt,"
Cries prating Balbus, "something will come out."
'Tis all in vain, deny it as I will.
"No, such a Genius never can lie still;"
And then for mine obligingly mistakes
The first Lampoon Sir Will or Bubo makes.
Poor guiltless I! and can I chuse but smile,
When ev'ry Coxcomb knows me by my *Style*?'

EPISTLE TO MISS BLOUNT
ON HER LEAVING THE TOWN AFTER THE CORONATION[1]

Girls of good family, with ambitious parents, came to London or
Bath, duly chaperoned, for 'the Season'. Jane Austen's novels
describe the process in the eighteenth century; today it can still be
studied in the columns of *The Times* (compare W. M. Praed, p. 245).

As some fond Virgin, whom her mother's care
Drags from the Town to wholesome Country air,
Just when she learns to roll a melting eye,
And hear a spark, yet think no danger nigh;
From the dear man unwilling she must sever,
Yet takes one kiss before she parts for ever:
Thus from the world fair Zephalinda flew,
Saw others happy, and with sighs withdrew;
Not that their pleasures caused her discontent,
She sighed not that they stayed, but that she went.
    She went, to plain-work, and to purling brooks,
Old-fashioned halls, dull Aunts, and croaking rooks:
She went from Op'ra, Park, Assembly, Play,
To morning walks, and pray'rs three hours a day;
To part her time 'twixt reading and bohea,
To muse, and spill her solitary tea,
Or o'er cold coffee trifle with the spoon,
Count the slow clock, and dine exact at noon;

---

[1] of George I in 1715.

Divert her eyes with pictures in the fire,
Hum half a tune, tell stories to the squire;
Up to her godly garret after sev'n,
There starve and pray, for that's the way to heav'n.
    Some Squire, perhaps, you take delight to rack;
Whose game is Whisk,[1] whose treat a toast in sack;[2]
Who visits with a Gun, presents you birds,
Then gives a smacking buss,[3] and cries,—'No words!'
Or with his hound comes hallowing from the stable,
Makes love with nods, and knees beneath a table;
Whose laughs are hearty, tho' his jests are coarse,
And loves you best of all things—but his horse.
    In some fair ev'ning, on your elbow laid,
You dream of Triumphs in the rural shade;
In pensive thought recall the fancy'd scene,
See Coronations rise on ev'ry green;
Before you pass th'imaginary sights
Of Lords, and Earls, and Dukes, and gartered Knights,
While the spread fan o'ershades your closing eyes;
Then give one flirt, and all the vision flies.
Thus vanish sceptres, coronets, and balls,
And leave you in lone woods, or empty walls!
    So when your Slave, at some dear idle time,
(Not plagued with head-aches, or the want of rhyme)
Stands in the streets, abstracted from the crew,
And while he seems to study, thinks of you;
Just when his fancy points your sprightly eyes,
Or sees the blush of soft Parthenia rise,
Gay[4] pats my shoulder, and you vanish quite,
Streets, Chairs, and Coxcombs rush upon my sight;
Vexed to be still in town, I knit my brow,
Look sour, and hum a Tune, as you may now.

---

[1] a card game.
[2] wine.
[3] kiss.
[4] the poet Gay.

Dr. Samuel Johnson (1709-1784)

From **LONDON**

Dr. Johnson—like Blake and Wordsworth—was a poet with a social conscience. That is, he was concerned with the fortunes of his fellow men, unlike his contemporary Pope, who was concerned only with the upper class and a very narrow section of that. Compare Blake, p. 132; Wordsworth, p. 157 and Goldsmith, p. 129.

By numbers here from shame or censure free,
All crimes are safe, but hated poverty.
This, only this, the rigid law pursues,
This, only this, provokes the snarling muse.
The sober trader at a tattered cloak,
Wakes from his dream, and labours for a joke;
With brisker air the silken courtiers gaze,
And turn the varied taunt a thousand ways.
Of all the griefs that harrass the distress'd,
Sure the most bitter is a scornful jest;
Fate never wounds more deep the gen'rous heart,
Than when a blockhead's insult points the dart.
Has heaven reserved, in pity to the poor,
No pathless waste, or undiscovered shore;
No secret island in the boundless main?
No peaceful desart yet unclaimed by Spain?
Quick let us rise, the happy seats explore,
And bear oppression's insolence no more.
This mournful truth is ev'rywhere confessed,
Slow rises Worth, by Poverty depress'd:
But here more slow, where all are slaves to gold,
Where looks are merchandise, and smiles are sold;
Where won by bribes, by flatteries implored,
The groom retails the favours of his lord.

Isaac Watts (1674-1748)

THE SLUGGARD

This is one of the poems which Lewis Carroll parodied in *Alice in Wonderland*:
'Tis the voice of the lobster: I heard him declare
'You have baked me too brown, I must sugar my hair.'
Watts was one of the first writers of hymns; there was no regular hymn-singing in any church before the eighteenth century.

'Tis the voice of the Sluggard; I heard him complain,
'You have wak'd me too soon; I must slumber again.'
And the door on its hinges, so he on his bed,
Turns his sides, and his shoulders, and his heavy head.

'A little more sleep, and a little more slumber,'
Thus he wastes half his days, and his hours without number,
And when he gets up, he sits folding his hands,
Or walks about saunt'ring, or trifling he stands.

I passed by his garden, and saw the wild brier,
The thorn and the thistle grow broader and higher;
The clothes that hang on him are turning to rags;
And his money still wastes, till he starves, or he begs.

I made him a visit, still hoping to find
He had took better care for improving his mind:
He told me his dreams, talked of eating and drinking;
But he scarce reads his Bible, and never loves thinking.

Said I then to my heart, 'Here's a lesson for me,
That man's but a picture of what I might be.
But thanks to my friends for their care in my breeding,
Who taught me betimes to love working and reading.'

Charles Wesley (1707-1788)

IN TEMPTATION

Jesu, Lover of my soul,
　　Let me to Thy bosom fly,
While the nearer waters roll,
　　While the tempest still is high.
Hide me, O my Saviour, hide,
　　Till the storm of life is past:
Safe into the haven guide;
　　O receive my soul at last.

Other refuge have I none:
　　Hangs my helpless soul on Thee.
Leave, ah leave me not alone,
　　Still support and comfort me.
All my trust on Thee is stayed,
　　All my help from Thee I bring;
Cover my defenceless head
　　With the shadow of Thy wing.

Wilt Thou not regard my call?
　　Wilt Thou not accept my prayer?
Lo, I sink, I faint, I fall!
　　Lo, on Thee I cast my care.
Reach me out Thy gracious hand!
　　While I of Thy strength receive,
Hoping against hope I stand,
　　Dying, and behold I live!

Thou, O Christ, art all I want;
　　More than all in Thee I find.
Raise the fallen, cheer the faint,
　　Heal the sick, and lead the blind.
Just and holy is Thy Name;
　　I am all unrighteousness:
False and full of sin I am;
　　Thou art full of truth and grace.

Plenteous grace with Thee is found,
Grace to cover all my sin:
Let the healing streams abound,
Make and keep me pure within.
Thou of Life the Fountain art:
Freely let me take of Thee:
Spring Thou up within my heart
Rise to all eternity.

Thomas Gray (1716-1771)

ELEGY WRITTEN IN A COUNTRY CHURCH-YARD

This *Elegy,* with Keats's *Ode to a Nightingale*:
   My heart aches, and a drowsy numbness pains
   My sense, as though of hemlock I had drunk,
—is probably the best-known poem in the language. Yet, when Gray
sent it to his friend Horace Walpole in 1750, he roughly called it just
'a thing with an end to it'. The fact is, Gray wrote very few poems at
all, and finished fewer. There is hardly a line of this poem which has
not some classical parallel, yet it is unique. It is worth noticing the
number of adjectives in it and how far the poem depends upon them.
Gray didn't care twopence about publication; nearly everything was
in MS at his death. He was idiosyncratic in his life and work, and his
work should never be linked, as it has been, with that of William
Collins. Compare with Charles Cotton's *Evening*, p. 84.

The Curfew tolls the knell of parting day,
The lowing herd wind slowly o'er the lea,
The plowman homeward plods his weary way,
And leaves the world to darkness and to me.

Now fades the glimmering landscape on the sight,
And all the air a solemn stillness holds,
Save where the beetle wheels his droning flight,
And drowsy tinklings lull the distant folds;

Save that from yonder ivy-mantled tow'r
The mopeing owl does to the moon complain
Of such, as wand'ring near her secret bow'r,
Molest her ancient solitary reign.

Beneath those rugged elms, that yew-tree's shade,
Where heaves the turf in many a mould'ring heap,
Each in his narrow cell for ever laid,
The rude Forefathers of the hamlet sleep.

The breezy call of incense-breathing Morn,
The swallow twitt'ring from the straw-built shed,
The cock's shrill clarion, or the echoing horn,
No more shall rouse them from their lowly bed.

For them no more the blazing hearth shall burn,
Or busy housewife ply her evening care:
No children run to lisp their sire's return,
Or climb his knees the envied kiss to share.

Oft did the harvest to their sickle yield,
Their furrow oft the stubborn glebe has broke;
How jocund did they drive their team afield!
How bowed the woods beneath their sturdy stroke!

Let not Ambition mock their useful toil,
Their homely joys, and destiny obscure;
Nor Grandeur hear with a disdainful smile,
The short and simple annals of the poor.

The boast of heraldry, the pomp of pow'r,
And all that beauty, all that wealth e'er gave,
Awaits alike th' inevitable hour.
The paths of glory lead but to the grave.

Nor you, ye Proud, impute to These the fault,
If Mem'ry o'er their Tomb no Trophies raise,
Where thro' the long-drawn aisle and fretted vault
The pealing anthem swells the note of praise.

Can storied urn or animated bust
Back to its mansion call the fleeting breath?
Can Honour's voice provoke the silent dust,
Or Flatt'ry sooth the dull cold ear of Death?

Perhaps in this neglected spot is laid
Some heart once pregnant with celestial fire;
Hands, that the rod of empire might have sway'd,
Or wak'd to extasy the living lyre.

But Knowledge to their eyes her ample page
Rich with the spoils of time did ne'er unroll;
Chill Penury repress'd their noble rage,
And froze the genial current of the soul.

Full many a gem of purest ray serene,
The dark unfathomed caves of ocean bear:
Full many a flower is born to blush unseen,
And waste its sweetness on the desert air.

Some village-Hampden, that with dauntless breast
The little Tyrant of his fields withstood;
Some mute inglorious Milton here may rest,
Some Cromwell guiltless of his country's blood.

Th' applause of list'ning senates to command,
The threats of pain and ruin to despise,
To scatter plenty o'er a smiling land,
And read their hist'ry in a nation's eyes,

Their lot forbad: nor circumscrib'd alone
Their growing virtues, but their crimes confin'd;
Forbad to wade through slaughter to a throne,
And shut the gates of mercy on mankind,

The struggling pangs of conscious truth to hide,
To quench the blushes of ingenuous shame,
Or heap the shrine of Luxury and Pride
With incense kindled at the Muse's flame.

Far from the madding crowd's ignoble strife,
Their sober wishes never learn'd to stray;
Along the cool sequestered vale of life
They kept the noiseless tenor of their way.

Yet ev'n these bones from insult to protect
Some frail memorial still erected nigh,
With uncouth rhymes and shapeless sculpture deck'd,
Implores the passing tribute of a sigh.

Their name, their years, spelt by th' unletter'd muse,
The place of fame and elegy supply:
And many a holy text around she strews,
That teach the rustic moralist to die.

For who to dumb Forgetfulness a prey,
This pleasing anxious being e'er resign'd,
Left the warm precincts of the chearful day,
Nor cast one longing ling'ring look behind?

On some fond breast the parting soul relies,
Some pious drops the closing eye requires;
Ev'n from the tomb the voice of Nature cries,
Ev'n in our Ashes live their wonted Fires.

For thee, who mindful of th' unhonoured Dead
Dost in these lines their artless tale relate;
If chance, by lonely contemplation led,
Some kindred Spirit shall inquire thy fate,

Haply some hoary-headed Swain may say,
'Oft have we seen him at the peep of dawn
Brushing with hasty steps the dews away
To meet the sun upon the upland lawn.

'There at the foot of yonder nodding beech
That wreathes its old fantastic roots so high,
His listless length at noontide would he stretch,
And pore upon the brook that babbles by.

'Hard by yon wood, now smiling as in scorn,
Mutt'ring his wayward fancies he would rove,
Now drooping, woeful wan, like one forlorn,
Or crazed with care, or crossed in hopeless love.

'One morn I missed him on the 'custom'd hill,
Along the heath and near his fav'rite tree;
Another came; nor yet beside the rill,
Nor up the lawn, nor at the wood was he;

'The next with dirges due in sad array
Slow thro' the church-way path we saw him born.
Approach and read (for thou can'st read) the lay,
Grav'd on the stone beneath yon aged thorn.'

The Epitaph

Here rests his head upon the lap of Earth
A Youth to Fortune and to Fame unknown.
Fair Science frown'd not on his humble birth,
And Melancholy mark'd him for her own.

Large was his bounty, and his soul sincere,
Heav'n did a recompence as largely send:
He gave to Mis'ry all he had, a tear,
He gain'd from Heav'n ('twas all he wish'd) a friend.

No farther seek his merits to disclose,
Or draw his frailties from their dread abode,
(There they alike in trembling hope repose,)
The bosom of his Father and his God.

Christopher Smart (1722-1771)

From **JUBILATE AGNO**

For I will consider my Cat Jeoffry

Smart was shut up in a mad-house. From reading his poems, would
you think he was mad?

For I will consider my Cat Jeoffry.
For he is the servant of the Living God, duly and daily serving
him.
For at the first glance of the glory of God in the East he
worships in his way.
For is this done by wreathing his body seven times round with
elegant quickness.
For then he leaps up to catch the musk, which is the blessing of
God upon his prayer.
For he rolls upon prank to work it in.
For having done duty and received blessing he begins to
consider himself.
For this he performs in ten degrees.
For first he looks upon his fore-paws to see if they are clean.
For secondly he kicks up behind to clear away there.
For thirdly he works it upon stretch with the fore-paws
extended.
For fourthly he sharpens his paws by wood.

For fifthly he washes himself.

For sixthly he rolls upon wash.

For seventhly he fleas himself, that he may not be interrupted upon the beat.

For eighthly he rubs himself against a post.

For ninthly he looks up for his instructions.

For tenthly he goes in quest of food.

For having considered God and himself he will consider his neighbour.

For if he meets another cat he will kiss her in kindness.

For when he takes his prey he plays with it to give it chance.

For one mouse in seven escapes by his dallying.

For when his day's work is done his business more properly begins.

For he keeps the Lord's watch in the night against the adversary.

For he counteracts the powers of darkness by his electrical skin and glaring eyes.

For he counteracts the Devil, who is death, by brisking about the life.

For in his morning orisons he loves the sun and the sun loves him.

For he is of the tribe of Tiger.

For the Cherub Cat is a term of the Angel Tiger.

For he has the subtlety and hissing of a serpent, which in goodness he suppresses.

For he will not do destruction, if he is well-fed, neither will he spit without provocation.

For he purrs in thankfulness, when God tells him he's a good Cat.

For he is an instrument for the children to learn benevolence upon.

For every house is incompleat without him and a blessing is lacking in the spirit.

He sung of God—the mighty source
Of all things—the stupendous force
    On which all strength depends;
From whose right arm, beneath whose eyes,
All period, pow'r, and enterprize
    Commences, reigns, and ends.

Angels—their ministry and meed,
Which to and fro with blessings speed,
    Or with their citterns[1] wait;
Where Michael with his millions bows,
Where dwells the seraph and his spouse,
    The cherub and her mate.

Of man—the semblance and effect
Of God and Love—the Saint elect
    For infinite applause—
To rule the land, and briny broad,
To be laborious in his laud,
    And heroes in his cause.

The world—the clust'ring spheres he made,
The glorious light, the soothing shade,
    Dale, champaign, grove, and hill;
The multitudinous abyss,
Where secrecy remains in bliss,
    And wisdom hides her skill.

Trees, plants, and flow'rs—of virtuous root;
Gem yielding blossom, yielding fruit,
    Choice gums and precious balm;
Bless ye the nosegay in the vale,
And with the sweetness of the gale
    Enrich the thankful psalm.

---

[1] zithers: stringed instruments.

Of fowl—e'en ev'ry beak and wing
Which cheer the winter, hail the spring,
　　That live in peace or prey;
They that make music, or that mock,
The quail, the brave domestic cock,
　　The raven, swan, and jay.

Of fishes—ev'ry size and shape,
Which Nature frames of light escape,
　　Devouring man to shun:
The shells are in the wealthy deep,
The shoals upon the surface leap,
　　And love the glancing sun.

Of beasts—the beaver plods his task;
While the sleek tigers roll and bask,
　　Nor yet the shades arouse;
Her cave the mining coney scoops;
Where o'er the mead the mountain stoops.
　　The kids exult and brouse.

Of gems—their virtue and their price,
Which hid in earth from man's device,
　　Their darts of lustre sheathe;
The jasper of the master's stamp,
The topaz blazing like a lamp
　　Among the mines beneath.

Blest was the tenderness he felt
When to his graceful harp he knelt,
　　And did for audience call;
When satan with his hand he quell'd,
And in serene suspense he held
　　The frantic throes of Saul. . . .

Strong is the horse upon his speed;
Strong in pursuit the rapid glede,
　　Which makes at once his game;
Strong the tall ostrich on the ground;
Strong through the turbulent profound
　　Shoots xiphias to his aim.

Strong is the lion—like a coal
His eyeball—like a bastion's mole
　　His chest against the foes;
Strong, the gier-eagle on his sail,
Strong against tide, th' enormous whale
　　Emerges as he goes.

But stronger still, in earth and air,
And in the sea, the man of pray'r,
　　And far beneath the tide;
And in the seat to faith assign'd,
Where ask is have, where seek is find
　　Where knock is open wide.

Beauteous the fleet before the gale;
Beauteous the multitudes in mail,
　　Rank'd arms and crested heads:
Beauteous the garden's umbrage mild,
Walk, water, meditated wild,
　　And all the bloomy beds.

Beauteous the moon full on the lawn;
And beauteous, when the veil's withdrawn,
　　The virgin to her spouse:
Beauteous the temple decked and filled,
When to the heav'n of heav'ns they build
　　Their heart-directed vows.

Beauteous, yea beauteous more than these,
The shepherd king upon his knees,
    For his momentous trust;
With wish of infinite conceit,
For man, beast, mute, the small and great,
    And prostrate dust to dust.

Precious the bounteous widow's mite;
And precious, for extreme delight,
    The largess from the churl:
Precious the ruby's blushing blaze,
And alba's blest imperial rays,
    And pure cerulean pearl.

Precious the penitential tear;
And precious is the sigh sincere,
    Acceptable to God:
And precious are the winning flow'rs,
In gladsome Israel's feast of bow'rs,
    Bound on the hallow'd sod.

More precious that diviner part
Of David, ev'n the Lord's own heart,
    Great, beautiful, and new:
In all things where it was intent,
In all extremes, in each event,
    Proof—answ'ring true to true.

Glorious the sun in mid career;
Glorious th'assembled fires appear;
    Glorious the comet's train:
Glorious the trumpet and alarm;
Glorious th'almighty stretched-out arm;
    Glorious th'enraptured main:

Glorious the northern lights a-stream;
Glorious the song, when God's the theme;
  Glorious the thunder's roar;
Glorious hosannah from the den;
Glorious the catholic amen;
  Glorious the martyr's gore:

Glorious—more glorious, is the crown
Of Him that brought salvation down
  By meekness, called thy Son;
Thou that stupendous truth believed,
And now the matchless deed's achieved,
  Determin'd, dar'd, *and* done.

William Cowper (1731-1800)

I AM MONARCH OF ALL I SURVEY

Verses supposed to be written by Alexander Selkirk, during his Solitary
Abode in the Island of Juan Fernandez.

Alexander Selkirk was the original of Daniel Defoe's *Robinson Crusoe*.
At the turn of the century, a Captain Woodes Rogers wrote an
account of finding Selkirk on Juan Fernandez in 1709.

I am monarch of all I survey,
  My right there is none to dispute;
From the centre all round to the sea,
  I am lord of the fowl and the brute.
O Solitude! where are the charms
  That sages have seen in thy face?
Better dwell in the midst of alarms,
  Than reign in this horrible place.

I am out of humanity's reach,
    I must finish my journey alone,
Never hear the sweet music of speech;
    I start at the sound of my own.
The beasts, that roam over the plain,
    My form with indifference see;
They are so unacquainted with man,
    Their tameness is shocking to me.

Society, friendship, and love,
    Divinely bestowed upon man,
Oh, had I the wings of a dove,
    How soon would I taste you again!
My sorrows I then might assuage
    In the ways of religion and truth,
Might learn from the wisdom of age,
    And be cheered by the sallies of youth.

Religion! what treasure untold
    Resides in that heavenly word!
More precious than silver and gold,
    Or all that this earth can afford.
But the sound of the church-going bell
    These valleys and rocks never heard,
Never sighed at the sound of a knell,
    Or smiled when a sabbath appeared.

Ye winds, that have made me your sport,
    Convey to this desolate shore
Some cordial endearing report
    Of a land I shall visit no more.
My friends, do they now and then send
    A wish or a thought after me?
Oh, tell me I yet have a friend,
    Though a friend I am never to see.

How fleet is a glance of the mind!
    Compared with the speed of its flight,
The tempest itself lags behind,
    And the swift-wing'd arrows of light.
When I think of my own native land,
    In a moment I seem to be there;
But alas! recollection at hand
    Soon hurries me back to despair.

But the sea-fowl is gone to her nest,
    The beast is laid down in his lair,
Even here is a season of rest,
    And I to my cabin repair.
There's mercy in every place;
    And mercy, encouraging thought!
Gives even affliction a grace,
    And reconciles man to his lot.

THE CONTRITE HEART

Isaiah, 57:15

The Lord will happiness divine
    On contrite hearts bestow;
Then tell me, gracious God, is mine
    A contrite heart, or no?

I hear, but seem to hear in vain,
    Insensible as steel;
If ought is felt, 'tis only pain,
    To find I cannot feel.

I sometimes think myself inclined
    To love thee, if I could;
But often feel another mind,
    Averse to all that's good.

My best desires are faint and few,
    I fain would strive for more;
But when I cry, 'My strength renew!'
    Seem weaker than before.

Thy saints are comforted, I know,
    And love thy house of prayer;
I therefore go where others go,
    But find no comfort there.

O make this heart rejoice, or ache;
    Decide this doubt for me;
And if it be not broken, break,—
    And heal it if it be!

THE CASTAWAY

This is probably the last poem that Cowper wrote. All his life he was subject to fits of increasing melancholy and, as poets often do, in this poem he is saying something at two levels—about being a real castaway and about being a spiritual castaway himself. He *was* 'whelmed in deep gulfs', what we would now call medically 'a manic depressive'. He was a very tender gentle man and this is reflected in many of his poems; yet everybody knows him by a poem called *The Diverting History of John Gilpin,* though nothing could really be further from what he was like as a person.

Obscurest night involved the sky,
    Th'Atlantic billows roared,
When such a destined wretch as I,
    Washed headlong from on board,
Of friends, of hope, of all bereft,
His floating home forever left.

No braver chief could Albion boast
    Than he with whom he went,
Nor ever ship left Albion's coast
    With warmer wishes sent.
He loved them both, but both in vain,
Nor him beheld, nor her again.

Not long beneath the whelming brine,
    Expert to swim, he lay;
Nor soon he felt his strength decline,
    Or courage die away;
But waged with death a lasting strife,
Supported by despair of life.

He shouted: nor his friends had failed
    To check the vessel's course,
But so the furious blast prevailed
    That, pitiless perforce,
They left their outcast mate behind,
And scudded still before the wind.

Some succour yet they could afford;
    And, such as storms allow,
The cask, the coop, the floated cord,
    Delayed not to bestow.
But he (they knew) nor ship nor shore,
Whate'er they gave, should visit more.

Nor, cruel as it seemed, could he
    Their haste himself condemn,
Aware that flight, in such a sea,
    Alone could rescue them;
Yet bitter felt it still to die
Deserted, and his friends so nigh.

He long survives, who lives an hour
    In ocean, self-upheld;
And so long he, with unspent pow'r,
    His destiny repelled;
And ever, as the minutes flew,
Entreated help, or cried—'Adieu!'

At length, his transient respite past,
    His comrades, who before
Had heard his voice in ev'ry blast,
    Could catch the sound no more.
For then, by toil subdued, he drank
The stifling wave, and then he sank.

No poet wept him: but the page
    Of narrative sincere,
That tells his name, his worth, his age,
    Is wet with Anson's[1] tear;
And tears by bards or heroes shed
Alike immortalize the dead.

I therefore purpose not, or dream,
    Descanting on his fate,
To give the melancholy theme
    A more enduring date;
But misery still delights to trace
Its semblance in another's case.

No voice divine the storm allayed,
    No light propitious shone;
When, snatched from all effectual aid,
    We perished, each alone:
But I beneath a rougher sea,
And whelmed in deeper gulfs than he.

---

[1] Cowper read this story in *Anson's Voyages*.

Oliver Goldsmith (1728-1774)

From THE DESERTED VILLAGE

Contrast *A Christmas Carrol*, p. 52 and Compare *Glenaradale*, p. 308.

Ill fares the land

Sweet smiling village, loveliest of the lawn,
Thy sports are fled, and all thy charms withdrawn;
Amidst thy bowers the tyrant's hand is seen,
And desolation saddens all thy green:
One only master grasps the whole domain,
And half a tillage stints thy smiling plain;
No more thy glassy brook reflects the day,
But choaked with sedges, works its weedy way;
Along thy glades, a solitary guest,
The hollow-sounding bittern guards its nest;
Amidst thy desert walks the lapwing flies,
And tires their ecchoes with unvaried cries.
Sunk are thy bowers, in shapeless ruin all,
And the long grass o'ertops the mouldering wall;
And, trembling, shrinking from the spoiler's hand,
Far, far away, thy children leave the land.
    Ill fares the land, to hastening ills a prey,
Where wealth accumulates, and men decay:
Princes and lords may flourish, or may fade;
A breath can make them, as a breath has made;
But a bold peasantry, their country's pride,
When once destroyed, can never be supplied.

Barren Splendour

Ye friends to truth, ye statesmen, who survey
The rich man's joys encrease, the poor's decay,
'Tis yours to judge, how wide the limits stand
Between a splendid and a happy land.
Proud swells the tide with loads of freighted ore,
And shouting Folly hails them from her shore;
Hoards even beyond the miser's wish abound,
And rich men flock from all the world around.

E*   129

Yet count our gains. This wealth is but a name
That leaves our useful products still the same.
Not so the loss. The man of wealth and pride
Takes up a space that many poor supplied;
Space for his lake, his park's extended bounds,
Space for his horses, equipage, and hounds;
The robe that wraps his limbs in silken sloth,
Has robbed the neighbouring fields of half their growth;
His seat, where solitary sports are seen,
Indignant spurns the cottage from the green;
Around the world each needful product flies,
For all the luxuries the world supplies.
While thus the land, adorned for pleasure, all
In barren splendour feebly waits the fall.

William Blake (1757-1827)

THE DIVINE IMAGE

William Blake was an eccentric, a man quite unlike other men of his
time, or any other. He was a painter as well as a poet, and he literally
made his books by hand. He engraved the words and designs; he
'printed' them, bound them, coloured the pages himself and,
occasionally, sold them! He was a man who saw 'visions' of God and
the angels, in which he entirely believed; in truth he was a Christian
of a very rare sort—a man whose beliefs in the teaching of the New
Testament controlled his life.

To Mercy, Pity, Peace, and Love
All pray in their distress;
And to these virtues of delight
Return their thankfulness.

For Mercy, Pity, Peace, and Love
Is God, our father dear,
And Mercy, Pity, Peace, and Love
Is Man, his child and care.

For Mercy has a human heart,
Pity a human face,
And Love, the human form divine,
And Peace, the human dress.

Then every man, of every clime,
That prays in his distress,
Prays to the human form divine,
Love, Mercy, Pity, Peace.

And all must love the human form,
In heathen, turk, or jew;
Where Mercy, Love, and Pity dwell
There God is dwelling too.

A POISON TREE

I was angry with my friend:
I told my wrath, my wrath did end.
I was angry with my foe:
I told it not, my wrath did grow.

And I watered it in fears,
Night and morning with my tears;
And I sunnèd it with smiles,
And with soft deceitful wiles.

And it grew both day and night,
Till it bore an apple bright;
And my foe beheld it shine,
And he knew that it was mine,

And into my garden stole
When the night had veiled the pole:
In the morning glad I see
My foe outstretched beneath the tree.

William Blake

LONDON

Compare with poems by Johnson, etc., p. 109, 162 and 364.

I wander thro' each chartered street,
Near where the chartered Thames does flow,
And mark in every face I meet
Marks of weakness, marks of woe.

In every cry of every Man,
In every Infant's cry of fear,
In every voice, in every ban,
The mind-forged manacles I hear.

How the Chimney-sweeper's cry
Every black'ning Church appalls;
And the hapless Soldier's sigh
Runs in blood down Palace walls.

But most thro' midnight streets I hear
How the youthful Harlot's curse
Blasts the new born Infant's tear,
And blights with plagues the Marriage hearse.

IF YOU TRAP THE MOMENT

If you trap the moment before it's ripe,
The tears of repentance you'll certainly wipe;
But if once you let the ripe moment go
You can never wipe off the tears of woe.

O LAPWING

O Lapwing, thou fliest around the heath,
Nor seest the net that is spread beneath.
Why dost thou not fly among the corn fields?
They cannot spread nets where a harvest yields.

I ASKED A THIEF

I askèd a thief to steal me a peach:
He turned up his eyes.
I asked a lithe lady to lie her down:
Holy and meek she cries.

As soon as I went an angel came:
He winked at the thief
And smiled at the dame,
And without one word spoke
Had a peach from the tree,
And 'twixt earnest and joke
Enjoyed the Lady.

ETERNITY

He who binds to himself a joy
Does the wingèd life destroy;
But he who kisses the joy as it flies
Lives in eternity's sun rise.

William Blake

From THE EVERLASTING GOSPEL

Was Jesus humble?

Was Jesus Humble? or did he
Give any proofs of Humility?
When but a Child he ran away
And left his Parents in dismay.
When they had wondered three days long
These were the words upon his Tongue:
'No Earthly Parents I confess:
I am doing my Father's business.'
When the rich learned Pharisee
Came to consult him secretly,
Upon his heart with Iron pen
He wrote, 'Ye must be born again.'
He was too Proud to take a bribe;
He spoke with authority, not like a Scribe.
He says with most consummate Art,
'Follow me, I am meek and lowly of heart,'
As that is the only way to Escape
The Miser's net and the Glutton's trap.
He who loves his Enemies, hates his Friends;
This is surely not what Jesus intends;
He must mean the meer love of Civility,
And so he must mean concerning Humility;
But he acts with triumphant, honest pride,
And this is the Reason Jesus died.
If he had been Antichrist, Creeping Jesus,
He'd have done anything to please us:
Gone sneaking into the Synagogues
And not used the Elders and Priests like Dogs,
But humble as a Lamb or an Ass,
Obey himself to Caiaphas.

Enion's Song

In Blake's long poems, called *Prophetic Books,* he invented a strange
mythical world peopled with symbolic characters very difficult to
understand without much study and reading. But much of what he
said in the poems can be read and understood without the necessity
of knowing who the characters represent.

'I am made to sow the thistle for wheat, the nettle for a
 nourishing dainty.
I have planted a false oath in the earth; it has brought forth a
 poison tree.
I have chosen the serpent for a councillor, and the dog
 for a schoolmaster to my children.
I have blotted out from light and living the dove and
 nightingale,
And I have caused the earth worm to beg from door to door.

'I have taught the thief a secret path into the house of the just.
I have taught pale artifice to spread his nets upon the morning.
My heavens are brass, my earth is iron, my moon a clod of clay,
My sun a pestilence burning at noon and a vapour of death in
 night.

'What is the price of Experience? do men buy it for a song?
Or wisdom for a dance in the street? No, it is bought with the
 price
Of all that a man hath, his house, his wife, his children.
Wisdom is sold in the desolate market where none come to buy,
And in the withered field where the farmer plows for bread in
 vain.

'It is an easy thing to triumph in the summer's sun
And in the vintage and to sing on the waggon loaded with corn.
It is an easy thing to talk of patience to the afflicted,
To speak the laws of prudence to the houseless wanderer,

To listen to the hungry raven's cry in wintry season
When the red blood is filled with wine and with the marrow of
lambs.

'It is an easy thing to laugh at wrathful elements,
To hear the dog howl at the wintry door, the ox in the slaughter-
house moan;
To see a god on every wind and a blessing on every blast;
To hear sounds of love in the thunderstorm that destroys our
enemies' house;
To rejoice in the blight that covers his field, and the sickness
that cuts off his children,
While our olive and vine sing and laugh round our door, and
our children bring fruits and flowers.

'Then the groan and the dolor are quite forgotten, and the slave
grinding at the mill,
And the captive in chains, and the poor in the prison, and the
soldier in the field
When the shattered bone hath laid him groaning among the
happier dead.

'It is an easy thing to rejoice in the tents of prosperity:
Thus could I sing and thus rejoice: but it is not so with me.'

The English have always had a penchant for the 'Epigram'—a short pithy saying of two or four lines (sometimes expanded to six) often of personal criticism, but always with a kind of social wit. Dr. Johnson, author of our greatest dictionary, could write of a very fat friend:

> When Tadlow walks the streets the paviours cry
> 'God bless you, sir!' and lay their rammers by.

Blake is often called 'mad'; Johnson is the essence of commonsense. Either could have written:

> A petty sneaking knave I knew—
> O Mr. Cromek, how do ye do?

Blake's epigrams show him in a sharp light—shrewd, witty, caustic and gay. The epigram is a verse form anyone can try to use, and should. In Blake you will find some of the best ever written.

> I mock thee not, though I by thee am mockèd,
> Thou call'st me madman, but I call thee blockhead.

I

Great things are done when Men and Mountains meet;
This is not done by Jostling in the Street.

II

If you play a Game of Chance, know, before you begin,
If you are benevolent you will never win.

Robert Burns did not come from the 'educated' class either in London or Edinburgh; he was simply a man of 'independent mind' with a natural genius for writing poetry. It is not enough to think of him as the national poet of Scotland, for this is to diminish his greatness. He was a great lyric poet and he drew on the country life he found round him and on his own philosophy of life. He wrote his own words to existing folk or popular tunes sometimes, but in everything he did his own words apply: 'rank is not the guinea stamp'. He was a poet who set his own stamp upon everything he wrote, whether it was in dialect or in 'correct' English. In the Age of Reason he was able to express the deepest emotions in a way that has made his love-songs universal and timeless. Like Blake he is a truly original writer and, as with Blake, critics have always tried to fit him into some movement or other. If anyone anticipated the Romantic Revival, it was Burns; but if you'd asked him what that meant, it is unlikely he would have known.

A MAN'S A MAN FOR A' THAT

Is there, for honest poverty,
    That hangs his head, and a' that?
The coward slave, we pass him by,
    We dare be poor for a' that!
For a' that, and a' that,
    Our toil's obscure, and a' that;
The rank is but the guinea-stamp,
    The man's the gowd[1] for a' that.

What though on hamely fare we dine,
    Wear hodden gray, and a' that;
Gi'e fools their silks, and knaves their wine,
    A man's a man for a' that!
For a' that, and a' that,
    Their tinsel show, and a' that;
The honest man, though e'er sae poor,
    Is king o' men for a' that.

---

[1] gold.

Ye see yon birkie, ca'd a lord,
    Wha struts, and stares, and a' that;
Though hundreds worship at his word,
    He's but a coof[1] for a' that!
For a' that, and a' that,
    His riband, star, and a' that;
The man of independent mind,
    He looks and laughs at a' that.

A king can mak a belted knight,
    A marquis, duke, and a' that;
But an honest man's aboon his might—
    Guid faith, he maunna fa' that!
For a' that, and a' that,
    Their dignities, and a' that,
The pith o' sense, and pride o' worth,
    Are higher ranks than a' that.

Then let us pray that come it may—
    As come it will for a' that—
That sense and worth, o'er a' the earth,
    May bear the gree,[2] and a' that.
For a' that, and a' that,
    It's comin' yet, for a' that,
That man to man, the warld o'er,
    Shall brothers be for a' that!

---

[1] fool.
[2] take the prize.

THE FAREWELL

It was a' for our rightfu' king
    We left fair Scotland's strand;
It was a' for our rightfu' king,
      We e'er saw Irish land, my dear,
      We e'er saw Irish land.

Now a' is done that men can do,
    And a' is done in vain:
My Love and Native Land fareweel,
      For I maun cross the main, my dear,
      For I maun cross the main.

He turned him reet and roun' about,
    Upon the Irish shore,
And gae his bridle-reins a shake,
      With, adieu for evermore, my dear,
      With, adieu for evermore!

The soger[1] frae the wars returns,
    The sailor frae the main;
But I hae parted frae my Love,
      Never to meet again, my dear,
      Never to meet again!

When day is gane, and night is come,
    And a' folk boun' to sleep;
I think on him that's far awa,
      The lee-lang nicht, and weep, my dear,
      The lee-lang nicht and weep.

---

[1] soldier.

TO A MOUSE

Wee, sleekit, cowrin', tim'rous beastie,
Oh, what a panic's in thy breastie!
Thou needna start awa' sae hasty,
      Wi' bick'ring brattle;
I wad be laith to rin and chase thee
      Wi' murd'ring pattle![1]

I'm truly sorry man's dominion
Has broken nature's social union,
And justifies that ill opinion
      Which maks thee startle
At me, thy poor earth-born companion
      And fellow-mortal.

I doubt na, whyles, but thou may thieve;
What then? poor beastie, thou maun[2] live!
A daimen icker[3] in a thrave[4]
      'S a sma' request:
I'll get a blessin' wi' the lave,
      And never miss't!

Thy wee bit housie, too, in ruin!
Its silly wa's the win's are strewin'!
And naething now to big[5] a new ane
      O' foggage green!
And bleak December's winds ensuin',
      Baith snell and keen!

---

[1] tool for cleaning a plough share.
[2] must.
[3] ear of corn.
[4] bundle of twenty-four sheaves.
[5] build.

Thou saw the fields laid bare and waste,
And weary winter comin' fast,
And cozie here, beneath the blast,
      Thou thought to dwell,
Till, crash! the cruel coulter past
      Out through thy cell.

That wee bit heap o' leaves and stibble
Has cost thee mony a weary nibble!
Now thou's turned out for a' thy trouble,
      But house or hald,
To thole the winter's sleety dribble,
      And cranreuch[1] cauld!

But, Mousie, thou art no thy lane
In proving foresight may be vain;
The best-laid schemes o' mice and men
      Gang aft a-gley,
And lea'e us nought but grief and pain
      For promised joy.

Still thou art blest, compared wi' me!
The present only toucheth thee;
But, och! I backward cast my ee
      On prospects drear;
And forward, though I canna see,
      I guess and fear.

---

[1] hoar frost.

From **THE JOLLY BEGGARS**

See! the smoking bowl before us,
Mark our jovial ragged ring!
Round and round take up the chorus,
And in raptures let us sing,

A fig for those by law protected!
Liberty's a glorious feast!
Courts for cowards were erected,
Churches built to please the priest.

What is title? what is treasure?
What is reputation's care?
If we lead a life of pleasure,
'Tis no matter how or where!

With the ready trick and fable,
Round we wander all the day;
And at night, in barn or stable,
Hug our doxies on the hay.

Does the train-attended carriage
Through the country lighter rove?
Does the sober bed of marriage
Witness brighter scenes of love?

Life is all a *variorum,*
We regard not how it goes;
Let them cant about *decorum*
Who have characters to lose.

Here's to budgets, bags and wallets!
Here's to all the wandering train!
Here's our ragged brats and callets!
One and all cry out, Amen!

A fig for those by law protected!
Liberty's a glorious feast!
Courts for cowards were erected,
Churches built to please the priest.

WHISTLE, AND I'LL COME TO YE, MY LAD

O whistle, and I'll come to ye, my lad;
O whistle, and I'll come to ye, my lad:
Though father and mither and a' should gae mad,
O whistle, and I'll come to ye, my lad.

But warily tent when ye come to court me,
And come na unless the back-yett[1] be a-jee;[2]
Syne up the back-stile, and let naebody see,
And come as ye were na comin' to me,
And come as ye were na comin' to me.

At kirk, or at market, whene'er ye meet me,
Gang by me as though that ye cared na a flie;
But steal me a blink o' your bonnie black ee,
Yet look as ye were na lookin' at me,
Yet look as ye were na lookin' at me.

---

[1] back gate.
[2] ajar.

Aye vow and protest that ye care na for me,
And whyles ye may lightly my beauty a wee;
But court na anither, though jokin' ye be,
For fear that she wyle your fancy frae me,
For fear that she wyle your fancy frae me.

O whistle, and I'll come to ye, my lad;
O whistle, and I'll come to ye, my lad:
Though father and mither and a' should gae mad,
O whistle, and I'll come to ye, my lad.

THE DISCREET HINT

'Lass, when your mither is frae hame,
　　May I but be sae bauld
As come to your bower window,
　　And creep in frae the cauld?
As come to your bower window,
　　And when it's cauld and wat,
Warm me in thy fair bosom—
　　Sweet lass, may I do that?'

'Young man, gin ye should be sae kind,
　　When our gudewife's frae hame,
As come to my bower window,
　　Whar I am laid my lane,[1]
To warm thee in my bosom—
　　Tak tent,[2] I'll tell thee what,
The way to me lies through the kirk—
　　Young man, do ye hear that!'

―――――――

[1] alone.
[2] Take note.

THE TARBOLTON LASSES

If ye gae up to yon hill-tap,
    Ye'll there see bonny Peggy;
She kens her faither is a laird,
    And she forsooth's a leddy.

There Sophy tight, a lassie bright,
    Besides a handsome fortune—
Wha canna win her in a night,
    Has little art in courting.

Gae down by Faile, and taste the ale,
    And tak a look o' Mysie;
She's dour and din, a de'il within,
    But aiblins[1] she may please ye.

If she be shy, her sister try,
    Ye'll maybe fancy Jenny;
If ye'll dispense wi' want o' sense—
    She kens hersel' she's bonny.

As ye gae up by yon hillside,
    Speer[2] in for bonnie Bessie;
She'll gi'e ye a beck, and bid ye licht,
    And handsomely address ye.

There's few sae bonnie, nane sae guid,
    In a' King George' dominion;
If ye should doubt the truth o' this—
    It's Bessie's ain opinion.

---

[1] perhaps.
[2] look.

THE BANKS OF DOON

Ye flowery banks o' bonnic Doon,
    How can ye bloom sae fair?
How can ye chant, ye little birds,
    And I sae fu' o' care?

Thou'll break my heart, thou bonnie bird
    That sings upon the bough;
Thou minds me o' the happy days
    When my fause love was true.

Thou'll break my heart, thou bonnie bird
    That sings beside thy mate;
For sae I sat, and sae I sang,
    And wist na o' my fate.

Aft ha'e I roved by bonnie Doon,
    To see the woodbine twine;
And ilka bird sang o' its love,
    And sae did I o' mine.

Wi' lightsome heart I pu'd a rose
    Frae aff its thorny tree;
And my fause lover staw[1] the rose,
    But left the thorn wi' me.

---

[1] stole.

Robert Burns

MY BONNIE MARY

Go, fetch to me a pint o' wine,
 An' fill it in a silver tassie,[1]
That I may drink before I go
 A service[2] to my bonnie lassie.
The boat rocks at the pier o' Leith;
 Fu' loud the wind blaws frae the ferry;
The ship lies by the Berwick Law,
 And I maun leave my bonnie Mary.

The trumpets sound, the banners fly,
 The glittering spears are rankèd ready;
The shouts o' war are heard afar,
 The battle closes thick and bloody;
But it's not the roar o' sea or shore
 Wad make me langer wish to tarry;
Nor shouts o' war that's heard afar—
 It's leaving thee, my bonnie Mary.

---

[1] drinking-cup.
[2] health.

III

The Romantic Revival

Towards the end of the eighteenth century, as at the beginning of the seventeenth century, there was a new stirring in men's minds. Just as previously, men had thrown off the rule of the Church, and government became secular in fact, so now it was felt that the powers of government were too narrowly confined; that all men had a right to liberty and freedom. This went with a new awareness of the countryside and the movement away from the court and from purely town and social values. The stirring of new ideas and new thoughts was not confined to England. It was strongest in France where the difference between the ruling class and the poor was more flagrantly obvious. Thus Wordsworth, especially in *The Prelude,* hailed the French Revolution as a new dawn of freedom for all mankind.

Naturally, with these new feelings there arose a new desire for expression. The mannered, narrowly artificial language of Dryden and Pope was *not* how ordinary men spoke to each other. The pendulum swung again, away from written language to spoken language.

But one must always beware of the way in which critics group poets who are really very different. 'The Romantic Revival', as it is called, means particularly the poetry of Wordsworth, Coleridge, Keats and Shelley. But on the Continent, *the* poet of the Romantic Revival is Byron whose poetical view looked back:

Thou shalt believe in Milton, Dryden, Pope;

Thou shalt not set up Wordsworth, Coleridge, Southey . . .

The fact is that all these poets were very different, though when it came to politics, Byron and Shelley were equally anti-Royalist, and Keats was not a political poet at all. This is said only as a warning for there is no doubt that in their separate ways these poets did indeed revive and renew the language of poetry. Byron, the aristocrat, in his great satire *Don Juan,* his greatest poem, attacks the society of his time in brilliant, *talkative* verse which has never been matched. This is the true influencing of one poet by another, for Byron's master *was* Pope and Byron began by writing imitation Pope but flowered to write a form of satire entirely original and for his own age.

The disillusion which was felt so acutely by Wordsworth and his fellow poets after the failure of the ideals of the French Revolution is parallelled by the bitter disillusion of young poets with Spain in the 1930's and with Russia in the 1950's. The rise of Napoleon, and the failure of the Revolution to achieve its ideals filled men's minds with the question: What *is* liberty, what *is* true freedom? Shelley was deeply conscious of the problem, as you will see if you read *The Mask of Anarchy* (page 196) or his sonnet, *England in 1819* (page 195). Read the sonnets of Wordsworth, too (pages 165 to 169).

So—to make a generalisation—poets became more and more identified with the ordinary people of their time. Yet Keats's poetry is not social poetry, it is personal and mythological, an exception to the general trend. But one thing is certain: if poets could not actually liberate people—and Byron went to fight for the liberation of Greece and died there—they could and did influence people's ideas and actions. The Romantic Revival is a revival of feeling and a revival of the means to express feeling, in many different styles, which have this one element in common: it is the language of men speaking rather than writing.

> What is Freedom?—ye can tell
> That which slavery is, too well—
> For its very name has grown
> To an echo of your own . . .

Thomas Campbell (1777-1844)

THE PARROT

Poets live with words. All through our literature, from Skelton
onwards, poets have been fascinated by the idea of creatures who
speak or can be taught to speak. Poets would like to talk to lions and
cows and mice and snails. Hence, parrots, as birds that can simulate
man's speech, have a peculiar fascination. There must be hundreds
of poems about parrots (compare Bridges, p. 345).

The deep affections of the breast
    That Heaven to living things imparts
Are not exclusively possessed
    By human hearts.

A parrot from the Spanish Main,
    Full young and early caged, came o'er
With bright wings to the bleak domain
    Of Mulla's shore.

To spicy groves where he had won
    His plumage of resplendent hue,
His native fruits and skies and sun,
    He bade adieu.

For these he changed the smoke of turf,
    A heathery land and misty sky,
And turned on rocks and raging surf
    His golden eye.

But, petted, in our climate cold
    He lived and chattered many a day;
Until with age from green and gold
    His wings grew gray.

At last, when blind and seeming dumb,
    He scolded, laughed, and spoke no more,
A Spanish stranger chanced to come
    To Mulla's shore;

He hailed the bird in Spanish speech;
The bird in Spanish speech replied,
Flapped round his cage with joyous screech,
Dropt down, and died.

Sir Walter Scott (1771-1832)

From MARMION

Flodden's Fatal Field

This was a period when romantic tales in verse, such as Scott wrote,
filled the place now taken by historical novels. Byron, indeed, was
far more popular for his tales—*The Corsair, The Giaour, The Bride of
Abydos*—than for his satire, and Tom Moore was as famed for *Lalla
Rookh, an Oriental Romance,* as for his *Irish Melodies.*

But as they left the darkening heath
More desperate grew the strife of death.
The English shafts in volleys hailed,
In headlong charge their horse assailed;
Front, flank, and rear, the squadrons sweep
To break the Scottish circle deep
        That fought around their king.
But yet, though thick the shafts as snow,
Though charging knights like whirlwinds go,
Though billmen ply the ghastly blow,
        Unbroken was the ring;
The stubborn spearmen still made good
Their dark impenetrable wood,
Each stepping where his comrade stood
        The instant that he fell.
No thought was there of dastard flight;
Linked in the serried phalanx tight,
Groom fought like noble, squire like knight,
        As fearlessly and well;

Till utter darkness closed her wing
O'er their thin host and wounded King.
Then skilful Surrey's sage commands
Led back from strife his shattered bands;
    And from the charge they drew,
As mountain-waves from wasted lands
    Sweep back to ocean blue.
Then did their loss his foemen know;
Their King, their lords, their mightiest low,
They melted from the field, as snow,
When streams are swoln and south winds blow,
    Dissolves in silent dew.
Tweed's echoes heard the ceaseless plash,
    While many a broken band
Disordered through her currents dash,
    To gain the Scottish land;
To town and tower, to down and dale,
To tell red Flodden's dismal tale,
And raise the universal wail.
Tradition, legend, tune, and song
Shall many an age that wail prolong:
Still from the sire the son shall hear
Of the stern strife and carnage drear
    Of Flodden's fatal field,
Where shivered was fair Scotland's spear
    And broken was her shield!

William Wordsworth (1770-1850)

INFLUENCE OF NATURAL OBJECTS IN CALLING FORTH AND STRENGTHENING THE IMAGINATION IN BOYHOOD AND EARLY YOUTH

Wordsworth grew up in the Lake District but he certainly was not just a 'Nature poet' or a country boy. He was intensely interested in the politics not only of England but of Europe; and indeed of any place in the world which was struggling for freedom against tyranny. He travelled widely in France and Germany.

Wisdom and Spirit of the universe!
The Soul, that art the Eternity of thought!
And giv'st to forms and images a breath
And everlasting motion! not in vain,
By day or star-light, thus from my first dawn
Of childhood didst thou intertwine for me
The passions that build up our human soul;
Not with the mean and vulgar works of Man;
But with high objects, with enduring things,
With life and nature; purifying thus
The elements of feeling and of thought,
And sanctifying by such discipline
Both pain and fear,—until we recognise
A grandeur in the beatings of the heart.

Nor was this fellowship vouchsafed to me
With stinted kindness. In November days,
When vapours rolling down the valleys made
A lonely scene more lonesome; among woods
At noon; and 'mid the calm of summer nights,
When, by the margin of the trembling lake,
Beneath the gloomy hills, homeward I went
In solitude, such intercourse was mine:
Mine was it in the fields both day and night,
And by the waters, all the summer long.
And in the frosty season, when the sun
Was set, and, visible for many a mile,
The cottage-windows through the twilight blazed,

I heeded not the summons: happy time
It was indeed for all of us; for me
It was a time of rapture! Clear and loud
The village-clock tolled six—I wheeled about,
Proud and exulting like an untired horse
That cares not for his home.—All shod with steel
We hissed along the polished ice, in games
Confederate, imitative of the chase
And woodland pleasures,—the resounding horn,
The pack loud-chiming, and the hunted hare.
So through the darkness and the cold we flew,
And not a voice was idle: with the din
Smitten, the precipices rang aloud;
The leafless trees and every icy crag
Tinkled like iron; while far-distant hills
Into the tumult sent an alien sound
Of melancholy, not unnoticed while the stars,
Eastward, were sparkling clear, and in the west
The orange sky of evening died away.

    Not seldom from the uproar I retired
Into a silent bay, or sportively
Glanced sideway, leaving the tumultuous throng,
To cut across the reflex of a star;
Image that, flying still before me, gleamed
Upon the glassy plain: and oftentimes,
When we had given our bodies to the wind,
And all the shadowy banks on either side
Came sweeping through the darkness, spinning still
The rapid line of motion, then at once
Have I, reclining back upon my heels,
Stopped short; yet still the solitary cliffs
Wheeled by me—even as if the earth had rolled
With visible motion her diurnal round!
Behind me did they stretch in solemn train,
Feebler and feebler, and I stood and watched
Till all was tranquil as a summer sea.

William Wordsworth

From THE PRELUDE

Boyhood in Cumberland

>   Fair seed-time had my soul, and I grew up
> Fostered alike by beauty and by fear:
> Much favoured in my birthplace, and no less
> In that belovèd Vale to which erelong
> We were transplanted—there were we let loose
> For sports of wider range. Ere I had told
> Ten birth-days, when among the mountain-slopes
> Frost, and the breath of frosty wind, had snapped
> The last autumnal crocus, 'twas my joy
> With store of springes o'er my shoulder hung
> To range the open heights where wood-cocks run
> Among the smooth green turf. Through half the night,
> Scudding away from snare to snare, I plied
> That anxious visitation;—moon and stars
> Were shining o'er my head. I was alone,
> And seemed to be a trouble to the peace
> That dwelt among them. Sometimes it befell
> In these night wanderings, that a strong desire
> O'erpowered my better reason, and the bird
> Which was the captive of another's toil
> Became my prey; and when the deed was done
> I heard among the solitary hills
> Low breathings coming after me, and sounds
> Of undistinguishable motion, steps
> Almost as silent as the turf they trod.
>   Nor less when spring had warmed the cultured Vale,
> Moved we as plunderers where the mother-bird
> Had in high places built her lodge; though mean
> Our object and inglorious, yet the end
> Was not ignoble. Oh! when I have hung
> Above the raven's nest, by knots of grass
> And half-inch fissures in the slippery rock
> But ill sustained, and almost (so it seemed)

Suspended by the blast that blew amain,
Shouldering the naked crag, oh, at that time
While on the perilous ridge I hung alone,
With what strange utterance did the loud dry wind
Blow through my ear! the sky seemed not a sky
Of earth—and with what motion moved the clouds!

London: St. Bartholomew's Fair

What say you, then,
To times, when half the city shall break out
Full of one passion, vengeance, rage, or fear?
To executions, to a street on fire,
Mobs, riots, or rejoicings? From these sights
Take one,—that ancient festival, the Fair,
Holden where martyrs suffered in past time,
And named of St. Bartholomew . . .
What a shock
For eyes and ears! what anarchy and din,
Barbarian and infernal,—a phantasma,
Monstrous in colour, motion, shape, sight, sound!
Below, the open space, through every nook
Of the wide area, twinkles is alive
With heads; the midway region, and above,
Is thronged with staring pictures and huge scrolls,
Dumb proclamations of the Prodigies;
With chattering monkeys dangling from their poles,
And children whirling in their roundabouts;
With those that stretch the neck and strain the eyes,
And crack the voice in rivalship, the crowd
Inviting; with buffoons against buffoons
Grimacing, writhing, screaming—him who grinds
The hurdy-gurdy, at the fiddle weaves,
Rattles the salt-box, thumps the kettle-drum,
And him who at the trumpet puffs his cheeks,
The silver-collared Negro with his timbrel,
Equestrians, tumblers, women, girls, and boys,
Blue-breeched, pink-vested, with high-towering plumes:
All moveables of wonder, from all parts,

And here—Albinos, painted Indians, Dwarfs,
The Horse of knowledge, and the learned Pig,
The Stone-eater, the man that swallows fire,
Giants, Ventriloquists, the Invisible Girl,
The Bust that speaks and moves its goggling eyes,
The Wax-work, Clock-work, all the marvellous craft
Of modern Merlins, Wild Beasts, Puppet-shows,
All out-o'-the-way, far-fetched, perverted things,
All freaks of nature, all Promethean thoughts
Of man, his dullness, madness, and their feats
All jumbled up together, to compose
A Parliament of Monsters. Tents and Booths
Meanwhile, as if the whole were one vast mill,
Are vomiting, receiving, on all sides,
Men, Women, three-years' Children, Babes in arms.

The French Revolution

Wordsworth is often accused of being a turncoat. But to him, and to
many young men and women, the *beginning* of the French Revolution
promised real freedom for the people of France and was a symbol of
Freedom—just as was the Russian Revolution in 1917. Had
Wordsworth been alive then he might well have written with the
same enthusiasm and lived to face the same disillusion and dis-
appointment.

Oh! pleasant exercise of hope and joy!
For mighty were the auxiliars which then stood
Upon our side, we who were strong in love!
Bliss was it in that dawn to be alive,
But to be young was very heaven!—Oh! times,
In which the meagre, stale, forbidding ways
Of custom, law, and statute, took at once
The attraction of a country in romance!
When reason seemed the most to assert her rights,

When most intent on making of herself
A prime enchantress—to assist the work
Which then was going forward in her name!
Not favoured spots alone, but the whole earth,
The beauty wore of promise, that which sets
(As at some moment might not be unfelt
Among the bowers of paradise itself)
The budding rose above the rose full blown.
What temper at the prospect did not wake
To happiness unthought of? The inert
Were roused, and lively natures rapt away!
They who had fed their childhood upon dreams,
The playfellows of fancy, who had made
All powers of swiftness, subtilty, and strength
Their ministers,—who in lordly wise had stirred
Among the grandest objects of the sense,
And dealt with whatsoever they found there
As if they had within some lurking right
To wield it;—they, too, who, of gentle mood,
Had watched all gentle motions, and to these
Had fitted their own thoughts, schemers more mild,
And in the region of their peaceful selves;—
Now was it that both found, the meek and lofty
Did both find, helpers to their heart's desire,
And stuff at hand, plastic as they could wish;
Were called upon to exercise their skill,
Not in Utopia, subterranean fields,
Or some secreted island, Heaven knows where!
But in the very world, which is the world
Of all of us,—the place where, in the end,
We find our happiness, or not at all!

Wordsworth in Paris after the September Massacres of 1792

Cheered with this hope, to Paris I returned,
And ranged, with ardour heretofore unfelt,
The spacious city, and in progress passed
The prison where the unhappy Monarch lay,
Associate with his children and his wife
In bondage; and the palace, lately stormed
With roar of cannon by a furious host.
I crossed the square (an empty area then!)
Of the Carrousel, where so late had lain
The dead, upon the dying heaped, and gazed
On this and other spots, as doth a man
Upon a volume whose contents he knows
Are memorable, but from him locked up,
Being written in a tongue he cannot read,
So that he questions the mute leaves with pain,
And half upbraids their silence. But that night
I felt most deeply in what world I was,
What ground I trod on, and what air I breathed.
High was my room and lonely, near the roof
Of a large mansion or hotel, a lodge
That would have pleased me in more quiet times;
Nor was it wholly without pleasure then.
With unextinguished taper I kept watch,
Reading at intervals; the fear gone by
Pressed on me almost like a fear to come.
I thought of those September massacres,
Divided from me by one little month,
Saw them and touched: the rest was conjured up
From tragic fictions or true history,
Remembrances and dim admonishments.
The horse is taught his manage, and no star
Of wildest course but treads back his own steps;
For the spent hurricane the air provides
As fierce a successor; the tide retreats
But to return out of its hiding-place

In the great deep; all things have second birth;
The earthquake is not satisfied at once;
And in this way I wrought upon myself,
Until I seemed to hear a voice that cried,
To the whole city, 'sleep no more.' The trance
Fled with the voice to which it had given birth;
But vainly comments of a calmer mind
Promised soft peace and sweet forgetfulness.
The place, all hushed and silent as it was,
Appeared unfit for the repose of night,
Defenceless as a wood where tigers roam.

Disillusion

Most melancholy at that time, O Friend!
Were my day-thoughts,—my nights were miserable;
Through months, through years, long after the last beat
Of those atrocities, the hour of sleep
To me came rarely charged with natural gifts,
Such ghastly visions had I of despair
And tyranny, and implements of death;
And innocent victims sinking under fear,
And momentary hope, and worn-out prayer,
Each in his separate cell, or penned in crowds
For sacrifice, and struggling with fond mirth
And levity in dungeons, where the dust
Was laid with tears. Then suddenly the scene
Changed, and the unbroken dream entangled me
In long orations, which I strove to plead
Before unjust tribunals,—with a voice
Labouring, a brain confounded, and a sense,
Death-like, of treacherous desertion, felt
In the last place of refuge—my own soul.

THE REVERIE OF POOR SUSAN

At the corner of Wood Street, when daylight appears,
Hangs a thrush that sings loud, it has sung for three years:
Poor Susan has passed by the spot, and has heard
In the silence of morning the song of the Bird.

'Tis a note of enchantment; what ails her? She sees
A mountain ascending, a vision of trees;
Bright volumes of vapour through Lothbury glide,
And a river flows on through the vale of Cheapside.

Green pastures she views in the midst of the dale,
Down which she so often has tripped with her pail;
And a single small cottage, a nest like a dove's,
The one only dwelling on earth that she loves.

She looks, and her heart is in heaven: but they fade,
The mist and the river, the hill and the shade:
The stream will not flow, and the hill will not rise,
And the colours have all passed away from her eyes!

ADMONITION

Intended more particularly for the perusal of those who may have happened
to be enamoured of some beautiful place of retreat, in the country of the
Lakes.

Compare the town week-ender today who has no real roots in the
country; compare, too, Goldsmith's *Deserted Village*, p. 129.

Well may'st thou halt—and gaze with brightening eye!
The lovely cottage in the guardian nook
Hath stirred thee deeply; with its own dear brook,
Its own small pasture, almost its own sky!
But covet not the abode;—forbear to sigh,
As many do, repining while they look;

Intruders—who would tear from Nature's book
This precious leaf, with harsh impiety.
Think what the home must be if it were thine,
Even thine, though few thy wants!—Roof, window, door,
The very flowers are sacred to the Poor,
The roses to the porch which they entwine:
Yea, all, that now enchants thee, from the day
On which it should be touched, would melt away.

WRITTEN IN GERMANY, ON ONE OF THE COLDEST DAYS OF THE CENTURY

The Reader must be apprised that the stoves in North Germany generally have the impression of a galloping horse upon them, this being part of the Brunswick Arms.

Suppose you did not know that these verses had been written by Wordsworth; would you be surprised? Poets suffer far too much from critics' labels; beware of them. This is *part* of the poet who wrote *The Prelude*—and a necessary part.

A plague on your languages, German and Norse!
Let me have the song of the kettle;
And the tongs and the poker, instead of that horse
That gallops away with such fury and force
On this dreary dull plate of black metal.

See that Fly,—a disconsolate creature! perhaps
A child of the field or the grove;
And, sorrow for him! the dull treacherous heat
Has seduced the poor fool from his winter retreat,
And he creeps to the edge of my stove.

Alas! how he fumbles about the domains
Which this comfortless oven environ!
He cannot find out in what track he must crawl,
Now back to the tiles, then in search of the wall,
And now on the brink of the iron.

Stock-still there he stands like a traveller bemazed:
The best of his skill he has tried;
His feelers, methinks, I can see him put forth
To the east and the west, to the south and the north,
But he finds neither guide-post nor guide.

His spindles sink under him, foot, leg, and thigh!
His eyesight and hearing are lost;
Between life and death his blood freezes and thaws;
And his two pretty pinions of blue dusky gauze
Are glued to his sides by the frost.

No brother, no mate has he near him—while I
Can draw warmth from the cheek of my Love;
As blest and as glad, in this desolate gloom,
As if green summer grass were the floor of my room,
And woodbines were hanging above.

Yet, God is my witness, thou small helpless Thing!
Thy life I would gladly sustain
Till summer come up from the south, and with crowds
Of thy brethren a march thou shouldst sound through the
     clouds,
And back to the forests again!

COMPOSED IN THE VALLEY NEAR DOVER, ON THE DAY OF LANDING
AUGUST 30th, 1802

Here, on our native soil, we breathe once more.
The cock that crows, the smoke that curls, that sound
Of bells;—those boys who in yon meadow-ground
In white-sleeved shirts are playing; and the roar
Of the waves breaking on the chalky shore;—
All, all are English. Oft have I looked round
With joy in Kent's green vales; but never found
Myself so satisfied in heart before.
Europe is yet in bonds; but let that pass,
Thought for another moment. Thou art free,
My Country! and 'tis joy enough and pride
For one hour's perfect bliss, to tread the grass
Of England once again, and hear and see,
With such a dear companion at my side.

SONNET: WHERE LIES THE LAND

Where lies the land to which yon ship must go?
Fresh as a lark mounting at break of day,
Festively she puts forth in trim array;
Is she for tropic suns, or polar snow?
What boots the enquiry?—Neither friend nor foe
She cares for; let her travel where she may,
She finds familiar names, a beaten way
Ever before her, and a wind to blow.
Yet still I ask, what haven is her mark?
And, almost as it was when ships were rare,
(From time to time, like Pilgrims, here and there
Crossing the waters) doubt, and something dark,
Of the old sea some reverential fear,
Is with me at thy farewell, joyous Bark![1]

---

[1] barque or ship.

SONNET: WITH SHIPS THE SEA WAS SPRINKLED FAR AND NIGH

With ships the sea was sprinkled far and nigh,
Like stars in heaven, and joyously it showed;
Some lying fast at anchor in the road,
Some veering up and down, one knew not why.
A goodly vessel did I then espy
Come like a giant from a haven broad;
And lustily along the bay she strode,
Her tackling rich, and of apparel high.
This ship was nought to me, nor I to her,
Yet I pursued her with a lover's look;
This ship to all the rest did I prefer:
When will she turn, and whither? She will brook
No tarrying; where she comes the winds must stir:
On went she, and due north her journey took.

SONNET: THE WORLD IS TOO MUCH WITH US

In Wordsworth's preface to the 1802 edition of the *Lyrical Ballads*,
you will find that he was one of the first to realise the danger to the
human spirit of great aggregations of men in big cities. It is always
to be remembered that Wordsworth set man in his proper relation
to nature. Here he is longing for the mythical past. You will find the
story of Proteus in Book IV of the *Georgics*, by Virgil.

The world is too much with us; late and soon,
Getting and spending, we lay waste our powers:
Little we see in Nature that is ours;
We have given our hearts away, a sordid boon!
This sea that bares her bosom to the moon;
The winds that will be howling at all hours,
And are up-gathered now like sleeping flowers;
For this, for everything, we are out of tune;
It moves us not.—Great God! I'd rather be
A Pagan suckled in a creed outworn;

So might I, standing on this pleasant lea,
Have glimpses that would make me less forlorn;
Have sight of Proteus rising from the sea;
Or hear old Triton blow his wreathèd horn.

TO TOUSSAINT L'OUVERTURE

This great poem breathes the very spirit of liberty. Toussaint, a
revolutionary leader in the West Indies against the great power of
imperial Spain and, later, Napoleon, symbolised for Wordsworth
that quality in man which refuses, even in defeat, to give in and be
bullied and dominated.

Toussaint, the most unhappy man of men!
Whether the whistling rustic tend his plough
Within thy hearing, or thy head be now
Pillowed in some deep dungeon's earless den;—
O miserable Chieftain! where and when
Wilt thou find patience! Yet die not; do thou
Wear rather in thy bonds a cheerful brow:
Though fallen thyself, never to rise again,
Live, and take comfort. Thou hast left behind
Powers that will work for thee; air, earth, and skies;
There's not a breathing of the common wind
That will forget thee; thou hast great allies;
Thy friends are exultations, agonies,
And love, and man's unconquerable mind.

NOVEMBER 1806

Here the foe is, again, Napoleon. Compare the words of Winston Churchill in 1940 and Shakespeare's Henry V, addressing the English troops on the eve of the Battle of Agincourt.

Another year!—another deadly blow!
Another mighty Empire[1] overthrown!
And we are left, or shall be left, alone;
The last that dare to struggle with the Foe.
'Tis well! from this day forward we shall know
That in ourselves our safety must be sought;
That by our own right hands it must be wrought;
That we must stand unpropped, or be laid low.
O dastard whom such foretaste doth not cheer!
We shall exult, if they who rule the land
Be men who hold its many blessings dear,
Wise, upright, valiant; not a servile band,
Who are to judge of danger which they fear,
And honour which they do not understand.

---

[1] The overthrow of Prussia in the Battle of Jena, October 14th, 1806.

THE FRENCH AND THE SPANISH GUERILLAS

Resistance movements were not confined to the Second World War.
These Spanish guerillas, in the Peninsular campaigns a century and
a half before, harassed the invading armies of Napoleon.

Hunger, and sultry heat, and nipping blast
From bleak hill-top, and length of march by night
Through heavy swamp, or over snow-clad height—
These hardships ill-sustained, these dangers past,
The roving Spanish Bands are reached at last,
Charged, and dispersed like foam: but as a flight
Of scattered quails by signs do reunite,
So these,—and, heard of once again, are chased
With combinations of long-practised art
And newly-kindled hope; but they are fled—
Gone are they, viewless as the buried dead:
Where now?—Their sword is at the foe-man's heart!
And thus from year to year his walk they thwart,
And hang like dreams around his guilty bed.

SONNET: IT IS NOT TO BE THOUGHT OF

It is not to be thought of that the flood
Of British freedom, which, to the open sea
Of the world's praise, from dark antiquity
Hath flowed, 'with pomp of waters, unwithstood,'
Roused though it be full often to a mood
Which spurns the check of salutary bands,
That this most famous stream in bogs and sands
Should perish; and to evil and to good
Be lost for ever. In our halls is hung
Armoury of the invincible knights of old:
We must be free or die, who speak the tongue
That Shakespeare spake; the faith and morals hold
Which Milton held.—In every thing we are sprung
Of Earth's first blood, have titles manifold.

Samuel Taylor Coleridge (1772-1834)

THE DUNGEON

This is one of the most Wordsworthian of Coleridge's poems. Written at a time when they were in close collaboration, it expresses very clearly the belief these poets had in the powers of Nature to heal, and also their horror at any loss of liberty. These beliefs are still in the forefront of the minds of present-day prison-reformers (in their advocacy, for example, of 'open' prisons) and of psychologists.

And this place our forefathers made for man!
This is the process of our love and wisdom,
To each poor brother who offends against us—
Most innocent, perhaps—and what if guilty?
Is this the only cure? Merciful God!
Each pore and natural outlet shrivelled up
By Ignorance and parching Poverty,
His energies roll back upon his heart,
And stagnate and corrupt; till changed to poison,
They break out on him, like a loathsome plague-spot;
Then we call in our pampered mountebanks—
And this is their best cure! uncomforted
And friendless solitude, groaning and tears,
And savage faces, at the clanking hour,
Seen through the steams and vapour of his dungeon,
By the lamp's dismal twilight! So he lies
Circled with evil, till his very soul
Unmoulds its essence, hopelessly deformed
By sights of ever more deformity!

With other ministrations thou, O Nature!
Healest thy wandering and distempered child:
Thou pourest on him thy soft influences,
Thy sunny hues, fair forms, and breathing sweets,
Thy melodies of woods, and winds, and waters,
Till he relent, and can no more endure
To be a jarring and a dissonant thing,
Amid this general dance and minstrelsy;

But, bursting into tears, wins back his way,
His angry spirit healed and harmonized
By the benignant touch of Love and Beauty.

From FEARS IN SOLITUDE

Written in April 1798, during the Alarm of an Invasion.

These are Coleridge's fears when an invasion of England by Napoleon
was thought to be imminent. His attitude to his fellow-countrymen
is particularly worth noticing.

A quiet spirit-healing nook

A green and silent spot, amid the hills,
A small and silent dell! O'er stiller place
No singing sky-lark ever poised himself.
The hills are heathy, save that swelling slope,
Which hath a gay and gorgeous covering on,
All golden with the never-bloomless furze,
Which now blooms most profusely: but the dell,
Bathed by the mist, is fresh and delicate
As vernal corn-field, or the unripe flax,
When, through its half-transparent stalks, at eve,
The level sunshine glimmers with green light.
Oh! 'tis a quiet spirit-healing nook!
Which all, methinks, would love; but chiefly he,
The humble man, who, in his youthful years,
Knew just so much of folly, as had made
His early manhood more securely wise!
Here he might lie on fern or withered heath,
While from the singing lark (that sings unseen
The minstrelsy that solitude loves best),
And from the sun, and from the breezy air,
Sweet influences trembled o'er his frame;
And he, with many feelings, many thoughts,
Made up a meditative joy, and found
Religious meanings in the forms of Nature!

And so, his senses gradually wrapt
In a half sleep, he dreams of better worlds,
And dreaming hears thee still, O singing lark,
That singest like an angel in the clouds!
  My God! it is a melancholy thing
For such a man, who would full fain preserve
His soul in calmness, yet perforce must feel
For all his human brethren—O my God!
It weighs upon the heart, that he must think
What uproar and what strife may now be stirring
This way or that way o'er these silent hills—
Invasion, and the thunder and the shout,
And all the crash of onset; fear and rage,
And undetermined conflict—even now,
Even now, perchance, and in his native isle:
Carnage and groans beneath this blessed sun!
We have offended, Oh! my countrymen!
We have offended very grievously,
And been most tyrannous. From east to west
A groan of accusation pierces Heaven!
The wretched plead against us; multitudes
Countless and vehement, the sons of God,
Our brethren! Like a cloud that travels on,
Steamed up from Cairo's swamps of pestilence,
Even so, my countrymen! have we gone forth
And borne to distant tribes slavery and pangs,
And, deadlier far, our vices, whose deep taint
With slow perdition murders the whole man,
His body and his soul! Meanwhile, at home,
All individual dignity and power
Engulfed in Courts, Committees, Institutions,
Associations and Societies,
A vain, speech-mouthing, speech-reporting Guild,
One Benefit-Club for mutual flattery,
We have drunk up, demure as at a grace,
Pollutions from the brimming cup of wealth;
Contemptuous of all honourable rule,
Yet bartering freedom and the poor man's life

For gold, as at a market! The sweet words
Of Christian promise, words that even yet
Might stem destruction, were they wisely preached,
Are muttered o'er by men, whose tones proclaim
How flat and wearisome they feel their trade:
Rank scoffers some, but most too indolent
To deem them falsehoods or to know their truth.
Oh! blasphemous! the Book of Life is made
A superstitious instrument, on which
We gabble o'er the oaths we mean to break;
For all must swear—all and in every place,
College and wharf, council and justice-court;
All, all must swear, the briber and the bribed,
Merchant and lawyer, senator and priest,
The rich, the poor, the old man and the young;
All, all make up one scheme of perjury,
That faith doth reel; the very name of God
Sounds like a juggler's charm; and, bold with joy,
Forth from his dark and lonely hiding-place,
(Portentous sight!) the owlet Atheism,
Sailing on obscene wings athwart the noon,
Drops his blue-fringèd lids, and holds them close,
And hooting at the glorious sun in Heaven,
Cries out, 'Where is it?'

The desolation and the agony

Thankless too for peace,
(Peace long preserved by fleets and perilous seas)
Secure from actual warfare, we have loved
To swell the war-whoop, passionate for war!
Alas! for ages ignorant of all
Its ghastlier workings, (famine or blue plague,
Battle, or siege, or flight through wintry snows,)
We, this whole people, have been clamorous
For war and bloodshed; animating sports,
The which we pay for as a thing to talk of,
Spectators and not combatants! No guess
Anticipative of a wrong unfelt,
No speculation on contingency,

However dim and vague, too vague and dim
To yield a justifying cause; and forth,
(Stuffed out with big preamble, holy names,
And adjurations of the God in Heaven,)
We send our mandates for the certain death
Of thousands and ten thousands! Boys and girls,
And women, that would groan to see a child
Pull off an insect's leg, all read of war,
The best amusement for our morning meal!
The poor wretch, who has learnt his only prayers
From curses, who knows scarcely words enough
To ask a blessing from his Heavenly Father,
Becomes a fluent phraseman, absolute
And technical in victories and defeats,
And all our dainty terms for fratricide;
Terms which we trundle smoothly o'er our tongues
Like mere abstractions, empty sounds to which
We join no feeling and attach no form!
As if the soldier died without a wound;
As if the fibres of this godlike frame
Were gored without a pang; as if the wretch,
Who fell in battle, doing bloody deeds,
Passed off to Heaven, translated and not killed;
As though he had no wife to pine for him,
No God to judge him! Therefore, evil days
Are coming on us, O my countrymen!
And what if all-avenging Providence,
Strong and retributive, should make us know
The meaning of our words, force us to feel
The desolation and the agony
Of our fierce doings?

MIGNON'S SONG FROM WILHELM MEISTER

From the German of Goethe

Coleridge was a very fine German scholar. His translations of the plays of Schiller are still among the best. He was, too, one of the most widely read men of his age.

Know'st thou the land where the pale citrons grow,
The golden fruits in darker foliage glow?
Soft blows the wind that breathes from that blue sky!
Still stands the myrtle and the laurel high!
Know'st thou it well, that land, belovèd Friend?
Thither with thee, O, thither would I wend!

APOLOGIA PRO VITA SUA

Seeing things in proportion—setting them in proportion and making order out of chaos—is one of the poet's greatest gifts; and saying something which is at once both gay and serious is another. In his famous poem on the daffodils, Wordsworth speaks of 'that inward eye, which is the bliss of solitude'—here is Coleridge offering the same idea and asking you to make fun of it. Poets are realists. They are apt to say exactly what they mean to. This is a poem to take wholly seriously—for what it is.

The poet in his lone yet genial hour
Gives to his eyes a magnifying power:
Or rather he emancipates his eyes
From the black shapeless accidents of size—
In unctuous cones of kindling coal,
Or smoke upwreathing from the pipe's trim bole,
 His gifted ken can see
 Phantoms of sublimity.

Samuel Taylor Coleridge

AN ODE TO THE RAIN

Composed before daylight, on the morning appointed for the departure
of a very worthy, but not very pleasant visitor, whom it was feared the rain
might detain.

I know it is dark; and though I have lain,
Awake, as I guess, an hour or twain,
I have not once opened the lids of my eyes,
But I lie in the dark, as a blind man lies.
O Rain! that I lie listening to,
You're but a doleful sound at best:
I owe you little thanks, 'tis true,
For breaking thus my needful rest!
Yet if, as soon as it is light,
O Rain! you will but take your flight,
I'll neither rail, nor malice keep,
Though sick and sore for want of sleep.
But only now, for this one day,
Do go, dear Rain! do go away!

O Rain! with your dull two-fold sound,
The clash hard by, and the murmur all round!
You know, if you know aught, that we,
Both night and day, but ill agree:
For days and months, and almost years,
Have limped on through this vale of tears,
Since body of mine, and rainy weather,
Have lived on easy terms together.
Yet if, as soon as it is light,
O Rain! you will but take your flight,
Though you should come again to-morrow,
And bring with you both pain and sorrow;
Though stomach should sicken and knees should swell—
I'll nothing speak of you but well.
But only now for this one day,
Do go, dear Rain! do go away!

Dear Rain! I ne'er refused to say
You're a good creature in your way;
Nay, I could write a book myself,
Would fit a parson's lower shelf,
Showing how very good you are.—
What then? sometimes it must be fair
And if sometimes, why not to-day?
Do go, dear Rain! do go away!

Dear Rain! if I've been cold and shy,
Take no offence! I'll tell you why.
A dear old Friend e'en now is here,
And with him came my sister dear;
After long absence now first met,
Long months by pain and grief beset—
We three dear friends! in truth, we groan
Impatiently to be alone.
We three, you mark! and not one more!
The strong wish makes my spirit sore.
We have so much to talk about,
So many sad things to let out;
So many tears in our eye-corners,
Sitting like little Jacky Horners—
In short, as soon as it is day,
Do go, dear Rain! do go away.

And this I'll swear to you, dear Rain!
Whenever you shall come again,
Be you as dull as e'er you could
(And by the bye 'tis understood,
You're not so pleasant as you're good)
Yet, knowing well your worth and place,
I'll welcome you with cheerful face;
And though you stayed a week or more,
Were ten times duller than before;
Yet with kind heart, and right good will,
I'll sit and listen to you still;

Nor should you go away, dear Rain!
Uninvited to remain.
But only now, for this one day,
Do go, dear Rain! do go away.

THE DELINQUENT TRAVELLERS

Some are home-sick—some two or three,
Their third year on the Arctic Sea—
Brave Captain Lyon tells us so—
Spite of those charming Esquimaux.
But O, what scores are sick of Home,
Agog for Paris or for Rome!
Nay! tho' contented to abide,
You should prefer your own fireside;
Yet since grim War has ceas'd its madding,
And Peace has set John Bull agadding,
'Twould such a vulgar taste betray,
For very shame you must away!
'What? not yet seen the coast of France!
The folks will swear, for lack of bail,
You've spent your last five years in jail!'

Keep moving! Steam, or Gas, or Stage,[1]
Hold, cabin, steerage, hencoop's cage—
Tour, Journey, Voyage, Lounge, Ride, Walk,
Skim, Sketch, Excursion, Travel-talk—
For move you must! 'Tis now the rage,
The law and fashion of the Age.

---

[1] stage coach.

If you but perch, where Dover tallies,
So strangely with the coast of Calais,
With a good glass[1] and knowing look,
You'll soon get matter for a book!
Or else, in Gas-car, take your chance
Like that adventurous king of France,
Who, once, with twenty thousand men
Went up—and then came down again;
At least, he moved if nothing more:
And if there's nought left to explore,
Yet while your well-greased wheels keep spinning,
The traveller's honoured name you're winning,
And, snug as Jonas in the Whale,
You may loll back and dream a tale.
Move, or be moved—there's no protection,
Our Mother Earth has ta'en the infection—
(That rogue Copernicus, 'tis said
First put the whirring in her head,)
A planet She, and can't endure
T'exist without her annual Tour:
The *name* were else a mere misnomer,
Since Planet is but Greek for *Roamer*.
The atmosphere, too, can do no less
Than ventilate her emptiness,
Bilks turn-pike gates, for no one cares,
And gives herself a thousand airs—
While streams and shopkeepers, we see,
Will have their run toward the sea—
And if, meantime, like old King Log,
Or ass with tether and a clog,
Must graze at home! to yawn and bray
'I guess we shall have rain to-day!'
Nor clog nor tether can be worse
Than the dead palsy of the purse.
Money, I've heard a wise man say,
Makes herself wings and flys away:

---

[1] telescope.

Ah! would She take it in her head
To make a pair for me instead!
At all events, the Fancy's free,
No traveller so bold as she.
From Fear and Poverty released
I'll saddle Pegasus, at least,
And when she's seated to her mind,
I within I can mount behind:
And since this outward I, you know,
Must stay because he cannot go,
My fellow-travellers shall be they
Who go because they cannot stay—
Rogues, rascals, sharpers, blanks and prizes,
Delinquents of all sorts and sizes,
Fraudulent bankrupts, Knights burglarious,
And demireps of means precarious—
All whom Law thwarted, Arms or Arts,
Compel to visit foreign parts,
All hail! No compliments, I pray,
I'll follow where you lead the way!
But ere we cross the main once more,
Methinks, along my native shore,
Dismounting from my steed I'll stray
Beneath the cliffs of Dumpton Bay,
Where, Ramsgate and Broadstairs between,
Rude caves and grated doors are seen:
And here I'll watch till break of day,
(For Fancy in her magic might
Can turn broad noon to starless night!)
When lo! methinks a sudden band
Of smock-clad smugglers round me stand.
Denials, oaths, in vain I try,
At once they gag me for a spy,
And stow me in the boat hard by.
Suppose us fairly now afloat,
Till Boulogne mouth receives our Boat.
But, bless us! what a numerous band
Of cockneys anglicise the strand!

Delinquent bankrupts, leg-bail'd debtors,
Some for the news, and some for letters—
With hungry look and tarnished dress,
French shrugs and British surliness.
Sick of the country for their sake
Of them and France *French leave* I take—
And lo! a transport comes in view
I hear the merry motley crew,
Well skill'd in pocket to make entry,
Of Dieman's Land the elected Gentry,
And founders of Australian Races.—
The Rogues! I see it in their faces!
Receive me, Lads! I'll go with you,
Hunt the black swan and kangaroo,
And that New Holland we'll presume
Old England with some elbow-room.
Across the mountains we will roam,
And each man make himself a home:
Or, if old habits ne'er forsaking,
Like clock-work of the Devil's making,
Ourselves inveterate rogues should be,
We'll have a virtuous progeny;
And on the dunghill of our vices
Raise human pine-apples and spices.
Of all the children of John Bull
With empty heads and bellies full,
Who ramble East, West, North and South,
With leaky purse and open mouth,
In search of varieties exotic
The usefullest and most patriotic,
And merriest, too, believe me, Sirs!
Are your Delinquent Travellers!

John Keats (1795-1821)

KEEN, FITFUL GUSTS ARE WHISP'RING HERE AND THERE

The little cottage was Leigh Hunt's (see p. 220) in the Vale of Health in the village of Hampstead. Keats had a long *country* walk home to London. The two young men were talking of the poetry of the past, of Milton's *Lycidas* and of the love sonnets Petrarch wrote for Laura in the fourteenth century.

Keen, fitful gusts are whisp'ring here and there
    Among the bushes half leafless, and dry;
    The stars look very cold about the sky,
And I have many miles on foot to fare.
Yet feel I little of the cool bleak air,
    Or of the dead leaves rustling drearily,
    Or of those silver lamps that burn on high,
Or of the distance from home's pleasant lair:
For I am brimfull of the friendliness
    That in a little cottage I have found;
Of fair-haired Milton's eloquent distress,
    And all his love for gentle Lycid drowned;
Of lovely Laura in her light green dress,
    And faithful Petrarch gloriously crowned.

HAPPY IS ENGLAND

Happy is England! I could be content
    To see no other verdure than its own;
    To feel no other breezes than are blown
Through its tall woods with high romances blent:
Yet do I sometimes feel a languishment
    For skies Italian, and an inward groan
    To sit upon an Alp as on a throne,
And half forget what world or worldling meant.
Happy is England, sweet her artless daughters;

Enough their simple loveliness for me,
    Enough their whitest arms in silence clinging:
Yet do I often warmly burn to see
    Beauties of deeper glance, and hear their singing,
And float with them about the summer waters.

ON FIRST LOOKING INTO CHAPMAN'S HOMER

George Chapman lived from about 1559 to 1634. In an age when most educated men knew all the Latin and Greek poets, Chapman's translation of Homer stands out as a great original work. It was published in 1624, with the title of *The Whole Workes of Homer, Prince of Poets,* and was the first complete translation of the Greek poet into English. Keats, like Shakespeare, had 'small Latin and less Greek' and was lent it to read by his friend, George Armitage Brown.

Much have I travelled in the realms of gold,
    And many goodly states and kingdoms seen;
    Round many western islands have I been
Which bards in fealty to Apollo hold.
Oft of one wide expanse had I been told
    That deep-browed Homer ruled as his demesne;
    Yet did I never breathe its pure serene
Till I heard Chapman speak out loud and bold:
Then felt I like some watcher of the skies
    When a new planet swims into his ken;
Or like stout Cortez when with eagle eyes
    He stared at the Pacific—and all his men
Looked at each other with a wild surmise—
    Silent, upon a peak in Darien.

John Keats

From ENDYMION

A Poetic Romance, inscribed to the memory of Thomas Chatterton.

Thomas Chatterton, 'the marvellous boy', is an astonishing figure.
He lived from 1751 to 1770, at a time when the eighteenth century
intellectuals were re-discovering the old fourteenth century ballads,
and Thomas Percy was collecting his *Reliques of Ancient English
Poetry* (published in 1765). Chatterton wrote quite genuinely, in the
old style, poems said to be by 'Thomas Rowley'—and, despite their
imitation old spelling, they were true and excellent poetry. Poor
Chatterton, for all his success, was destitute and poisoned himself
when he was only seventeen. Such a sad and romantic figure was
bound to appeal to Keats.

A thing of beauty is a joy for ever:
Its loveliness increases; it will never
Pass into nothingness; but still will keep
A bower quiet for us, and a sleep
Full of sweet dreams, and health, and quiet breathing.
Therefore, on every morrow, are we wreathing
A flowery band to bind us to the earth,
Spite of despondence, of the inhuman dearth
Of noble natures, of the gloomy days,
Of all the unhealthy and o'er-darkened ways
Made for our searching: yes, in spite of all,
Some shape of beauty moves away the pall
From our dark spirits. Such the sun, the moon,
Trees old and young, sprouting a shady boon
For simple sheep; and such are daffodils
With the green world they live in; and clear rills
That for themselves a cooling covert make
'Gainst the hot season; the mid forest brake,
Rich with a sprinkling of fair musk-rose blooms:
And such too is the grandeur of the dooms
We have imagined for the mighty dead;
All lovely tales that we have heard or read:
An endless fountain of immortal drink,
Pouring unto us from the heaven's brink.

Nor do we merely feel these essences
For one short hour; no, even as the trees
That whisper round a temple become soon
Dear as the temple's self, so does the moon,
The passion poesy, glories infinite,
Haunt us till they become a cheering light
Unto our souls, and bound to us so fast,
That, whether there be shine, or gloom o'ercast,
They always must be with us, or we die.

THE SUN FROM MERIDIAN HEIGHT

The Sun from meridian height
Illumines the depth of the sea
And the fishes beginning to sweat
Cry 'Damn it, how hot we shall be!'

IN DREAR-NIGHTED DECEMBER

In drear-nighted December,
Too happy, happy tree,
Thy branches ne'er remember
Their green felicity:
The north cannot undo them
With a sleety whistle through them;
Nor frozen thawings glue them
From budding at the prime.

In drear-nighted December,
Too happy, happy brook,
Thy bubblings ne'er remember
Apollo's summer look;
But with a sweet forgetting,
They stay their crystal fretting,
Never, never petting
About the frozen time.

Ah! would 'twere so with many
A gentle girl and boy!
But were there ever any
Writhed not at passed joy?
The feel of not to feel it,
When there is none to heal it
Nor numbèd sense to steel it,
Was never said in rhyme!

WHEN I HAVE FEARS

Keats was only twenty-six when he died of consumption—TB, as
we would call it now. His studies in medicine at St. Thomas's gave
him an insight into the dangers of disease very early on. He nursed
his brother, Tom, who was dying of consumption for which he knew
there was no cure; and he must have known how likely he was to
catch it, which he did. His fears that he 'might cease to be' were only
too well founded.

When I have fears that I may cease to be
    Before my pen has gleaned my teeming brain,
Before high-pilèd books, in charact'ry,
    Hold like rich garners the full-ripened grain;
When I behold, upon the night's starred face,
    Huge cloudy symbols of a high romance,
And think that I may never live to trace
    Their shadows, with the magic hand of chance;
And when I feel, fair creature of an hour!
    That I shall never look upon thee more,
Never have relish in the faery power
    Of unreflecting love!—then on the shore
Of the wide world I stand alone, and think,
Till love and fame to nothingness do sink.

WHAT THE THRUSH SAID . . .

O thou whose face hath felt the Winter's wind,
Whose eye has seen the snow-clouds hung in mist,
And the black elm-tops 'mong the freezing stars,
To thee the Spring will be a harvest-time.
O thou, whose only book has been the light
Of supreme darkness, which thou feddest on
Night after night when Phœbus was away,
To thee the Spring shall be a triple morn.
O fret not after knowledge—I have none,
And yet my song comes native with the warmth.
O fret not after knowledge—I have none,
And yet the evening listens. He who saddens
At thought of idleness cannot be idle,
And he's awake who thinks himself asleep.

MODERN LOVE

Many people think the word 'modern' applies only to now, in the
twentieth century. 'Wellington' boots—popularised by the great
Duke—were not made of rubber in 1818, but they were both fashion-
able and modern.

And what is love? It is a doll dressed up
For idleness to cosset, nurse, and dandle;
A thing of soft misnomers, so divine
That silly youth doth think to make itself
Divine by loving too, and so goes on
Yawning and doting a whole summer long,
Till Miss's comb is made a pearl tiara,
And common Wellingtons turn Romeo boots;
Then Cleopatra lives at number seven,
And Antony resides in Brunswick Square.

Fools! if some passions high have warmed the world,
If queens and soldiers have played deep for hearts,
It is no reason why such agonies
Should be more common than the growth of weeds.
Fools! make me whole again that weighty pearl
The Queen of Egypt melted, and I'll say
That ye may love in spite of beaver hats.

From EPISTLE TO JOHN HAMILTON REYNOLDS

It was not only Keats who wrote letters to his friends in verse. There
was a great vogue for it in the early nineteenth century.

O that our dreamings all, of sleep or wake,
Would all their colours from the sunset take:
From something of material sublime,
Rather than shadow our own soul's day time
In the dark void of night. For in the world
We jostle—but my flag is not unfurled
On the admiral-staff,—and to philosophize
I dare not yet! Oh, never will the prize,
High reason, and the lore of good and ill,
Be my award! Things cannot to the will
Be settled, but they tease us out of thought.
Or is it that imagination brought
Beyond its proper bound, yet still confined,—
Lost in a sort of Purgatory blind,
Cannot refer to any standard law
Of either earth or heaven? It is a flaw
In happiness, to see beyond our bourn—
It forces us in summer skies to mourn:
It spoils the singing of the nightingale.

No, no, go not to Lethe, neither twist
   Wolf's-bane, tight-rooted, for its poisonous wine;
Nor suffer thy pale forehead to be kissed
   By nightshade, ruby grape of Proserpine;
Make not your rosary of yew-berries,
     Nor let the beetle, nor the death-moth be
        Your mournful Psyche, nor the downy owl
A partner in your sorrow's mysteries;
     For shade to shade will come too drowsily,
       And drown the wakeful anguish of the soul.

But when the melancholy fit shall fall
   Sudden from heaven like a weeping cloud,
That fosters the droop-headed flowers all,
   And hides the green hill in an April shroud;
Then glut thy sorrow on a morning rose,
     Or on the rainbow of the salt sand-wave,
       Or on the wealth of globèd peonies;
Or if thy mistress some rich anger shows,
     Emprison her soft hand, and let her rave,
       And feed deep, deep upon her peerless eyes.

She dwells with Beauty—Beauty that must die;
   And Joy, whose hand is ever at his lips
Bidding adieu; and aching Pleasure nigh,
   Turning to poison while the bee-mouth sips:
Ay, in the very temple of Delight
     Veil'd Melancholy has her sovran shrine,
       Though seen of none save him whose strenuous tongue
Can burst Joy's grape against his palate fine;
     His soul shall taste the sadness of her might,
       And be among her cloudy trophies hung.

John Keats

From THE FALL OF HYPERION: A DREAM

Nearly all poets return again and again to the same themes and ideas.
So do painters and composers. Keats never lived to finish this second
attempt at the myth of Hyperion.

Fanatics have their dreams, wherewith they weave
A paradise for a sect; the savage, too,
From forth the loftiest fashion of his sleep
Guesses at Heaven; pity these have not
Trac'd upon vellum or wild Indian leaf
The shadows of melodious utterance.
But bare of laurel they live, dream and die;
For Poesy alone can tell her dreams,—
With the fine spell of words alone can save
Imagination from the sable charm
And dumb enchantment. Who alive can say,
'Thou art no poet—mayst not tell thy dreams?'
Since every man whose soul is not a clod
Hath visions, and would speak, if he had loved,
And been well nurtured in his mother tongue.
Whether the dream now purposed to rehearse
Be poet's or fanatic's will be known
When this warm scribe, my hand, is in the grave.
        Methought I stood where trees of every clime,
Palm, myrtle, oak, and sycamore, and beech,
With plantain, and spice-blossoms, made a screen;
In neighbourhood of fountains, by the noise
Soft-showering in mine ears; and, by the touch
Of scent, not far from roses. Turning round
I saw an arbour with a drooping roof
Of trellis vines, and bells, and larger blooms,
Like floral censers swinging light in air;
Before its wreathed doorway, on a mound
Of moss, was spread a feast of summer fruits,
Which, nearer seen, seemed refuse of a meal
By angel tasted, or our Mother Eve;

For empty shells were scattered on the grass,
And grape-stalks but half bare, and remnants more
Sweet smelling, whose pure kinds I could not know.
Still was more plenty than the fabled horn
Thrice emptied could pour forth, at banqueting
For Proserpine returned to her own fields,
Where the white heifers low. And appetite,
More yearning than on earth I ever felt,
Growing within, I ate deliciously;
And, after not long, thirsted; for thereby
Stood a cool vessel of transparent juice,
Sipped by the wandered bee, the which I took,
And, pledging all the mortals of the world,
And all the dead whose names are in our lips,
Drank. That full draught is parent of my theme.
No Asian poppy nor elixir fine
Of the soon-fading jealous Caliphat;
No poison gendered in close monkish cell
To thin the scarlet conclave of old men,
Could so have rapt unwilling life away.
Among the fragrant husks and berries crushed,
Upon the grass I struggled hard against
The domineering potion; but in vain:
The cloudy swoon came on, and down I sunk,
Like a Silenus on an antique vase.
How long I slumbered 'tis a chance to guess.
When sense of life returned, I started up
As if with wings; but the fair trees were gone,
The mossy mound and arbour were no more;
I looked around upon the carvèd sides
Of an old sanctuary with roof august,
Builded so high, it seemed that filmèd clouds
Might spread beneath, as o'er the stars of heaven;
So old the place was, I remembered none
The like upon the earth: what I had seen
Of gray cathedrals, buttressed walls, rent towers,
The superannuations of sunk realms,
Or Nature's rocks toiled hard in waves and winds,
Seemed but the faulture of decrepit things
To that eternal domèd monument.

Upon the marble at my feet there lay
Store of strange vessels, and large draperies,
Which needs had been of dyed asbestos wove,
Or in that place the moth could not corrupt,
So white the linen; so, in some, distinct
Ran imageries from a sombre loom.
All in a mingled heap confused there lay
Robes, golden tongs, censer, and chafing-dish,
Girdles, and chains, and holy jewelries.

    Turning from these with awe, once more I raised
My eyes to fathom the space every way;
The embossèd roof, the silent massy range
Of columns north and south, ending in mist
Of nothing; then to eastward, where black gates
Were shut against the sunrise evermore.
Then to the west I looked, and saw far off
An image, huge of feature as a cloud,
At level of whose feet an altar slept,
To be approached on either side by steps,
And marble balustrade, and patient travail
To count with toil the innumerable degrees.
Towards the altar sober-paced I went,
Repressing haste, as too unholy there;
And, coming nearer, saw beside the shrine
One minist'ring; and there arose a flame.
When in mid-May the sickening east-wind
Shifts sudden to the south, the small warm rain
Melts out the frozen incense from all flowers,
And fills the air with so much pleasant health
That even the dying man forgets his shroud;—
Even so that lofty sacrificial fire,
Sending forth Maian incense, spread around
Forgetfulness of everything but bliss,
And clouded all the altar with soft smoke;
From whose white fragrant curtains thus I heard
Language pronounced: 'If thou canst not ascend
These steps, die on that marble where thou art.
Thy flesh, near cousin to the common dust,

Will parch for lack of nutriment—thy bones
Will wither in few years, and vanish so
That not the quickest eye could find a grain
Of what thou now art on that pavement cold.
The sands of thy short life are spent this hour
And no hand in the universe can turn
Thy hour glass, if these gummèd leaves be burnt
Ere thou canst mount up these immortal steps.'
I heard, I looked: two senses both at once,
So fine, so subtle, felt the tyranny
Of that fierce threat, and the hard task proposed.
Prodigious seem'd the toil; the leaves were yet
Burning,—when suddenly a palsied chill
Struck from the pavèd level up my limbs,
And was ascending quick to put cold grasp
Upon those streams that pulse beside the throat:
I shrieked; and the sharp anguish of my shriek
Stung my own ears—I strove hard to escape
The numbness; strove to gain the lowest step.
Slow, heavy, deadly was my pace: the cold
Grew stifling, suffocating, at the heart;
And when I clasped my hands I felt them not.
One minute before death, my iced foot touched
The lowest stair; and as it touched, life seemed
To pour in at the toes: I mounted up,
As once fair angels on a ladder flew
From the green turf to heaven.—'Holy Power',
Cried I, approaching near the hornèd shrine,
'What am I that should so be saved from death?
What am I that another death come not
To choke my utterance sacrilegious here?'
Then said the veilèd shadow: 'Thou hast felt
What 'tis to die and live again before
Thy fated hour; that thou hadst power to do so
Is thy own safety; thou hast dated on
Thy doom.' 'High Prophetess', said I, 'purge off,
Benign, if so it please thee, my mind's film.'
'None can usurp this height', returned that shade,
'But those to whom the miseries of the world
Are misery, and will not let them rest.

All else who find a haven in the world,
Where they may thoughtless sleep away their days,
If by a chance into this fane they come,
Rot on the pavement where thou rotted'st half.'
'Are there not thousands in the world', said I,
Encouraged by the sooth voice of the shade,
'Who love their fellows even to the death;
Who feel the giant agony of the world;
And more, like slaves to poor humanity,
Labour for mortal good? I sure should see
Other men here, but I am here alone.'
'Those whom thou spak'st of are no visionaries',
Rejoined that voice,—'they are no dreamers weak;
They seek no wonder but the human face,
No music but a happy-noted voice—
They come not here, they have no thought to come—
And thou art here, for thou art less than they.
What benefit canst thou do, or all thy tribe,
To the great world? Thou art a dreaming thing;
A fever of thyself—think of the earth;
What bliss even in hope is there for thee?
What haven? every creature hath its home;
Every sole man hath days of joy and pain,
Whether his labours be sublime or low—
The pain alone; the joy alone; distinct:
Only the dreamer venoms all his days,
Bearing more woe than all his sins deserve.
Therefore, that happiness be somewhat shared,
Such things as thou art are admitted oft
Into like gardens thou didst pass erewhile,
And suffered in these temples: for that cause
Thou standest safe beneath this statue's knees'.

Percy Bysshe Shelley (1792-1822)

OZYMANDIAS

I met a traveller from an antique land
Who said: Two vast and trunkless legs of stone
Stand in the desert . . . Near them, on the sand,
Half sunk, a shattered visage lies, whose frown,
And wrinkled lip, and sneer of cold command,
Tell that its sculptor well those passions read
Which yet survive, stamped on these lifeless things,
The hand that mocked them, and the heart that fed:
And on the pedestal these words appear:
'My name is Ozymandias, king of kings:
Look on my works, ye Mighty, and despair!'
Nothing beside remains, Round the decay
Of that colossal wreck, boundless and bare
The lone and level sands stretch far away.

ENGLAND IN 1819

George III, who died in 1820, had been mad for many years. This
was the time of the Regency—a time when society and politics were
notably corrupt.

An old, mad, blind, despised, and dying king,—
Princes, the dregs of their dull race, who flow
Through public scorn,—mud from a muddy spring,—
Rulers who neither see, nor feel, nor know,
But leech-like to their fainting country cling,
Till they drop, blind in blood, without a blow,—
A people starved and stabbed in the untilled field,—
An army, which liberticide[1] and prey
Makes as a two-edged sword to all who wield,—
Golden and sanguine laws which tempt and slay;
Religion Christless, Godless—a book sealed;
A Senate,—Time's worst statute unrepealed,—
Are graves, from which a glorious Phantom may
Burst, to illumine our tempestuous day.

---

[1] murder of liberty.

From THE MASK OF ANARCHY

Shelley was an Etonian, the son of Sir Timothy Shelley, a rich Tory landowner. He could hardly have been more of a renegade to his class, but nothing would stop him speaking his mind. He was quite fearless of the consequences. Luckily, he had enough money to live on.

'Men of England, heirs of Glory,
Heroes of unwritten story,
Nurslings of one mighty Mother,
Hopes of her, and one another;

'Rise like Lions after slumber
In unvanquishable number,
Shake your chains to earth like dew
Which in sleep had fallen on you—
Ye are many—they are few.

'What is Freedom?—ye can tell
That which slavery is, too well—
For its very name has grown
To an echo of your own.

' 'Tis to work and have such pay
As just keeps life from day to day
In your limbs, as in a cell
For the tyrants' use to dwell.

'So that ye for them are made
Loom, and plough, and sword, and spade,
With or without your own will bent
To their defence and nourishment.

' 'Tis to see your children weak
With their mothers pine and peak,
When the winter winds are bleak,—
They are dying whilst I speak.

' 'Tis to hunger for such diet
As the rich man in his riot
Casts to the fat dogs that lie
Surfeiting beneath his eye;

' 'Tis to let the Ghost of Gold
Take from Toil a thousandfold
More than e'er its substance could
In the tyrannies of old.

LINES: THE COLD EARTH SLEPT BELOW

The cold earth slept below,
    Above the cold sky shone;
And all around, with a chilling sound,
    From caves of ice and fields of snow,
    The breath of night like death did flow
      Beneath the sinking moon.

The wintry hedge was black,
    The green grass was not seen,
The birds did rest on the bare thorn's breast,
    Whose roots, beside the pathway track,
    Had bound their folds o'er many a crack
      Which the frost had made between.

Thine eyes glowed in the glare
    Of the moon's dying light;
As a fen-fire's beam on a sluggish stream
    Gleams dimly, so the moon shone there,
    And it yellowed the strings of thy raven hair,
      That shook in the wind of night.

The moon made thy lips pale, beloved—
    The wind made thy bosom chill—
The night did shed on thy dear head
    Its frozen dew, and thou didst lie
    Where the bitter breath of the naked sky
      Might visit thee at will.

SUMMER AND WINTER

It was a bright and cheerful afternoon,
Towards the end of the sunny month of June,
When the north wind congregates in crowds
The floating mountains of the silver clouds
From the horizon—and the stainless sky
Opens beyond them like eternity.
All things rejoiced beneath the sun; the weeds,
The river, and the corn-fields, and the reeds;
The willow leaves that glanced in the light breeze,
And the firm foliage of the larger trees.

It was a winter such as when birds die
In the deep forests; and the fishes lie
Stiffened in the translucent ice, which makes
Even the mud and slime of the warm lakes
A wrinkled clod as hard as brick; and when,
Among their children, comfortable men
Gather about great fires, and yet feel cold:
Alas, then, for the homeless beggar old!

GOOD-NIGHT

Good-night? ah! no; the hour is ill
    Which severs those it should unite;
Let us remain together still,
    Then it will be *good* night.

How can I call the lone night good,
    Though thy sweet wishes wing its flight?
Be it not said, thought, understood—
    Then it will be—*good* night.

To hearts which near each other move
    From evening close to morning light,
The night is good; because, my love,
    They never *say* good-night.

TO NIGHT

Swiftly walk o'er the western wave,
      Spirit of Night!
Out of the misty eastern cave,
Where, all the long and lone daylight,
Thou wovest dreams of joy and fear,
Which make thee terrible and dear,—
      Swift be thy flight!

Wrap thy form in a mantle gray,
      Star-inwrought!
Blind with thine hair the eyes of Day;
Kiss her until she be wearied out,
Then wander o'er city, and sea, and land,
Touching all with thine opiate wand—
      Come, long-sought!

When I arose and saw the dawn,
      I sighed for thee;
When light rode high, and the dew was gone,
And noon lay heavy on flower and tree,
And the weary Day turned to his rest,
Lingering like an unloved guest,
      I sighed for thee.

Thy brother Death came, and cried,
      Wouldst thou me?
Thy sweet child Sleep, the filmy-eyed,
Murmured like a noontide bee,
Shall I nestle near thy side?
Wouldst thou me?—And I replied,
      No, not thee!

Death will come when thou art dead,
　　　Soon, too soon—
Sleep will come when thou art fled;
Of neither would I ask the boon
I ask of thee, belovèd Night—
Swift be thine approaching flight,
　　　Come soon, soon!

TIME

Unfathomable Sea! whose waves are years,
　　　Ocean of Time, whose waters of deep woe
Are brackish with the salt of human tears!
　　　Thou shoreless flood, which in thy ebb and flow
Claspest the limits of mortality,
And sick of prey, yet howling on for more,
Vomitest thy wrecks on its inhospitable shore;
　　　Treacherous in calm, and terrible in storm,
　　　　Who shall put forth on thee,
　　　　Unfathomable Sea?

WHEN PASSION'S TRANCE IS OVERPAST

When passion's trance is overpast,
If tenderness and truth could last,
Or live, whilst all wild feelings keep
Some mortal slumber, dark and deep,
I should not weep, I should not weep!

It were enough to feel, to see,
Thy soft eyes gazing tenderly,
And dream the rest—and burn and be
The secret food of fires unseen,
Couldst thou but be as thou hast been.

After the slumber of the year
The woodland violets reappear;
All things revive in field or grove,
And sky and sea, but[1] two, which move
And form all others, life and love.

WHEN THE LAMP IS SHATTERED

This is a difficult and mysterious poem. Rhythmically and in the form of its verses it is most original and exciting—and it is not necessary to know exactly what it is *about*. Certainly it is a 'private' poem, the key to which lies in Shelley's own life and his loves.

When the lamp is shattered
The light in the dust lies dead—
When the cloud is scattered
The rainbow's glory is shed.
When the lute is broken,
Sweet tones are remembered not;
When the lips have spoken,
Loved accents are soon forgot.

As music and splendour
Survive not the lamp and the lute,
The heart's echoes render
No song when the spirit is mute:—
No song but sad dirges,
Like the wind through a ruined cell,
Or the mournful surges
That ring the dead seaman's knell.

---

[1] except.

When hearts have once mingled
Love first leaves the well-built nest;
   The weak one is singled
To endure what it once possessed.
   O Love! who bewailest
The frailty of all things here,
   Why choose you the frailest
For your cradle, your home, and your bier?

   Its passions will rock thee
As the storms rock the ravens on high;
   Bright reason will mock thee,
Like the sun from a wintry sky.
   From thy nest every rafter
Will rot, and thine eagle home
   Leave thee naked to laughter,
When leaves fall and cold winds come.

EVENING: PONTE AL MARE, PISA

English society, which disapproved of their ideas and the conduct of their private lives, succeeded in driving both Shelley and Byron out of England. They spent most of their lives in Italy.

The sun is set; the swallows are asleep;
   The bats are flitting fast in the gray air;
The slow soft toads out of damp corners creep,
   And evening's breath, wandering here and there
Over the quivering surface of the stream,
Wakes not one ripple from its summer dream.

There is no dew on the dry grass to-night,
　　Nor damp within the shadow of the trees;
The wind is intermitting, dry, and light;
　　And in the inconstant motion of the breeze
The dust and straws are driven up and down,
And whirled about the pavement of the town . . .

The chasm in which the sun has sunk is shut
　　By darkest barriers of cinereous cloud,
Like mountain over mountain huddled, but
　　Growing and moving upward in a crowd,
And over it a space of watery blue,
Which the keen evening star is shining through.

From PROMETHEUS UNBOUND

The story of Prometheus, the man who rebelled against the authority
of the old Greek gods of Mount Olympus, and who climbed up and
stole fire for men, is a story which has fascinated poets. Prometheus
is a potent symbol of man's independence. The gods punished
Prometheus, but here he is unbound, free and, in Shelley's mind, a
symbol of Freedom.

Final Chorus

This is the day, which down the void abysm
At the Earth-born's spell yawns for Heaven's despotism,
　　And Conquest is dragged captive through the deep:
Love, from its awful throne of patient power
In the wise heart, from the last giddy hour
　　Of dread endurance, from the slippery, steep,
And narrow verge of crag-like agony, springs
And folds over the world its healing wings.

Gentleness, Virtue, Wisdom, and Endurance,
These are the seals of that most firm assurance
   Which bars the pit over Destruction's strength;
And if, with infirm hand, Eternity,
Mother of many acts and hours, should free
   The serpent that would clasp her with his length;
These are the spells by which to reassume
An empire o'er the disentangled doom.

To suffer woes which Hope thinks infinite;
To forgive wrongs darker than death or night;
   To defy Power, which seems omnipotent;
To love, and bear; to hope till Hope creates
From its own wreck the thing it contemplates;
   Neither to change, nor falter, nor repent;
This, like thy glory, Titan, is to be
Good, great and joyous, beautiful and free;
This is alone Life, Joy, Empire, and Victory.

George Gordon, Lord Byron (1788-1824)

From **CHILDE HAROLD'S PILGRIMAGE**

The Eve of the Battle of Waterloo, June 1815

There was a sound of revelry by night,
And Belgium's capital had gathered then
Her Beauty and her Chivalry, and bright
The lamps shone o'er fair women and brave men;
A thousand hearts beat happily; and when
Music arose with its voluptuous swell,
Soft eyes looked love to eyes which spake again,
And all went merry as a marriage-bell;
But hush! hark! a deep sound strikes like a rising knell!

Did ye not hear it?—No; 'twas but the wind
Or the car rattling o'er the stony street;
On with the dance! let joy be unconfined;
No sleep till morn, when Youth and Pleasure meet
To chase the glowing Hours with flying feet—
But, hark!—that heavy sound breaks in once more,
As if the clouds its echo would repeat;
And nearer, clearer, deadlier than before!
Arm! Arm! it is—it is—the cannon's opening roar!

Within a windowed niche of that high hall
Sate Brunswick's fated chieftain; he did hear
That sound the first amidst the festival,
And caught its tone with Death's prophetic ear;
And when they smiled because he deemed it near,
His heart more truly knew that peal too well
Which stretched his father on a bloody bier,
And roused the vengeance blood alone could quell:
He rushed into the field, and, foremost fighting, fell.

Ah! then and there was hurrying to and fro,
And gathering tears, and tremblings of distress,
And cheeks all pale, which but an hour ago
Blushed at the praise of their own loveliness;
And there were sudden partings, such as press
The life from out young hearts, and choking sighs
Which ne'er might be repeated; who could guess
If ever more should meet those mutual eyes,
Since upon night so sweet such awful morn could rise!

And there was mounting in hot haste: the steed,
The mustering squadron, and the clattering car,
Went pouring forward with impetuous speed,
And swiftly forming in the ranks of war;
And the deep thunder peal on peal afar;
And near, the beat of the alarming drum
Roused up the soldier ere the morning star;
While throng'd the citizens with terror dumb,
Or whispering, with white lips—'The foe! They come!
They come!'

Death of a Gladiator

From mighty wrongs to petty perfidy
Have I not seen what human things could do?
From the loud roar of foaming calumny
To the small whisper of the as paltry few,
And subtler venom of the reptile crew,
The Janus glance of whose significant eye,
Learning to lie with silence, would *seem* true,
And without utterance, save the shrug or sigh,
Deal round to happy fools its speechless obloquy.

But I have lived, and have not lived in vain:
My mind may lose its force, my blood its fire,
And my frame perish even in conquering pain;
But there is that within me which shall tire
Torture and Time, and breathe when I expire;
Something unearthly, which they deem not of,
Like the remembered tone of a mute lyre,
Shall on their softened spirits sink, and move
In hearts all rocky now the late remorse of love.

The seal is set.—Now welcome, thou dread power!
Nameless, yet thus omnipotent, which here
Walk'st in the shadow of the midnight hour
With a deep awe, yet all distinct from fear;
Thy haunts are ever where the dead walls rear
Their ivy mantles, and the solemn scene
Derives from thee a sense so deep and clear
That we become a part of what has been,
And grow unto the spot, all-seeing but unseen.

And here the buzz of eager nations ran,
In murmured pity, or loud-roared applause,
As man was slaughtered by his fellow-man.
And wherefore slaughtered? wherefore, but because
Such were the bloody Circus' genial laws,
And the imperial pleasure.—Wherefore not?
What matters where we fall to fill the maws

Of worms—on battle-plains or listed spot?
Both are but theatres where the chief actors rot.

I see before me the Gladiator lie:
He leans upon his hand—his manly brow
Consents to death, but conquers agony,
And his drooped head sinks gradually low—
And through his side the last drops, ebbing slow
From the red gash, fall heavy, one by one,
Like the first of a thunder-shower; and now
The arena swims around him—he is gone,
Ere ceased the inhuman shout which hailed the wretch who won.

He heard it, but he heeded not—his eyes
Were with his heart, and that was far away;
He recked not of the life he lost nor prize,
But where his rude hut by the Danube lay,
There were his young barbarians all at play,
There was their Dacian mother—he, their sire,
Butchered to make a Roman holiday—
All this rushed with his blood—Shall he expire
And unavenged? Arise! ye Goths, and glut your ire!

But here, where Murder breathed her bloody steam;
And here, where buzzing nations choked the ways,
And roared or murmured like a mountain stream
Dashing or winding as its torrent strays;
Here, where the Roman million's blame or praise
Was death or life, the playthings of a crowd,
My voice sounds much—and fall the stars' faint rays
On the arena void—seats crushed—walls bowed—
And galleries, where my steps seem echoes strangely loud.

A ruin—yet what ruin! from its mass
Walls, palaces, half-cities, have been reared;
Yet oft the enormous skeleton ye pass,
And marvel where the spoil could have appeared.
Hath it indeed been plundered, or but cleared?

Alas! developed, opens the decay,
When the colossal fabric's form is neared:
It will not bear the brightness of the day,
Which streams too much on all, years, man, have reft away.

But when the rising moon begins to climb
Its topmost arch, and gently pauses there;
When the stars twinkle through the loops of time,
And the low night-breeze waves along the air
The garland-forest, which the grey walls wear,
Like laurels on the bald first Caesar's head;
When the light shines serene but doth not glare,
Then in this magic circle raise the dead:
Heroes have trod this spot—'tis on their dust ye tread.

From DON JUAN

Byron had a lively jackdaw mind. There was nothing new that didn't
interest him, and he brought all that interested him into his poems:
often with a mockery which made people afraid of him. Look, for
example, at the last verse of this extract.

The Patent Age of New Inventions

Man's a strange animal, and makes strange use
    Of his own nature, and the various arts,
And likes particularly to produce
    Some new experiment to show his parts;
This is the age of oddities let loose,
    Where different talents find their different marts;
You'd best begin with truth, and when you've lost your
Labour, there's a sure market for imposture.

What opposite discoveries we have seen!
    (Signs of true genius, and of empty pockets.)
One makes new noses, one a guillotine,
    One breaks your bones, one sets them in their sockets;
But vaccination certainly has been
    A kind antithesis to Congreve's rockets,
With which the Doctor paid off an old pox,
By borrowing a new one from an ox.

Bread has been made (indifferent) from potatoes;
    And galvanism has set some corpses grinning,
But has not answered like the apparatus
    Of the Humane Society's beginning,
By which men are unsuffocated gratis:
    What wondrous new machines have late been spinning!
I said the small pox has gone out of late;
Perhaps it may be followed by the great.

'Tis said the great came from America;
    Perhaps it may set out on its return,—
The population there so spreads, they say
    'Tis grown high time to thin it in its turn,
With war, or plague, or famine, any way,
    So that civilization they may learn;
And which in ravage the more loathsome evil is—
Their real lues, or our pseudo-syphilis?

This is the patent age of new inventions
    For killing bodies, and for saving souls,
All propagated with the best intentions;
    Sir Humphry Davy's lantern, by which coals
Are safely mined for in the mode he mentions;
    Tombuctoo travels, voyages to the Poles,
Are ways to benefit mankind, as true,
Perhaps, as shooting them at Waterloo.

Man's a phenomenon, one knows not what,
　　And wonderful beyond all wondrous measure;
'Tis pity though, in this sublime world, that
　　Pleasure's a sin, and sometimes sin's a pleasure;
Few mortals know what end they would be at,
　　But whether glory, power, or love, or treasure,
The path is through perplexing ways, and when
The goal is gained, we die, you know—and then—

What then?—I do not know, no more do you—
　　And so good night . . .

Thou Shalt Believe

If ever I should condescend to prose,
　　I'll write poetical commandments, which
Shall supersede beyond all doubt all those
　　That went before; in these I shall enrich
My text with many things that no one knows,
　　And carry precept to the highest pitch:
I'll call the work 'Longinus o'er a Bottle,
Or, Every Poet his *own* Aristotle'.

Thou shalt believe in Milton, Dryden, Pope;
　　Thou shalt not set up Wordsworth, Coleridge, Southey;
Because the first is crazed beyond all hope,
　　The second drunk, the third so quaint and mouthy:
With Crabbe it may be difficult to cope,
　　And Campbell's Hippocrene is somewhat drouthy:
Thou shalt not steal from Samuel Rogers, nor
Commit—flirtation with the muse of Moore.

Thou shalt not covet Mr. Sotheby's muse,
　　His Pegasus, nor anything that's his;
Thou shalt not bear false witness like 'the Blues'—
　　(There's one, at least, is very fond of this);
Thou shalt not write, in short, but what I choose;
　　This is true criticism, and you may kiss—
Exactly as you please, or not,—the rod;
But if you don't, I'll lay it on, by God!

Milton's the prince of poets—so we say;
    A little heavy, but no less divine:
An independent being in his day—
    Learn'd, pious, temperate in love and wine;
But his life falling into Johnson's way,
    We're told this great high priest of all the Nine
Was whipt at college—a harsh sire—odd spouse,
For the first Mrs. Milton left his house.

All these are, *certes*, entertaining facts,
    Like Shakespeare's stealing deer, Lord Bacon's bribes;
Like Titus' youth, and Caesar's earliest acts;
    Like Burns (whom Doctor Currie well describes);
Like Cromwell's pranks;—but although truth exacts
    These amiable descriptions from the scribes,
As most essential to their hero's story,
They do not much contribute to his glory.

All are not moralists, like Southey, when
    He prated to the world of 'Pantisocracy';
Or Wordsworth unexcised, unhired, who then
    Seasoned his pedlar poems with democracy;
Or Coleridge, long before his flighty pen
    Lent to the Morning Post its aristocracy;
When he and Southey, following the same path,
Espoused two partners (milliners, of Bath).

Such names at present cut a convict figure,
    The very Botany Bay in moral geography;
Their loyal treason, renegado rigour,
    Are good manure for their more bare biography,
Wordsworth's last quarto, by the way, is bigger
    Than any since the birthday of typography;
A drowsy, frowzy poem, called 'The Excursion',
Writ in a manner which is my aversion.

He there builds up a formidable dyke
    Between his own and others' intellect:
But Wordsworth's poem, and his followers, like
    Joanna Southcote's Shiloh, and her sect,
Are things which in this century don't strike
    The public mind,—so few are the elect;
And the new births of both their stale virginities
Have proved but dropsies, taken for divinities.

We learn from Horace

We learn from Horace, 'Homer sometimes sleeps;'
    We feel without him, Wordsworth sometimes wakes,—
To show with what complacency he creeps,
    With his dear 'Waggoners' around his lakes.
He wishes for a 'boat' to sail the deeps—
    Of ocean?—No, of air: and then he makes
Another outcry for 'a little boat',
And drivels seas to set it well afloat.

If he must fain sweep o'er the ethereal plain,
    And Pegasus runs restive in his 'Waggon',
Could he not beg the loan of Charles's Wain?
    Or pray Medea for a single dragon?
Or if, too classic for his vulgar brain,
    He feared his neck to venture such a nag on,
And he must needs mount nearer to the moon,
Could not the blockhead ask for a balloon?

'Pedlars', and 'Boats', and 'Waggons'! Oh! ye shades
    Of Pope and Dryden, are we come to this?
That trash of such sort not alone evades
    Contempt, but from the bathos' vast abyss
Floats scumlike uppermost, and these Jack Cades
    Of sense and song, above your graves may hiss—

The 'little boatman' and his 'Peter Bell'[1]
Can sneer at him who drew 'Achitophel'![2]

If here and there some transient trait of pity

If here and there some transient trait of pity   ·
    Was shown, and some more noble heart broke through
Its bloody bond, and saved, perhaps, some pretty
    Child, or an aged, helpless man or two—
What's this in one annihilated city,
    Where thousand loves, and ties, and duties, grew?
Cockneys of London! Muscadins of Paris!
Just ponder what a pious pastime war is.

Think how the joys of reading a Gazette
    Are purchased by all agonies and crimes:
Or if these do not move you, don't forget
    Such doom may be your own in after-times.
Meantime the Taxes, Castlereagh, and Debt,
    Are hints as good as sermons, or as rhymes.
Read your own hearts and Ireland's present story,
Then feed her famine fat with Wellesley's glory.

But still there is unto a patriot nation,
    Which loves so well its country and its king,
A subject of sublimest exultation—
    Bear it, ye Muses, on your brightest wing!
Howe'er the mighty locust, Desolation
    Strip your green fields, and to your harvest cling,
Gaunt famine never shall approach the throne—
Though Ireland starve, great George weighs twenty stone.

---

[1] *Peter Bell*, a poem by Wordsworth.
[2] *Absalom and Achitophel*, by Dryden.

George Gordon, Lord Byron: from DON JUAN

Portrait of Wellington[1]

Oh, Wellington! (or 'Villainton'—for Fame
    Sounds the heroic syllables both ways;
France could not even conquer your great name,
    But punn'd it down to this facetious phrase—
Beating òr beaten she will laugh the same),
    You have obtained great pensions and much praise:
Glory like yours should any dare gainsay,
Humanity would rise, and thunder 'Nay!'

I don't think that you used Kinnaird quite well
    In Marinet's affair—in fact, 'twas shabby,
And like some other things won't do to tell
    Upon your tomb in Westminster's old abbey.
Upon the rest 'tis not worth while to dwell,
    Such tales being for the tea-hours of some tabby;
But though your years as *man* tend fast to *zero*,
In fact your Grace is still but a *young hero*.

Though Britain owes (and pays you too) so much,
    Yet Europe doubtless owes you greatly more;
You have repaired Legitimacy's crutch,
    A prop not quite so certain as before:
The Spanish, and the French, as well as Dutch,
    Have seen, and felt, how strongly you *restore*;
And Waterloo has made the world your debtor
(I wish your bards would sing it rather better).

You are 'the best of cut-throats':—do not start;
    The phrase is Shakespeare's, and not misapplied:—
War's a brain-spattering, windpipe-slitting art,
    Unless her cause by right be sanctified.
If you have acted *once* a generous part,
    The world, not the world's masters, will decide,
And I shall be delighted to learn who,
Save you and yours, have gained by Waterloo?

---

[1] Compare Swift, p. 92.

When Newton saw an apple fall, he found
    In that slight startle from his contemplation—
'Tis *said* (for I'll not answer above ground
    For any sage's creed or calculation)—
A mode of proving that the earth turned round
    In a most natural whirl, called 'gravitation';
And this is the sole mortal who could grapple,
Since Adam, with a fall, or with an apple.

Man fell with apples, and with apples rose,
    If this be true; for we must deem the mode
In which Sir Isaac Newton could disclose
    Through the then unpaved stars the turnpike road,
A thing to counterbalance human woes:
    For, ever since, immortal man hath glowed
With all kinds of mechanics, and full soon
Steam-engines will conduct him to the moon.

SO, WE'LL GO NO MORE A ROVING

So, we'll go no more a roving
    So late into the night,
Though the heart be still as loving,
    And the moon be still as bright.

For the sword outwears its sheath,
    And the soul wears out the breast,
And the heart must pause to breathe,
    And love itself have rest.

Though the night was made for loving,
    And the day returns too soon,
Yet we'll go no more a roving
    By the light of the moon.

George Gordon, Lord Byron

ON THIS DAY I COMPLETE MY THIRTY-SIXTH YEAR

Missolonghi. January 22, 1824

Like Shelley, Byron was a rebel against society, but, unlike Shelley, he had entered London society and been greatly pursued by many young women; although he was, as an unsuccessful one said, 'mad, bad and dangerous to know'. But he was also very good looking. Like Shelley, he preferred to live in Italy. Like him, he had a passion for freedom and in 1824 went to help the Greeks fight to free themselves from the Ottoman Empire, and died in Greece. Incidentally, he was a magnificent swimmer and tried out the legend of Hero and Leander by swimming the Hellespont.

'Tis time this heart should be unmoved,
        Since others it hath ceased to move:
Yet, though I cannot be beloved,
        Still let me love!

My days are in the yellow leaf;
        The flowers and fruits of love are gone;
The worm, the canker, and the grief
        Are mine alone!

The fire that on my bosom preys
        Is lone as some volcanic isle;
No torch is kindled at its blaze—
        A funeral pile.

The hope, the fear, the jealous care,
        The exalted portion of the pain
And power of love, I cannot share,
        But wear the chain.

But 'tis not *thus*—and 'tis not *here*—
        Such thoughts should shake my soul, nor *now*,
Where glory decks the hero's bier,
        Or binds his brow.

The sword, the banner, and the field,
    Glory and Greece, around me see!
The Spartan, borne upon his shield,
      Was not more free.

Awake! (not Greece—she *is* awake!)
    Awake, my spirit! Think through *whom*
Thy life-blood tracks its parent lake,
      And then strike home!

Tread those reviving passions down,
    Unworthy manhood!—unto thee
Indifferent should the smile or frown
      Of beauty be.

If thou regret'st thy youth, *why live?*
    The land of honourable death
Is here:—up to the field, and give
      Away thy breath!

Seek out—less often sought than found—
    A soldier's grave, for thee the best;
Then look around, and choose thy ground,
      And take thy rest.

OFT, IN THE STILLY NIGHT

Thomas Moore's *Irish Melodies* brought back into poetry the same element as Robert Burns had brought—the use of ballads and popular tunes.

Oft, in the stilly night,
    Ere Slumber's chain has bound me,
Fond Memory brings the light
    Of other days around me;
        The smiles, the tears,
        Of boyhood's years,
    The words of love then spoken;
        The eyes that shone,
        Now dimmed and gone,
    The cheerful hearts now broken!
Thus, in the stilly night,
    Ere Slumber's chain has bound me,
Sad Memory brings the light
    Of other days around me.

When I remember all
    The friends so linked together
I've seen around me fall,
    Like leaves in wintry weather;
        I feel like one
        Who treads alone
    Some banquet-hall deserted,
        Whose lights are fled,
        Whose garlands dead,
    And all but he departed!
Thus, in the stilly night,
    Ere Slumber's chain has bound me,
Sad Memory brings the light
    Of other days around me.

They may rail at this life—from the hour I began it,
    I've found it a life full of kindness and bliss;
And until they can show me some happier planet,
    More social and bright, I'll content me with this.
As long as the world has such lips and such eyes,
    As before me this moment enraptured I see,
They may say what they will of the orbs in the skies,
    But this earth is the planet for you, love, and me.

In Mercury's star, where each minute can bring them
    New sunshine and wit from the fountain on high,
Though the nymphs may have livelier poets to sing them,
    They've none, even there, more enamoured than I.
And as long as this harp can be wakened to love,
    And that eye its divine inspiration shall be,
They may talk as they will of their Edens above,
    But this earth is the planet for you, love, and me.

In that star of the west, by whose shadowy splendour
    At twilight so often we've roamed through the dew,
There are maidens, perhaps, who have bosoms as tender,
    And look, in their twilights, as lovely as you.
But though they were even more bright than the queen
    Of that isle they inhabit in heaven's blue sea,
As I never those fair young celestials have seen,
    Why,—this earth is the planet for you, love, and me.

As for those chilly orbs on the verge of creation,
    Where sunshine and smiles must be equally rare,
Did they want a supply of cold hearts for that station,
    Heaven knows we have plenty on earth we could spare.
Oh! think what a world we should have of it here,
    If the haters of peace, of affection, and glee,
Were to fly up to Saturn's comfortless sphere,
    And leave earth to such spirits as you, love, and me.

THE FISH, THE MAN, AND THE SPIRIT

To a Fish

You strange, astonished-looking, angle-faced,
　　Dreary-mouthed, gaping wretches of the sea,
　　Gulping salt-water everlastingly,
Cold-blooded, though with red your blood be graced,
And mute, though dwellers in the roaring waste;
　　And you, all shapes beside, that fishy be,—
　　Some round, some flat, some long, all devilry,
Legless, unloving, infamously chaste:—

O scaly, slippery, wet, swift, staring wights,
　　What is't ye do? What life lead? eh, dull goggles?
How do ye vary your vile days and nights?
　　How pass your Sundays? Are ye still but joggles
In ceaseless wash? Still nought but gapes and bites,
　　And drinks, and stares, diversified with boggles?

A Fish Answers

Amazing monster! that, for aught I know,
　　With the first sight of thee didst make our race
　　For ever stare! O flat and shocking face,
Grimly divided from the breast below!
Thou that on dry land horribly dost go
　　With a split body and most ridiculous pace,
　　Prong after prong, disgracer of all grace,
Long-useless-finned, haired, upright, unwet, slow!

O breather of unbreathable, sword-sharp air,
　　How canst exist? How bear thyself, thou dry
And dreary sloth? What particle canst share
　　Of the only blessed life, the watery?
I sometimes see of ye an actual *pair*
　　Go by! linked fin by fin! most odiously.

The Fish turns into a Man, and then into a Spirit, and again speaks

Indulge thy smiling scorn, if smiling still,
    O man! and loathe, but with a sort of love;
    For difference must its use by difference prove,
And, in sweet clang, the spheres with music fill.
One of the spirits am I, that at his will
    Live in whate'er has life—fish, eagle, dove—
    No hate, no pride, beneath nought, nor above,
A visitor of the rounds of God's sweet skill.

Man's life is warm, glad, sad, 'twixt loves and graves,
    Boundless in hope, honoured with pangs austere,
Heaven-gazing; and his angel-wings he craves:—
    The fish is swift, small-needing, vague yet clear,
A cold, sweet, silver life, wrapped in round waves,
    Quickened with touches of transporting fear.

John Clare (1793-1864)

John Clare was a wholly self-taught country boy, who wrote of the scene around him. He was 'taken up' by London society and enjoyed a brief period of sensational popularity but, once the novelty wore off, he was dropped again and returned to obscurity. He, like Smart, spent many of his later years in an asylum. His poetry was very little known until the twentieth century—indeed many of his poems have only recently been published.

WITH GARMENTS FLOWING

Come, come, my love, the bush is growing,
    The linnet sings the tune again
He sung when thou with garments flowing
    Went talking with me down the lane,
Dreaming of beauty ere I found thee,
    And musing by the bushes green;
The wind, enamoured, streaming round thee
    Painted the visions I had seen.

I guessed thy face without the knowing
    Was beautiful as e'er was seen;
I thought so by thy garments flowing
    And gait as airy as a queen;
Thy shape, thy size, could not deceive me;
    Beauty seemed hid in every limb;
And then thy face, when seen, believe me,
    Made every former fancy dim.

Yes, when thy face in beauty brightened
    The music of a voice divine,
Upon my heart thy sweetness lightened;
    Life, love, that moment, all were thine;
All I imagined musing lonely,
    When dreaming 'neath the greenwood tree,
Seeming to fancy visions only,
    Breathed living when I met with thee.

I wander oft, not to forget thee
    But just to feel those joys again,
When by the hawbush stile I met thee
    And heard thy voice adown the lane
Return me its good-humoured greeting;
    And oh, what music met my ear!
And then thy looks of wonder meeting,
    To see me come and talk so near!

Thy face that held no sort of scorning,
    Thy careless jump to reach the may;
That bush—I saw it many a morning
    And hoped to meet thee many a day;
Till winter came and stripped the bushes,
    The thistle withered on the moors,
Hopes sighed like winds along the rushes—
    I could not meet thee out of doors.

But winter's gone and spring is going
    And by thy own fireside I've been,
And told thee, dear, with garments flowing
    I met thee when the spring was green;
When travellers through snow-deserts rustle,
    Far from the strife of humankind,
How little seems the noise and bustle
    Of places they have left behind!

And on that long-remembered morning
    When first I lost this heart of mine,
Fame, all I'd hoped for, turned to scorning
    And love and hope lived wholly thine;
I told thee, and with rapture glowing
    I heard thee more than once declare,
That down the lane with garments flowing
    Thou with the spring wouldst wander there.

John Clare

MARRIED TO A SOLDIER

It is unlikely that A. E. Housman read this poem. The coincidence in
tone and rhythm of this poem and Housman's *In Valleys Green and
Still* (p. 339) is therefore all the more interesting.

The pride of all the village,
    The fairest to be seen,
The pride of all the village
    That might have been a queen,
Has bid good-bye to neighbours
    And left the dance and play
And married to a soldier
    And wandered far away.

The cottage is neglected,
    Where young men used to go
And talk about her beauty
    And see her come and go;
The bench agen her cottage
    Where she used to work at eve
Is vanished with the woodbine;
    And all are taken leave.

Her cottage is neglected,
    Her garden gathers green,
The summer comes unnoticed,
    Her flowers are never seen;
There's none to tie a blossom up
    Or clean a weed away;
She's married to a soldier
    And wandered far away.

The neighbours wonder at her,
    And surely well they may,
To think one so could flatter
    Her heart to go away.

But the cocked hat and feather
    Appeared so very gay,
She bundled clothes together
    And married far away.

AFTER-FAME

Time's stream in light is flowing,
    Where fame goes stirring on,
Where the mighty are agoing—
    Yet they never shall be gone.

Their names are earth's for ever,
    A breath for every mind,
Everlasting as the river,
    Never-ceasing as the wind.

A HILL-SIDE HOUSE

There is a house stands in a lonely way,
The hill seems falling on it all the day;
It seems half-hidden, like a robber's den,
And seems more safe for robbers than for men.
The trees look bushes scarcely half as big,
Seem taking root and growing on the rig.[1]
The cows that travel up with little heed
Seem looking down upon the roof to feed,
And if they take a step or stumble more
They seem in danger then of tumbling o'er.
The cocks and hens that fill a little space
Are all that look like home about the place.
The woods seem ready on the house to drop,
And rabbits breed above the chimney-top.

---

[1] ridge, roof.

O SILLY LOVE! O CUNNING LOVE!

O silly love! O cunning love!
    An old maid to trepan:
I cannot go about my work
    For loving of a man.
I cannot bake, I cannot brew,
    And, do the best I can,
I burn the bread and chill the mash,
    Through loving of a man.

Shrove Tuesday last I tried and tried
    To turn the cakes in pan,
And dropt the batter on the floor,
    Through thinking of a man.
My mistress screamed, my master swore,
    Boys cursed me in a troop;
The cat was all the friends I had,
    Who helped to clean it up.

Last Christmas Eve, from off the spit
    I took the goose to table,
Or should have done, but teasing love
    Did make me quite unable;
And down slipt dish, and goose, and all,
    With din and clitter-clatter;
All but the dog fell foul on me;
    He licked the broken platter.

Although I'm ten years past a score,
    Too long to play the fool,
My mistress says I must turn o'er
    My service for a school.
Good feth! what must I do, and do,
    To keep my service still?
I'll give the winds my thoughts to lose,
    Indeed and so I will.

And if the wind my love should lose,
    Right foolish were the play,
For I should mourn what I had lost,
    And love another day.
With crosses and with losses
    Right double were the ill,
So I'll e'en bear with love and all,
    Alack, and so I will.

PEGGY

Peggy said good morning and I said good-bye,
When farmers dib the corn and laddies sow the rye.
Young Peggy's face was commonsense and I was rather shy
When I met her in the morning when the farmers sow the rye.

Her half-laced boots fit tightly as she tripped along the grass,
And she set her foot so lightly where the early bee doth pass.
Oh, Peggy was a young thing, her face was commonsense,
I courted her about the spring and loved her ever thence.

Oh, Peggy was the young thing and bonny as to size;
Her lips were cherries of the spring and hazel were her eyes.
Oh, Peggy she was straight and tall as is the poplar-tree,
Smooth as the freestone of the wall, and very dear to me.

Oh, Peggy's gown was chocolate and full of cherries white;
I keep a bit on't for her sake and love her day and night.
I drest myself just like a prince and Peggy went to woo,
But she's been gone some ten years since, and I know not what
    to do.

John Clare

APPROACHING NIGHT

Oh, take this world away from me!
Its strife I cannot bear to see,
Its very praises hurt me more
Than e'en its coldness did before,
Its hollow ways torment me now
And start a cold sweat on my brow,
Its noise I cannot bear to hear,
Its joy is trouble to my ear,
Its ways I cannot bear to see,
Its crowds are solitudes to me.
Oh, how I long to be agen
That poor and independent man,
With labour's lot from morn to night
And books to read at candle-light;
That followed labour in the field
From light to dark when toil could yield
Real happiness with little gain,
Rich thoughtless health unknown to pain:
Though leaning on my spade to rest,
I've thought how richer folks were blest
And knew not quiet was the best.

Walter Savage Landor (1775-1864)

Landor lived to the age of 89, and his life spans many generations of poets. Young Swinburne went to see the old man, to pay court, and Landor with great ceremony gave the young poet a picture (which Swinburne later found to be worthless!). Landor was a man who lived among books, particularly the classics of Greek and Latin. He, like Shelley, lived in Italy; he was extremely well off. He, too, was an eccentric, a liberally-minded aristocrat, someone who does not fit in to any pigeon-hole.

DEATH STANDS ABOVE ME

Death stands above me, whispering low
    I know not what into my ear:
Of this strange language all I know
    Is, there is not a word of fear.

THAT CRITIC MUST INDEED BE BOLD

That critic must indeed be bold
Who pits new authors against old.
Only the ancient coin is prized,
The dead alone are canonized:
What was even Shakespeare until then?
A poet scarce compared with Ben:
And Milton in the streets no taller
Than sparkling easy-ambling Waller.
Waller now walks with rhyming crowds,
While Milton sits above the clouds,
Above the stars, his fixt abode,
And points to men their way to God.

PLAYS

Alas, how soon the hours are over,
Counted us out to play the lover!
And how much narrower is the stage,
Allotted us to play the sage!
But when we play the fool, how wide
The theatre expands; beside,
How long the audience sits before us!
How many prompters! what a chorus!

DYING SPEECH OF AN OLD PHILOSOPHER

I strove with none, for none was worth my strife:
    Nature I loved, and, next to Nature, Art:
I warmed both hands before the fire of Life;
    It sinks; and I am ready to depart.

ON THOMAS HOOD: CONFESSION OF JEALOUSY

Jealous, I own it, I was once,
That wickedness I here renounce.
I tried at wit . . . it would not do . . .
At tenderness . . . that failed me too,
Before me on each path there stood
The witty and the tender Hood.

IV

The Victorians

The adjective 'Victorian' in fact defines a period of over sixty years in which there were the profoundest changes in English life. Early Victorian—around 1845—has little in common with late Victorian—say 50 years later, 1895—yet if you read Hood's *Song of the Shirt,* published in 1843, and John Davidson's *Thirty Bob a Week,* published fifty years later, you will find them very close together in sentiment.

Two very different but overpowering figures dominated the long Victorian scene: Tennyson and Browning. Both wrote prolifically and both need to be read at length. Browning's masterpiece, *The Ring and the Book,* is far longer than the average novel and far more concentrated. It was a period in which poets, particularly Tennyson, aroused almost the same emotions as filmstars or pop-singers do now. Poetry, too, was expected to have a message, to exert moral influence. It is perhaps difficult for us, looking back, to understand how doubtful and melancholy the Victorians were in the midst of tremendous material prosperity which was the fruit of the Industrial Revolution. You read Matthew Arnold speaking of 'this strange disease of modern life' and yearning for the time of the scholar gipsy, whose story had been told by Glanvil in 1661. You have Clough mocking the materialism of the time in *The Latest Decalogue,* or a little known poet, Walter C. Smith, bitterly lamenting the depopulation of the Highlands in his poem *Glenaradale.* On the whole there is no movement or pattern of poetry one can truly say is essentially Victorian. Instead, there are many individuals writing in a variety of styles. After the Romantic Movement, which was, broadly speaking, the assertion of the individual, each poet sought his own style. There was no single accepted mode of writing as in the Elizabethan age or in the age of Pope. But the pervading tone, whether it be Coventry Patmore or Sydney Dobell, is one of melancholy, of personal melancholy.

It is important to remember that the one great artistic movement of the Victorian age—the Pre-Raphaelite movement—was based on a longing to return to a remote, entirely primitive and romantic age—to escape from machinery and commerce and the materialism that went with them, to a mythical, pre-Elizabethan era of chivalry, belief and simplicity: an era which never really existed.

Whereas Byron could incorporate galvanism (there was, in reality, a Signor Galvani) and Sir Humphrey Davy's safety lamp into his poetry, the Victorians found themselves overwhelmed by mechanism in all its forms—from photography to flying machines. When Tennyson wrote his splendid line about 'the ringing grooves of change' he really thought railway-wheels ran in grooves because he had, then, only once been in a train, and at night. In fifty years the landscape of England was changed. The whole basis of religious belief was also changed. The new science of geology and the publication of Darwin's *Origin of Species* in 1859, made simple Christian belief in the seven days of creation, as told in Genesis, impossible to accept literally. In face of such violence it is not surprising that men turned inward to think of and write about themselves or turned for reassurance to the past.

Everyone has heard of the 'nineties, and in the final decade of the century there was a sudden and intense activity. The theory of 'art for art's sake' propounded by Edgar Allan Poe in America in the 'forties and seized upon by Charles Baudelaire in France, at last percolated to England. Here was something to set against Tennyson's moral purpose and Arnold's 'high seriousness'. Poetry was to be for the sake of poetry alone. So Ernest Dowson could write *Cynara* without, as it were, meaning a word of it. The artificial brilliance of Wilde's wit recalls Pope: literature is again larger than life. But side by side with the aesthetes were the realists such as Davidson and the young Thomas Hardy. The plays of the Norwegian, Henrik Ibsen, were performed in London for the first time and the poet W. B. Yeats cursed *A Doll's House*; 'Art is art,' he said, 'because it is *not* life.' Can one imagine Wordsworth saying that a hundred years earlier as he pondered about poetry being the natural language of men speaking to each other? Add to this, too, such a young writer as Kipling—the first artist of any stature able to celebrate and enjoy machines for what they were.

It is no use pretending that any clear image emerges from the Victorian era. The 'romantic' and personal attitudes remain and harden. It is difficult to see how it could have been otherwise. But it was bound to lead, and rightly, to a change of taste in the twentieth century, as it has done.

Thomas Hood (1799-1845)

SONG: THE STARS ARE WITH THE VOYAGER

The stars are with the voyager
  Wherever he may sail;
The moon is constant to her time;
  The sun will never fail;
But follow, follow round the world,
  The green earth and the sea;
So love is with the lover's heart,
  Wherever he may be.

Wherever he may be, the stars
  Must daily lose their light;
The moon will veil her in the shade;
  The sun will set at night.
The sun may set, but constant love
  Will shine when he's away;
So that dull night is never night,
  And day is brighter day.

THE DOUBLE KNOCK

Notice the brilliance of Hood's device whereby the rhymes come at
the beginning of the lines, and are double rhymes, too. In the next
poem he dazzles with a treble rhyme at the *end* of each line. Fanny
Kemble and Edmund Kean were the star actress and actor of the day;
but the poem contains a whole catalogue of stage figures.
The opening line is a reference to the lion-shaped knockers you can
still see on many old front doors.

Rat-tat it went upon the lion's chin,
'That hat, I know it!' cried the joyful girl;
'Summer's it is, I know him by his knock,
Comers like him are welcome as the day!

Lizzy! go down and open the street-door,
Busy I am to any one but *him*.
Know him you must—he has been often here;
Show him up stairs, and tell him I'm alone.'

Quickly the maid went tripping down the stair;
Thickly the heart of Rose Matilda beat;
'Sure he has brought me tickets for the play—
Drury—or Covent Garden—darling man!—
Kemble will play—or Kean who makes the soul
Tremble; in Richard or the frenzied Moor—
Farren, the stay and prop of many a farce
Barren beside—or Liston, Laughter's Child—
Kelly the natural, to witness whom
Jelly is nothing to the public's jam—
Cooper, the sensible—and Walter Knowles
Super, in William Tell, now rightly told.
Better—perchance, from Andrews, brings a box,
Letter of boxes for the Italian stage—
Brocard! Donzelli! Taglioni! Paul!
No card,—thank heaven—engages me to-night!
Feathers, of course—no turban, and no toque—
Weather's against it, but I'll go in curls.
Dearly I dote on white—my satin dress,
Merely one night—it won't be much the worse—
Cupid—the New Ballet I long to see—
Stupid! why don't she go and ope the door!'

Glisten'd her eye as the impatient girl
Listen'd, low bending o'er the topmost stair,
Vainly, alas! she listens and she bends,
Plainly she hears this question and reply:
'Axes your pardon, Sir, but what d'ye want?'
'Taxes,' says he, 'and shall not call again!'

A NOCTURNAL SKETCH

Even is come; and from the dark Park, hark,
The signal of the setting sun—one gun!
And six is sounding from the chime, prime time
To go and see the Drury-Lane Dane[1] slain,—
Or hear Othello's jealous doubt spout out,—
Or Macbeth raving at that shade-made blade,
Denying to his frantic clutch much touch;—
Or else to see Ducrow with wide stride ride
Four horses as no other man can span;
Or in the small Olympic Pit, sit split
Laughing at Liston, while you quiz his phiz.

Anon Night comes, and with her wings brings things
Such as, with his poetic tongue, Young sung;
The gas up-blazes with its bright white light,
And paralytic watchmen prowl, howl, growl,
About the streets and take up Pall-Mall Sal,
Who, hasting to her nightly jobs, robs fobs.

Now thieves to enter for your cash, smash, crash,
Past drowsy Charley in a deep sleep, creep,
But frightened by Policeman B. 3, flee,
And while they're going, whisper low, 'No go!'
Now puss, while folks are in their beds, treads leads,
And sleepers waking, grumble—'Drat that cat!'
Who in the gutter caterwauls, squalls, mauls
Some feline foe, and screams in shrill ill-will.

Now Bulls of Bashan, of a prize size, rise
In childish dreams, and with a roar gore poor
Georgy, or Charley, or Billy, willy-nilly;—
But Nursemaid in a nightmare rest, chest-press'd,

---

[1] reference to *Hamlet* at Drury Lane Theatre.

Dreameth of one of her old flames, James Games,
And that she hears—what faith is man's—Ann's banns
And his, from Reverend Mr. Rice, twice, thrice:
White ribbons flourish, and a stout shout out,
That upward goes, shows Rose knows those bows' woes!

OUR VILLAGE: BY A VILLAGER

Mary Russell Mitford (1787–1855) was famous for her novel, *Our Village*, published in five volumes between 1824 and 1832.
This sort of verse, of irregular rhythms and long lines, but always ending in a rhyme however dragged in, prefigures the present-day American comic writer, Ogden Nash. Contrast Goldsmith, p. 129.

'Sweet Auburn, loveliest village of the plain'—Goldsmith.

Our village, that's to say not Miss Mitford's village, but our
    village of Bullock Smithy,
Is come into by an avenue of trees, three oak pollards, two
    elders, and a withy;
And in the middle, there's a green of about not exceeding an acre
    and a half;
It's common to all, and fed off by nineteen cows, six ponies,
    three horses, five asses, two foals, seven pigs, and a calf!
Besides a pond in the middle, as is held by a similar sort of
    common law lease,
And contains twenty ducks, six drakes, three ganders, two dead
    dogs, four drown'd kittens, and twelve geese.
Of course the green's cropt very close, and does famous for
    bowling when the little village boys play at cricket;
Only some horse, or pig, or cow, or great jackass, is sure to come
    and stand right before the wicket.
There's fifty-five private houses, let alone barns and workshops,
    and pigstyes, and poultry huts, and suchlike sheds;
With plenty of public-houses—two Foxes, one Green Man, three
    Bunch of Grapes, one Crown, and six King's Heads.

The Green Man is reckon'd the best, as the only one that for love
or money can raise

A postilion, a blue jacket, two deplorable lame white horses, and
a ramshackled 'neat postchaise.'

There's one parish church for all the people, whatsoever may be
their ranks in life or their degrees,

Except one very damp, small, dark, freezing-cold, little Methodist
chapel of Ease;

And close by the church-yard there's a stone-mason's yard, that
when the time is seasonable

Will furnish with afflictions sore and marble urns and cherubims
very low and reasonable.

There's a cage, comfortable enough; I've been in it with old Jack
Jeffrey and Tom Pike;

For the Green Man next door will send you in ale, gin, or any
thing else you like.

I can't speak of the stocks, as nothing remains of them but the
upright post;

But the pound is kept in repairs for the sake of Cob's horse, as is
always there almost.

There's a smithy of course, where that queer sort of a chap in his
way, Old Joe Bradley,

Perpetually hammers and stammers, for he stutters and shoes
horses very badly.

There's a shop of all sorts, that sells every thing, kept by the
widow of Mr. Task;

But when you go there it's ten to one she's out of every thing you
ask.

You'll know her house by the swarm of boys, like flies, about the
old sugary cask:

There are six empty houses, and not so well paper'd inside as out.

For bill-stickers won't beware, but sticks notices of sales and
election placards all about.

That's the Doctor's with a green door, where the garden pots in
the windows is seen;

A weakly monthly rose that don't blow, and a dead geranium,
and a tea-plant with five black leaves and one green.

As for hollyoaks at the cottage doors, and honeysuckles and
   jasmines, you may go and whistle;
But the Tailor's front garden grows two cabbages, a dock, a
   ha'porth of pennyroyal, two dandelions, and a thistle.
There are three small orchards—Mr. Busby's the schoolmaster's
   is the chief—
With two pear-trees that don't bear; one plum and an apple, that
   every year is stripped by a thief.
There's another small day-school too, kept by the respectable
   Mrs. Gaby.
A select establishment, for six little boys and one big, and four
   little girls and a baby;
There's a rectory, with pointed gables and strange odd chimneys
   that never smokes,
For the rector don't live on his living like other Christian sort of
   folks;
There's a barber's, once a week well filled with rough black-
   bearded, shock-headed churls,
And a window with two feminine men's heads, and two masculine
   ladies in false curls;
There's a butcher's, and a carpenter's, and a plumber's, and a
   small green-grocer's, and a baker,
But he won't bake on a Sunday, and there's a sexton that's a
   coal-merchant besides, and an undertaker;
And a toy-shop, but not a whole one, for a village can't compare
   with the London shops;
One window sells drums, dolls, kites, carts, bats, Clout's balls, and
   the other sells malt and hops.
And Mrs. Brown, in domestic economy not to be a bit behind
   her betters,
Lets her house to a milliner, a watchmaker, a rat-catcher, a
   cobbler, lives in it herself, and it's the post-office for letters.
Now I've gone through all the village—ay, from end to end, save
   and except one more house,
But I haven't come to that—and I hope I never shall—and that's
   the Village Poor House!

The imagination and memory play curious tricks. No doubt Hood *did* think that this was the house he was born in, but it wasn't! It was the house he moved to when he was just over two—so it is a pretty good feat of memory all the same.

I remember, I remember,
The house where I was born,
The little window where the sun
Came peeping in at morn;
He never came a wink too soon,
Nor brought too long a day,
But now, I often wish the night
Had borne my breath away!

I remember, I remember,
The roses, red and white,
The vi'lets, and the lily-cups,
Those flowers made of light!
The lilacs where the robin built,
And where my brother set
The laburnum on his birthday,—
The tree is living yet!

I remember, I remember,
Where I was used to swing,
And thought the air must rush as fresh
To swallows on the wing;
My spirit flew in feathers then,
That is so heavy now,
And summer pools could hardly cool
The fever on my brow!

I remember, I remember,
The fir trees dark and high;
I used to think their slender tops
Were close against the sky:

It was a childish ignorance,
But now 'tis little joy
To know I'm farther off from heav'n
Than when I was a boy.

THE SONG OF THE SHIRT

This poem was published in the Christmas number of *Punch,* 1843
A woman had been charged at Lambeth Police Court 'with pawning
her master's goods, for which she had to give £2 security. He
husband had died by an accident and had left her with two childre
to support and she obtained by her needle for the maintenance o
herself and family what her master called "the good living" of seve
shillings a week.'
Hood's poem shocked many people into realising the condition o
the poor. It is worth reflecting on the social changes since, and als
on the difference between *Punch* as it began and as it has become
When Hood wrote, there was no unemployment pay, no sick benefit
no National Assistance to help those in need. Hood's contemporary
Charles Dickens, was attacking the same social evils in his grea
novels.

With fingers weary and worn,
    With eyelids heavy and red,
A Woman sat, in unwomanly rags,
    Plying her needle and thread—
        Stitch! stitch! stitch!
In poverty, hunger, and dirt,
And still with a voice of dolorous pitch
She sang the 'Song of the Shirt!'

'Work! work! work!
While the cock is crowing aloof!
    And work—work—work,
Till the stars shine through the roof!
It's O! to be a slave
    Along with the barbarous Turk,
Where woman has never a soul to save,
    If this is Christian work!

'Work—work—work
    Till the brain begins to swim;
        Work—work—work
    Till the eyes are heavy and dim!
Seam, and gusset, and band,
        Band, and gusset, and seam,
    Till over the buttons I fall asleep,
        And sew them on in a dream!

'O! Men with Sisters dear!
        O! Men! with Mothers and Wives!
It is not linen you're wearing out,
        But human creatures' lives!
            Stitch—stitch—stitch,
        In poverty, hunger, and dirt,
Sewing at once, with a double thread,
        A Shroud as well as a Shirt.

'But why do I talk of Death?
        That Phantom of grisly bone,
I hardly fear his terrible shape,
        It seems so like my own—
        It seems so like my own,
        Because of the fasts I keep,
Oh! God! that bread should be so dear,
        And flesh and blood so cheap!

'Work—work—work!
        My labour never flags;
And what are its wages? A bed of straw,
        A crust of bread—and rags.
That shatter'd roof,—and this naked floor—
        A table—a broken chair—
And a wall so blank, my shadow I thank
        For sometimes falling there!

'Work—work—work!
From weary chime to chime,
    Work—work—work—
As prisoners work for crime!
Band, and gusset, and seam,
    Seam, and gusset, and band,
Till the heart is sick, and the brain benumb'd,
    As well as the weary hand.

'Work—work—work,
In the dull December light,
    And work—work—work,
When the weather is warm and bright—
While underneath the eaves
    The brooding swallows cling
As if to show me their sunny backs
    And twit me with the spring.

'Oh! but to breathe the breath
Of the cowslip and primrose sweet—
    With the sky above my head,
And the grass beneath my feet,
For only one short hour
    To feel as I used to feel,
Before I knew the woes of want
    And the walk that costs a meal!

'Oh but for one short hour!
    A respite however brief!
No blessed leisure for Love or Hope,
    But only time for Grief!
A little weeping would ease my heart,
    But in their briny bed
My tears must stop, for every drop
    Hinders needle and thread!'

Seam, and gusset, and band,
Band, and gusset, and seam,
    Work, work, work,
Like the Engine that works by Steam!
A mere machine of iron and wood
        That toils for Mammon's sake—
Without a brain to ponder and craze
        Or a heart to feel—and break!

With fingers weary and worn,
        With eyelids heavy and red,
A woman sate in unworthy rags,
        Plying her needle and thread—
            Stitch! stitch! stitch!
    In poverty, hunger, and dirt,
And still with a voice of dolorous pitch,
Would that its tone could reach the Rich!—
        She sang this 'Song of the Shirt!'

SONNET: IT IS NOT DEATH

With the weakening of Christian belief, the poet becomes less
reconciled to death; compare the seventeenth century attitude to
death in such poems as those on pages 35 and 46.

It is not death, that sometime in a sigh
This eloquent breath shall take its speechless flight;
That sometime these bright stars, that now reply
In sunlight to the sun, shall set in night;
That this warm conscious flesh shall perish quite,
And all life's ruddy springs forget to flow;
That thoughts shall cease, and the immortal spright
Be lapp'd in alien clay and laid below;

It is not death to know this,—but to know
That pious thoughts, which visit at new graves
In tender pilgrimage, will cease to go
So duly and so oft,—and when grass waves
Over the past-away, there may be then
No resurrection in the minds of men.

William Barnes (1801-1886)

TROUBLES OF THE DAY

Most of William Barnes's poems are written in Dorset dialect which
at first sight makes them difficult. But they are no more difficult than
Burns, and well repay perseverance. Thomas Hardy wrote a beautiful
poem, *The Last Signal,* in memory of Barnes, who was his lifelong
friend.

As there, along the elmy hedge, I go
    By banksides white with parsley—parsley-bloom—
Where smell of new-mown hay comes wafted by
    On wind of dewy evening, evening gloom,
And homeward take my shaded way between
The hedge's high-tipped wood, and barley green,
       I sing, or mean,
'O troubles of the day. Flee to the west,
Come not my homeward way. I seek my rest.'

The dairy cows, by meadow trees, lie free,
    Of calls to milkers' pails—the milkmaids' calls;
The horses now have left their rolling wheels
    And reel'd in home to stable, to their stalls,
And down the grey-pool'd stream the fish awhile
Are free from all the prowling angler's guile,
       And o'er the stile
I sink, and sing or say, 'Flee to the west
O troubles of the day. I seek my rest.'

My boy—whose little high-rigged boat, athwart
    The windy pool, by day, at afternoon,
Has fluttered, tippling like a bird
    That tries to fly unfledged—to fly too soon—
Now sleeps forgetful of the boat and fond
Old dog that he has taught to swim the pond.
      So flee beyond
The edge of sinking day, towards the west,
Ye troubles, flee away. I seek my rest.

A star is o'er the tower on the hill
    Whence rings no clanging knell; no evening peal,
The mill stands dark beside the flouncing foam;
    But still is all its gear, its mossy wheel.
No rooks now sweep along the darkened sky,
And o'er the road few feet or wheels go by.
      So fly, O fly
Ye troubles, with the day, adown the west,
Come not along my way. I seek my rest.

Winthrop Mackworth Praed (1802-1839)

GOOD-NIGHT TO THE SEASON

Compare this *vers de société,* as it is called—or light verse—with poems
by Pope and Hood.

So runs the world away.—Hamlet

Good-night to the Season! 'tis over!
    Gay dwellings no longer are gay;
The courtier, the gambler, the lover,
    Are scattered like swallows away;
There's nobody left to invite one,
    Except my good uncle and spouse;

My mistress is bathing at Brighton,
    My patron is sailing at Cowes;
For want of a better employment,
    Till Ponto and Don can get out,
I'll cultivate rural enjoyment,
    And angle immensely for trout.

Good-night to the Season! the lobbies,
    Their changes, and rumours of change,
Which startled the rustic Sir Bobbies,
    And made all the Bishops look strange;
The breaches, and battles, and blunders,
    Performed by the Commons and Peers;
The Marquis's eloquent thunders,
    The Baronet's eloquent ears;
Denouncings of Papists and treasons,
    Of foreign dominion, and oats;
Misrepresentations of reasons,
    And misunderstandings of notes.

Good-night to the Season! the building's
    Enough to make Inigo sick;
The paintings, and plasterings, and gildings
    Of stucco, and marble, and brick;
The orders deliciously blended,
    From love of effect, into one;
The club-houses only intended,
    The palaces only begun;
The hell, where the fiend in his glory
    Sits staring at putty and stones,
And scrambles from story to story,
    To rattle at midnight his bones.

Good-night to the Season! the dances,
    The fillings of hot little rooms,
The glancings of rapturous glances
    The fancyings of fancy costumes;

The pleasures which fashion makes duties,
    The praisings of fiddles and flutes,
The luxury of looking at beauties,
    The tedium of talking to mutes;
The female diplomatists, planners
    Of matches for Laura and Jane,
The ice of her Ladyship's manners,
    The ice of his Lordship's champagne.

Good-night to the Season! the rages
    Led off by the chiefs of the throng,
The Lady Matilda's new pages,
    The Lady Eliza's new song,
Miss Fennel's macaw, which at Boodle's
    Was held to have something to say;
Mrs. Splenetic's musical poodles,
    Which bark 'Batti—Batti!' all day;
The pony Sir Araby sported,
    As hot and as black as a coal,
And the lion his mother imported,
    In bearskins and grease, from the Pole.

Good-night to the Season! the Toso,
    So very majestic and tall;
Miss Ayton, whose singing was so-so,
    And Pasta, divinest of all;
The labour in vain of the ballet,
    So sadly deficient in stars;
The foreigners thronging the Alley,
    Exhaling the breath of cigars;
The *loge*, where some heiress, how killing,
    Environed with exquisites, sits,
The lovely one out of her drilling,
    The silly ones out of their wits.

Good-night to the Season! the splendour
    That beamed in the Spanish bazaar,
Where I purchased—my heart was so tender—
    A card-case,—a pasteboard guitar,—
A bottle of perfume,—a girdle,—
    A lithographed Riego, full-grown,
Whom bigotry drew on a hurdle,
    That artists might draw him on stone,—
A small panorama of Seville,—
    A trap for demolishing flies,—
A caricature of the Devil,—
    And a look from Miss Sheridan's eyes.

Good-night to the Season! the flowers
    Of the grand horticultural fete,
When boudoirs were quitted for bowers,
    And the fashion was, not to be late;
When all who had money and leisure
    Grew rural o'er ices and wines,
All pleasantly toiling for pleasure,
    All hungrily pining for pines,
And making of beautiful speeches,
    And marring of beautiful shows,
And feeding on delicate peaches,
    And treading on delicate toes.

Good-night to the Season! another
    Will come with its trifles and toys,
And hurry away, like its brother,
    In sunshine, and odour, and noise.
Will it come with a rose, or a brier?
    Will it come with a blessing, or curse?
Will its bonnets be lower, or higher?
    Will its morals be better, or worse?
Will it find me grown thinner, or fatter,
    Or fonder of wrong or of right,
Or married, or buried?—no matter,—
    Good-night to the Season!—Good-night!

THE SEA RITUAL

Prayer unsaid, and mass unsung,
Deadman's dirge must still be rung:
    Dingle-dong, the dead-bells sound!
    Mermen chant his dirge around!

Wash him bloodless, smoothe him fair,
Stretch his limbs, and sleek his hair:
    Dingle-dong, the dead-bells go!
    Mermen swing them to and fro!

In the wormless sands shall he
Feast for no foul gluttons be:
    Dingle-dong, the dead-bells chime!
    Mermen keep the tone and time!

We must with a tombstone brave
Shut the shark out from his grave:
    Dingle-dong, the dead-bells toll!
    Mermen dirgers ring his knoll!

Such a slab will we lay o'er him
All the dead shall rise before him!
    Dingle-dong, the dead-bells boom;
    Mermen lay him in his tomb!

Thomas Lovell Beddoes (1803-1849)

WOLFRAM'S SONG

Beddoes, like Chatterton, was an extraordinary and eccentric genius
He wrote fragments, and long bits of plays, in such brilliant imitatior
Elizabethan or Jacobean English that they deceived many people
He finally committed suicide, leaving to his doctor a stomach-pump
and a case of champagne! This is a song from one of his plays.

Old Adam, the carrion crow,
    The old crow of Cairo;
He sat in the shower, and let it flow
    Under his tail and over his crest;
        And through every feather
        Leaked the wet weather;
And the bough swung under his nest;
For his beak it was heavy with marrow.
    Is that the wind dying? O no;
    It's only two devils, that blow
    Through a murderer's bones, to and fro,
    In the ghosts' moonshine.

Ho! Eve, my grey carrion wife,
    When we have supped on kings' marrow,
Where shall we drink and make merry our life?
    Our nest it is queen Cleopatra's skull,
        'Tis cloven and cracked,
        And battered and hacked,
But with tears of blue eyes it is full:
Let us drink then, my raven of Cairo!
    Is that the wind dying? O no;
    It's only two devils, that blow
    Through a murderer's bones, to and fro,
    In the ghosts' moonshine.

ARK ROSALEEN

Sometimes—as in Shelley's *When the Lamp is Shattered* (p. 201)—it is impossible to 'explain' a poem or even to want to. In this poem it is not necessary to know that dark Rosaleen is Ireland, and it does not necessarily help if you do. What is there is marvellous sound and rhythm like an incantation. This poem, if you read it aloud, is like a spell.

O my Dark Rosaleen,
    Do not sigh, do not weep!
The priests are on the ocean green,
    They march along the deep.
There's wine from the royal Pope,
    Upon the ocean green;
And Spanish ale shall give you hope,
    My Dark Rosaleen!
    My own Rosaleen!
Shall glad your heart, shall give you hope,
Shall give you health, and help, and hope,
    My Dark Rosaleen!

Over hills, and thro' dales,
    Have I roamed for your sake;
All yesterday I sailed with sails
    On river and on lake.
The Erne, at its highest flood,
    I dashed across unseen,
For there was lightning in my blood,
    My dark Rosaleen!
    My own Rosaleen!
O, there was lightning in my blood,
Red lightning lightened thro' my blood,
    My Dark Rosaleen!

All day long, in unrest,
    To and fro do I move.
The very soul within my breast
    Is wasted for you, love!

The heart in my bosom faints
　　To think of you, my Queen,
My life of life, my saint of saints,
　　My Dark Rosaleen!
　　My own Rosaleen!
To hear your sweet and sad complaints,
My life, my love, my saint of saints,
　　My Dark Rosaleen!

Woe and pain, pain and woe,
　　Are my lot, night and noon,
To see your bright face clouded so,
　　Like to the mournful moon.
But yet will I rear your throne
　　Again in golden sheen;
'Tis you shall reign, shall reign alone,
　　My Dark Rosaleen!
　　My own Rosaleen!
'Tis you shall have the golden throne,
'Tis you shall reign, and reign alone,
　　My Dark Rosaleen!

Over dews, over sands,
　　Will I fly, for your weal:
Your holy delicate white hands
　　Shall girdle me with steel.
At home, in your emerald bowers,
　　From morning's dawn till e'en,
You'll pray for me, my flower of flowers,
　　My Dark Rosaleen!
　　My fond Rosaleen!
You'll think of me thro' daylight hours,
My virgin flower, my flower of flowers,
　　My Dark Rosaleen!

I could scale the blue air,
　　I could plough the high hills,
O, I could kneel all night in prayer,
　　To heal your many ills!
And one beamy smile from you
　　Would float like light between
My toils and me, my own, my true,
　　My Dark Rosaleen!
　　My fond Rosaleen!
Would give me life and soul anew,
A second life, a soul anew,
　　My Dark Rosaleen!

O, the Erne shall run red,
　　With redundance of blood,
The earth shall rock beneath our tread,
　　And flames wrap hill and wood,
And gun-peal and slogan-cry
　　Wake many a glen serene,
Ere you shall fade, ere you shall die,
　　My Dark Rosaleen!
　　My own Rosaleen!
The Judgement Hour must first be nigh,
Ere you can fade, ere you can die,
　　My Dark Rosaleen!

Emily Brontë (1818-1848)

THE VISIONARY

Silent is the house: all are laid asleep:
One alone looks out o'er the snow-wreaths deep,
Watching every cloud, dreading every breeze
That whirls the 'wildering drift, and bends the groaning trees.

Cheerful is the hearth, soft the matted floor;
Not one shivering gust creeps through pane or door;
The little lamp burns straight, its rays shoot strong and far:
I trim it well, to be the wanderer's guiding-star.

Frown, my haughty sire! chide, my angry dame!
Set your slaves to spy; threaten me with shame:
But neither sire nor dame, nor prying serf shall know
What angel nightly tracks that waste of frozen snow.

What I love shall come like visitant of air,
Safe in secret power from lurking human snare;
Who loves me, no word of mine shall e'er betray,
Though for faith unstained my life must forfeit pay.

Burn then, little lamp; glimmer straight and clear—
Hush! a rustling wing stirs, methinks, the air:
He for whom I wait thus ever comes to me;
Strange Power! I trust thy might; trust thou my constancy.

Alfred Lord Tennyson (1809-1892)

THE DYING SWAN

The plain was grassy, wild and bare,
Wide, wild, and open to the air,
Which had built up everywhere
    An under-roof of doleful gray.
With an inner voice the river ran,
Adown it floated a dying swan,
        And loudly did lament.
    It was the middle of the day.
Ever the weary wind went on,
        And took the reed-tops as it went.

Some blue peaks in the distance rose,
And white against the cold-white sky,
Shone out their crowning snows.
    One willow over the river wept,
And shook the wave as the wind did sigh;
Above in the wind was the swallow,
        Chasing itself at its own wild will,
        And far thro' the marish green and still
        The tangled water-courses slept,
Shot over with purple, and green, and yellow.

The wild swan's death-hymn took the soul
Of that waste place with joy
Hidden in sorrow: at first to the ear
The warble was low, and full and clear;
And floating about the under-sky,
Prevailing in weakness, the coronach stole
Sometimes afar, and sometimes anear;
But anon her awful jubilant voice,
With a music strange and manifold,
Flowed forth on a carol free and bold;
As when a mighty people rejoice
With shawms, and with cymbals, and harps of gold,
And the tumult of their acclaim is rolled

Thro' the open gates of the city afar,
To the shepherd who watcheth the evening star.
And the creeping mosses and clambering weeds,
And the willow-branches hoar and dank,
And the wavy swell of the soughing reeds,
And the wave-worn horns of the echoing bank,
And the silvery marish-flowers that throng
The desolate creeks and pools among,
Were flooded over with eddying song.

THE BROOK

This poem is usually only printed in part: the lyric about the Brook
—'I come from haunts of coot and hern'—but it is best to read it in
full, for it is most original and truly Tennysonian. You must
imagine a silent listener and a speaker, Lawrence Aylmer, whose
brother Edmund, a poet, is dead. It was Edmund who wrote the
poem about the Brook which Lawrence quotes, at intervals, as he
tells the story of the Willows family. Such a perfect and amusing,
evocation of country life could only have come from a country-bred
man, as Tennyson was.

'Here, by this brook, we parted; I to the East
And he for Italy—too late—too late:
One whom the strong sons of the world despise;
For lucky rhymes to him were scrip and share,
And mellow metres more than cent for cent;
Nor could he understand how money breeds,
Thought it a dead thing; yet himself could make
The thing that is not as the thing that is.
O had he lived! In our schoolbooks we say,
Of those that held their heads above the crowd,
They flourished then or then; but life in him
Could scarce be said to flourish, only touched
On such a time as goes before the leaf,
When all the wood stands in a mist of green,

And nothing perfect: yet the brook he loved,
For which, in branding summers of Bengal,
Or ev'n the sweet half-English Neilgherry air
I panted, seems, as I re-listen to it,
Prattling the primrose fancies of the boy,
To me that loved him; for "O brook," he says,
"O babbling brook," says Edmund in his rhyme,
"Whence come you?" and the brook, why not? replies.

I come from haunts of coot and hern,
    I make a sudden sally,
And sparkle out among the fern,
    To bicker down a valley.

By thirty hills I hurry down,
    Or slip between the ridges,
By twenty thorps, a little town,
    And half a hundred bridges.

Till last by Philip's farm I flow
    To join the brimming river,
For men may come and men may go,
    But I go on for ever.

'Poor lad, he died at Florence, quite worn out,
Travelling to Naples. There is Darnley bridge,
It has more ivy; there the river; and there
Stands Philip's farm where brook and river meet.

I chatter over stony ways,
    In little sharps and trebles,
I bubble into eddying bays,
    I babble on the pebbles.

With many a curve my banks I fret
    By many a field and fallow,
And many a fairy foreland set
    With willow-weed and mallow.

I chatter, chatter, as I flow
    To join the brimming river,
For men may come and men may go,
    But I go on for ever.

'But Philip chattered more than brook or bird;
Old Philip; all about the fields you caught
His weary daylong chirping, like the dry
High-elbowed grigs that leap in summer grass.

I wind about, and in and out,
    With here a blossom sailing,
And here and there a lusty trout,
    And here and there a grayling,

And here and there a foamy flake
    Upon me, as I travel
With many a silvery waterbreak
    Above the golden gravel,

And draw them all along, and flow
    To join the brimming river,
For men may come and men may go,
    But I go on for ever.

'O darling Katie Willows, his one child!
A maiden of our century, yet most meek;
A daughter of our meadows, yet not coarse;
Straight, but as lissome as a hazel wand;
Her eyes a bashful azure, and her hair
In gloss and hue the chestnut, when the shell
Divides threefold to show the fruit within.
    'Sweet Katie, once I did her a good turn,
Her and her far-off cousin and betrothed,
James Willows, of one name and heart with her.
For here I came, twenty years back—the week
Before I parted with poor Edmund; crossed
By that old bridge which, half in ruins then,

Still makes a hoary eyebrow for the gleam
Beyond it, where the waters marry—crossed,
Whistling a random bar of Bonny Doon,
And pushed at Philip's garden-gate. The gate,
Half-parted from a weak and scolding hinge,
Stuck; and he clamour'd from a casement, "Run"
To Katie somewhere in the walks below,
"Run, Katie!" Katie never ran: she moved
To meet me, winding under woodbine bowers,
A little fluttered, with her eyelids down,
Fresh apple-blossom, blushing for a boon.

    'What was it? less of sentiment than sense
Had Katie; not illiterate; nor of those
Who dabbling in the fount of fictive tears,
And nursed by mealy-mouthed philanthropies,
Divorce the Feeling from her mate the Deed.

    'She told me. She and James had quarrelled. Why?
What cause of quarrel? None, she said, no cause;
James had no cause: but when I prest the cause,
I learnt that James had flickering jealousies
Which angered her. Who angered James? I said.
But Katie snatched her eyes at once from mine,
And sketching with her slender pointed foot
Some figure like a wizard pentagram
On garden gravel, let my query pass
Unclaimed, in flushing silence, till I asked
If James were coming. "Coming every day,"
She answered, "ever longing to explain,
But evermore her father came across
With some long-winded tale, and broke him short;
And James departed vext with him and her."
How could I help her? "Would I—was it wrong?"
(Claspt hands and that petitionary grace
Of sweet seventeen subdued me ere she spoke)
"O would I take her father for one hour,
For one half-hour, and let him talk to me!"
And even while she spoke, I saw where James
Made toward us, like a wader in the surf,
Beyond the brook, waist-deep in meadow-sweet.

'O Katie, what I suffered for your sake!
For in I went, and called old Philip out
To show the farm: full willingly he rose:
He led me thro' the short sweet-smelling lanes
Of his wheat-suburb, babbling as he went.
He praised his land, his horses, his machines;
He praised his ploughs, his cows, his hogs, his dogs;
He praised his hens, his geese, his guinea-hens;
His pigeons, who in session on their roofs
Approved him, bowing at their own deserts:
Then from the plaintive mother's teat he took
Her blind and shuddering puppies, naming each,
And naming those, his friends, for whom they were:
Then crost the common into Darnley chase
To show Sir Arthur's deer. In copse and fern
Twinkled the innumerable ear and tail.
Then, seated on a serpent-rooted beech,
He pointed out a pasturing colt, and said:
"That was the four-year-old I sold the Squire."
And there he told a long long-winded tale
Of how the Squire had seen the colt at grass,
And how it was the thing his daughter wished,
And how he sent the bailiff to the farm
To learn the price, and what the price he asked,
And how the bailiff swore that he was mad,
But he stood firm; and so the matter hung;
He gave them line: and five days after that
He met the bailiff at the Golden Fleece,
Who then and there had offered something more,
But he stood firm; and so the matter hung;
He knew the man; the colt would fetch its price;
He gave them line: and how by chance at last
(It might be May or April, he forgot,
The last of April or the first of May)
He found the bailiff riding by the farm,
And, talking from the point, he drew him in,
And there he mellowed all his heart with ale,
Until they closed a bargain, hand in hand.

'Then, while I breathed in sight of haven, he,
Poor fellow, could he help it? recommenced,
And ran thro' all the coltish chronicle,
Wild Will, Black Bess, Tantivy, Tallyho,
Reform, White Rose, Bellerophon, the Jilt,
Arbaces, and Phenomenon, and the rest,
Till, not to die a listener, I arose,
And with me Philip, talking still; and so
We turned our foreheads from the falling sun,
And following our own shadows thrice as long
As when they followed us from Philip's door,
Arrived and found the sun of sweet content
Re-risen in Katie's eyes, and all things well.

I steal by lawns and grassy plots,
   I slide by hazel covers;
I move the sweet forget-me-nots
   That grow for happy lovers.

I slip, I slide, I gloom, I glance,
   Among my skimming swallows;
I make the netted sunbeam dance
   Against my sandy shallows.

I murmur under moon and stars
   In brambly wildernesses;
I linger by my shingly bars;
   I loiter round my cresses;

And out again I curve and flow
   To join the brimming river,
For men may come and men may go,
   But I go on for ever.

Yes, men may come and go; and these are gone,
All gone. My dearest brother, Edmund, sleeps,
Not by the well-known stream and rustic spire,
But unfamiliar Arno, and the dome
Of Brunelleschi; sleeps in peace: and he,
Poor Philip, of all his lavish waste of words

Remains the lean P. W. on his tomb:
I scraped the lichen from it: Katie walks
By the long wash of Australasian seas
Far off, and holds her head to other stars,
And breathes in April-autumns. All are gone.'
   So Lawrence Aylmer, seated on a stile
In the long hedge, and rolling in his mind
Old waifs of rhyme, and bowing o'er the brook
A tonsured head in middle age forlorn,
Mused, and was mute. On a sudden a low breath
Of tender air made tremble in the hedge
The fragile bindweed-bells and briony rings;
And he looked up. There stood a maiden near,
Waiting to pass. In much amaze he stared
On eyes a bashful azure, and on hair
In gloss and hue the chestnut, when the shell
Divides threefold to show the fruit within:
Then, wondering, asked her 'Are you from the farm?'
'Yes' answered she. 'Pray stay a little: pardon me;
What do they call you?' 'Katie.' 'That were strange.
What surname?' 'Willows.' 'No!' 'That is my name.'
'Indeed!' and here he looked so self-perplext,
That Katie laughed, and laughing blushed, till he
Laughed also, but as one before he wakes,
Who feels a glimmering strangeness in his dream.
Then looking at her; 'Too happy, fresh and fair,
Too fresh and fair in our sad world's best bloom,
To be the ghost of one who bore your name
About these meadows, twenty years ago.'
   'Have you not heard?' said Katie, 'we came back.
We bought the farm we tenanted before.
Am I so like her? so they said on board.
Sir, if you knew her in her English days,
My mother, as it seems you did, the days
That most she loves to talk of, come with me.
My brother James is in the harvest-field:
But she—you will be welcome—O, come in!'

From THE PRINCESS: A MEDLEY

This is an account of an actual early-Victorian fête, held in the grounds of Sir Henry Lushington's house near Maidstone. *The Princess* itself is not judged to be one of Tennyson's most successful poems, but its theme—the better education of women—was serious enough, and in later editions Tennyson added lyrics, such as *Tears, idle tears,* which are among his most famous poems. Compare *Penshurst,* p. 37.

So sang the gallant glorious chronicle

So sang the gallant glorious chronicle;
And, I all rapt in this, 'Come out,' he said,
'To the Abbey: there is Aunt Elizabeth
And sister Lilia with the rest.' We went
(I kept the book and had my finger in it)
Down thro' the park: strange was the sight to me;
For all the sloping pasture murmured, sown
With happy faces and with holiday.
There moved the multitude, a thousand heads:
The patient leaders of their Institute
Taught them with facts. One reared a font of stone
And drew, from butts of water on the slope,
The fountain of the moment, playing, now
A twisted snake, and now a rain of pearls,
Or steep-up spout whereon the gilded ball
Danced like a wisp: and somewhat lower down
A man with knobs and wires and vials fired
A cannon: Echo answered in her sleep
From hollow fields: and here were telescopes
For azure views; and there a group of girls
In circle waited, whom the electric shock
Dislink'd with shrieks and laughter: round the lake
A little clock-work steamer paddling plied
And shook the lilies: perch'd about the knolls
A dozen angry models jetted steam:
A petty railway ran: a fire-balloon
Rose gem-like up before the duskly groves
And dropt a fairy parachute and past:

And there thro' twenty posts of telegraph
They flashed a saucy message to and fro
Between the mimic stations; so that sport
Went hand in hand with Science; otherwhere
Pure sport; a herd of boys with clamour bowl'd
And stump'd the wicket; babies roll'd about
Like tumbled fruit in grass; and men and maids
Arranged a country dance, and flew thro' light
And shadow, while the twangling violin
Struck up with Soldier-laddie, and overhead
The broad ambrosial aisles of lofty lime
Made noise with bees and breeze from end to end.

'Tears, idle tears'

'Tears, idle tears, I know not what they mean,
Tears from the depth of some divine despair
Rise in the heart, and gather to the eyes,
In looking on the happy Autumn-fields,
And thinking of the days that are no more.

'Fresh as the first beam glittering on a sail,
That brings our friends up from the underworld,
Sad as the last which reddens over one
That sinks with all we love below the verge;
So sad, so fresh, the days that are no more.

'Ah, sad and strange as in dark summer dawns
The earliest pipe of half-awakened birds
To dying ears, when unto dying eyes
The casement slowly grows a glimmering square;
So sad, so strange, the days that are no more.

'Dear as remembered kisses after death,
And sweet as those by hopeless fancy feigned
On lips that are for others; deep as love,
Deep as first love, and wild with all regret;
O Death in Life, the days that are no more.'

From IN MEMORIAM A. H. H.

When Tennyson was at Cambridge, he was one of a set of brilliant young men of whom Arthur Henry Hallam (the A.H.H. of *In Memoriam*) was another. Hallam's very sudden death in Vienna (in 1833) at the early age of twenty-four was a terrible shock to Tennyson. For several years he brooded inconsolably over the loss of his friend. Oddly enough, his first *poetic* expression of his determination not to give in to grief is a poem which would seem to have nothing to do with Hallam. It is the famous *Ulysses,* which ends: 'to strive, to seek, to find, and not to yield'; but Tennyson tells us himself that he was thinking of Hallam. In 1850, *In Memoriam* was published. It was later to be read continuously by Queen Victoria after the death of the Prince Consort.

Old Yew

Old Yew, which graspest at the stones
    That name the under-lying dead,
    Thy fibres net the dreamless head,
Thy roots are wrapt about the bones.

The seasons bring the flower again,
    And bring the firstling to the flock;
    And in the dusk of thee, the clock
Beats out the little lives of men.

O not for thee the glow, the bloom,
    Who changest not in any gale,
    Nor branding summer suns avail
To touch thy thousand years of gloom:

And gazing on thee, sullen tree,
    Sick for thy stubborn hardihood,
    I seem to fail from out my blood
And grow incorporate into thee.

Alfred Lord Tennyson: from IN MEMORIAM

Dark House

Dark house, by which once more I stand
    Here in the long unlovely street,
    Doors, where my heart was used to beat
So quickly, waiting for a hand,

A hand that can be clasped no more—
    Behold me, for I cannot sleep,
    And like a guilty thing I creep
At earliest morning to the door.

He is not here; but far away
    The noise of life begins again,
    And ghastly thro' the drizzling rain
On the bald street breaks the blank day.

Calm is the morn

Calm is the morn without a sound,
    Calm as to suit a calmer grief,
    And only thro' the faded leaf
The chestnut pattering to the ground:

Calm and deep peace on this high wold,
    And on these dews that drench the furze,
    And all the silvery gossamers
That twinkle into green and gold:

Calm and still light on yon great plain
    That sweeps with all its autumn bowers,
    And crowded farms and lessening towers,
To mingle with the bounding main:

Calm and deep peace in this wide air,
    These leaves that redden to the fall;
    And in my heart, if calm at all,
If any calm, a calm despair:

Calm on the seas, and silver sleep,
    And waves that sway themselves in rest,
    And dead calm in that noble breast
Which heaves but with the heaving deep.

To-night the winds begin to rise

To-night the winds begin to rise
    And roar from yonder dropping day:
    The last red leaf is whirled away,
The rooks are blown about the skies;

The forest cracked, the waters curled,
    The cattle huddled on the lea;
    And wildly dashed on tower and tree
The sunbeam strikes along the world:

And but for fancies, which aver
    That all thy motions gently pass
    Athwart a plane of molten glass,
I scarce could brook the strain and stir

That makes the barren branches loud;
    And but for fear it is not so,
    The wild unrest that lives in woe
Would dote and pore on yonder cloud

That rises upward always higher,
    And onward drags a labouring breast,
    And topples round the dreary west,
A looming bastion fringed with fire.

Be near me when my light is low

Be near me when my light is low,
    When the blood creeps, and the nerves prick
    And tingle; and the heart is sick,
And all the wheels of Being slow.

Be near me when the sensuous frame
　　Is racked with pangs that conquer trust;
　　And Time, a maniac scattering dust,
And Life, a Fury slinging flame.

Be near me when my faith is dry,
　　And men the flies of latter spring,
　　That lay their eggs, and sting and sing
And weave their petty cells and die.

Be near me when I fade away,
　　To point the term of human strife,
　　And on the low dark verge of life
The twilight of eternal day.

Oh yet we trust

Until the nineteenth century, science had been largely employed in
the discovery of how man worked as a physical being (for example,
Harvey's discovery of the circulation of the blood), or in studying
the earth's place in the universe (as in the work of Galileo). The
beginnings of the new science of geology now made men really
curious about the earth itself. From 'scarpèd cliff and quarried stone'
came fossils which proved the earth millions of years old. New
sciences gave rise to religious doubts of a new and deeper kind.
Tennyson voiced the feelings and thoughts of his time honestly.

Oh yet we trust that somehow good
　　Will be the final goal of ill,
　　To pangs of nature, sins of will,
Defects of doubt, and taints of blood;

That nothing walks with aimless feet;
　　That not one life shall be destroyed,
　　Or cast as rubbish to the void,
When God hath made the pile complete;

That not a worm is cloven in vain;
    That not a moth with vain desire
    Is shrivelled in a fruitless fire,
Or but subserves another's gain.

Behold, we know not anything;
    I can but trust that good shall fall
    At last—far off—at last, to all,
And every winter change to spring.

So runs my dream: but what am I?
    An infant crying in the night:
    An infant crying for the light:
And with no language but a cry.

The wish, that of the living whole
    No life may fail beyond the grave,
    Derives it not from what we have
The likest God within the soul?

Are God and Nature then at strife,
    That Nature lends such evil dreams?
    So careful of the type she seems,
So careless of the single life;

That I, considering everywhere
    Her secret meaning in her deeds,
    And finding that of fifty seeds
She often brings but one to bear,

I falter where I firmly trod,
    And falling with my weight of cares
    Upon the great world's altar-stairs
That slope thro' darkness up to God,

I stretch lame hands of faith, and grope,
    And gather dust and chaff, and call
    To what I feel is Lord of all,
And faintly trust the larger hope.

'So careful of the type?' but no.
    From scarpèd cliff and quarried stone
    She cries, 'A thousand types are gone:
I care for nothing, all shall go.

'Thou makest thine appeal to me:
    I bring to life, I bring to death:
    The spirit does but mean the breath:
I know no more.' And he, shall he,

Man, her last work, who seemed so fair,
    Such splendid purpose in his eyes,
    Who rolled the psalm to wintry skies,
Who built him fanes of fruitless prayer,

Who trusted God was love indeed
    And love Creation's final law—
    Tho' Nature, red in tooth and claw
With ravine, shrieked against his creed—

Who loved, who suffered countless ills,
    Who battled for the True, the Just,
    Be blown about the desert dust,
Or sealed within the iron hills?

No more? A monster then, a dream,
    A discord. Dragons of the prime,
    That tear each other in their slime,
Were mellow music matched with him.

O life as futile, then, as frail!
    O for thy voice to soothe and bless!
    What hope of answer, or redress?
Behind the veil, behind the veil.

All his life Tennyson had been determined to write about the Arthurian legend. Two centuries before, Milton had thought there *ought* to be an English epic poem comparable with Virgil's Aeneid. He, too, planned to write about King Arthur but abandoned the idea in favour of *Paradise Lost*. Tennyson's *Idylls of the King* do not attempt the grand style of an epic. They are a series of narrative poems connected by a central theme.

From Pelleas and Ettarre

Up ran a score of damsels to the tower;
'Avaunt,' they cried, 'our lady loves thee not.'
But Gawain lifting up his vizor said,
'Gawain am I, Gawain of Arthur's court,
And I have slain this Pelleas whom ye hate:
Behold his horse and armour. Open gates,
And I will make you merry.'
                    And down they ran,
Her damsels, crying to their lady, 'Lo!
Pelleas is dead—he told us—he that hath
His horse and armour: will ye let him in?
He slew him! Gawain, Gawain of the court,
Sir Gawain—there he waits below the wall,
Blowing his bugle as who should say him nay.'
        And so, leave given, straight on thro' open door
Rode Gawain, whom she greeted courteously.
'Dead, is it so?' she asked. 'Ay, ay,' said he,
'And oft in dying cried upon your name.'
'Pity on him,' she answered, 'a good knight,
But never let me bide one hour at peace.'
'Ay,' thought Gawain, 'and you be fair enow:
But I to your dead man have given my troth,
That whom ye loathe, him will I make you love.'
        So those three days, aimless about the land,
Lost in a doubt, Pelleas wandering
Waited, until the third night brought a moon
With promise of large light on woods and ways.
        Hot was the night and silent; but a sound
Of Gawain ever coming, and this lay—

Which Pelleas had heard sung before the Queen,
And seen her sadden listening—vext his heart,
And marred his rest—'A worm within the rose.'

'A rose, but one, none other rose had I,
A rose, one rose, and this was wondrous fair,
One rose, a rose that gladdened earth and sky,
One rose, my rose, that sweetened all mine air—
I cared not for the thorns; the thorns were there.

'One rose, a rose to gather by and by,
One rose, a rose, to gather and to wear,
No rose but one—what other rose had I?
One rose, my rose; a rose that will not die,—
He dies who loves it,—if the worm be there.'

This tender rhyme, and evermore the doubt,
'Why lingers Gawain with his golden news?'
So shook him that he could not rest, but rode
Ere midnight to her walls, and bound his horse
Hard by the gates. Wide open were the gates,
And no watch kept; and in thro' these he past,
And heard but his own steps, and his own heart
Beating, for nothing moved but his own self,
And his own shadow. Then he crost the court,
And spied not any light in hall or bower,
But saw the postern portal also wide
Yawning; and up a slope of garden, all
Of roses white and red, and brambles mixt
And overgrowing them, went on, and found,
Here too, all hushed below the mellow moon,
Save that one rivulet from a tiny cave
Came lightening downward, and so spilt itself
Among the roses, and was lost again.

Then was he ware of three pavilions reared
Above the bushes, gilden-peakt: in one,
Red after revel, droned her lurdane[1] knights
Slumbering, and their three squires across their feet:

---

[1] heavy—from fr. lourde.

In one, their malice on the placid lip
Froz'n by sweet sleep, four of her damsels lay:
And in the third, the circlet of the jousts
Bound on her brow, were Gawain and Ettarre.
     Back, as a hand that pushes thro' the leaf
To find a nest and feels a snake, he drew:
Back, as a coward slinks from what he fears
To cope with, or a traitor proven, or hound
Beaten, did Pelleas in an utter shame
Creep with his shadow thro' the court again,
Fingering at his sword-handle until he stood
There on the castle-bridge once more, and thought,
'I will go back, and slay them where they lie.'
     And so went back, and seeing them yet in sleep
Said, 'Ye, that so dis-hallow the holy sleep,
Your sleep is death,' and drew the sword, and thought,
'What! slay a sleeping knight? the King hath bound
And sworn me to this brotherhood'; again,
'Alas that ever a knight should be so false.'
Then turned, and so returned, and groaning laid
The naked sword athwart their naked throats,
There left it, and them sleeping; and she lay,
The circlet of the tourney round her brows,
And the sword of the tourney across her throat.
     And forth he past, and mounting on his horse
Stared at her towers that, larger than themselves
In their own darkness, thronged into the moon.

From The Passing of Arthur

     But, as he walked, King Arthur panted hard,
Like one that feels a nightmare on his bed
When all the house is mute. So sighed the King,
Muttering and murmuring at his ear, 'Quick, quick!
I fear it is too late, and I shall die.'
But the other swiftly strode from ridge to ridge,
Clothed with his breath, and looking, as he walked,
Larger than human on the frozen hills.
He heard the deep behind him, and a cry

Before. His own thought drove him like a goad.
Dry clashed his harness in the icy caves
And barren chasms, and all to left and right
The bare black cliff clanged round him, as he based
His feet on juts of slippery crag that rang
Sharp-smitten with the dint of armèd heels—
And on a sudden, lo! the level lake,
And the long glories of the winter moon.

Then saw they how there hove a dusky barge,
Dark as a funeral scarf from stem to stern,
Beneath them; and descending they were ware
That all the decks were dense with stately forms,
Black-stoled, black-hooded, like a dream—by these
Three Queens with crowns of gold: and from them rose
A cry that shivered to the tingling stars,
And, as it were one voice, an agony
Of lamentation, like a wind that shrills
All night in a waste land, where no one comes,
Or hath come, since the making of the world.

Then murmured Arthur, 'Place me in the barge.'
So to the barge they came. There those three Queens
Put forth their hands, and took the King, and wept.
But she, that rose the tallest of them all
And fairest, laid his head upon her lap,
And loosed the shattered casque, and chafed his hands,
And called him by his name, complaining loud,
And dropping bitter tears against a brow
Striped with dark blood: for all his face was white
And colourless, and like the withered moon
Smote by the fresh beam of the springing east;
And all his greaves and cuisses dashed with drops
Of onset; and the light and lustrous curls—
That made his forehead like a rising sun
High from the daïs-throne—were parched with dust:
Or, clotted into points and hanging loose,
Mixed with the knightly growth that fringed his lips.
So like a shattered column lay the King;
Not like that Arthur who, with lance in rest,

From spur to plume a star of tournament,
Shot thro' the lists at Camelot, and charged
Before the eyes of ladies and of kings.

From THE ANCIENT SAGE

The Passion of the Past

To-day? but what of yesterday? for oft
On me, when boy, there came what then I called,
Who knew no books and no philosophies,
In my boy-phrase 'The Passion of the Past.'
The first gray streak of earliest summer-dawn,
The last long stripe of waning crimson gloom,
As if the late and early were but one—
A height, a broken grange, a grove, a flower
Had murmurs 'Lost and gone and lost and gone!'
A breath, a whisper—some divine farewell—
Desolate sweetness—far and far away—
What had he loved, what had he lost, the boy?
I know not and I speak of what has been.

And more, my son! for more than once when I
Sat all alone, revolving in myself
The word that is the symbol of myself,
The mortal limit of the Self was loosed,
And past into the Nameless, as a cloud
Melts into Heaven. I touched my limbs, the limbs
Were strange not mine—and yet no shade of doubt,
But utter clearness, and thro' loss of Self
The gain of such large life as matched with ours
Were Sun to spark—unshadowable in words,
Themselves but shadows of a shadow-world.
'And idle gleams will come and go,
But still the clouds remain;'
The clouds themselves are children of the Sun.
'And Night and Shadow rule below
When only Day should reign.'
And Day and Night are children of the Sun,
And idle gleams to thee are light to me.
Some say, the Light was father of the Night,
And some, the Night was father of the Light,

No night no day!—I touch thy world again—
No ill no good! such counter-terms, my son,
Are border-races, holding, each its own
By endless war: but night enough is there
In yon dark city: get thee back: and since
The key to that weird casket, which for thee
But holds a skull, is neither thine nor mine,
But in the hand of what is more than man,
Or in man's hand when man is more than man,
Let be thy wail and help thy fellow men,
And make thy gold thy vassal not thy king,
And fling free alms into the beggar's bowl,
And send the day into the darkened heart;
Nor list for guerdon in the voice of men,
A dying echo from a falling wall;
Nor care—for Hunger hath the Evil eye—
To vex the noon with fiery gems, or fold
Thy presence in the silk of sumptuous looms;
Nor roll thy viands on a luscious tongue,
Nor drown thyself with flies in honied wine;
Nor thou be rageful, like a handled bee,
And lose thy life by usage of thy sting;
Nor harm an adder thro' the lust for harm,
Nor make a snail's horn shrink for wantonness;
And more—think well! Do-well will follow thought,
And in the fatal sequence of this world
An evil thought may soil thy children's blood;
But curb the beast would cast thee in the mire,
And leave the hot swamp of voluptuousness
A cloud between the Nameless and thyself,
And lay thine uphill shoulder to the wheel,
And climb the Mount of Blessing, whence, if thou
Look higher, then—perchance—thou mayest—beyond
A hundred ever-rising mountain lines,
And past the range of Night and Shadow—see
The high-heaven dawn of more than mortal day
Strike on the Mount of Vision!

So, farewell.

TWO IN THE CAMPAGNA

Robert Browning's whirlwind elopement with Elizabeth Barrett is well known. But were they happy? Not always; and here is a poem in which Browning is putting down his doubts and fears, honestly and directly, but in such a way that these doubts and fears can apply to anyone not entirely at ease in their love.

I wonder do you feel to-day
    As I have felt since, hand in hand,
We sat down on the grass, to stray
    In spirit better through the land,
This morn of Rome and May?

For me, I touched a thought, I know,
    Has tantalized me many times,
(Like turns of thread the spiders throw
    Mocking across our path) for rhymes
To catch at and let go.

Help me to hold it! First it left
    The yellowing fennel, run to seed
There, branching from the brickwork's cleft,
    Some old tomb's ruin: yonder weed
Took up the floating weft,

Where one small orange cup amassed
    Five beetles,—blind and green they grope
Among the honey-meal: and last,
    Everywhere on the grassy slope
I traced it. Hold it fast!

The champaign with its endless fleece
    Of feathery grasses everywhere!
Silence and passion, joy and peace,
    An everlasting wash of air—
Rome's ghost since her decease.

Such life here, through such lengths of hours,
　　Such miracles performed in play,
Such primal naked forms of flowers,
　　Such letting nature have her way
While heaven looks from its towers!

How say you? Let us, O my dove,
　　Let us be unashamed of soul,
As earth lies bare to heaven above!
　　How is it under our control
To love or not to love?

I would that you were all to me,
　　You that are just so much, no more.
Nor yours nor mine, nor slave nor free!
　　Where does the fault lie? What the core
O' the wound, since wound must be?

I would I could adopt your will,
　　See with your eyes, and set my heart
Beating by yours, and drink my fill
　　At your soul's springs,—your part my part
In life, for good and ill.

No. I yearn upward, touch you close,
　　Then stand away. I kiss your cheek,
Catch your soul's warmth,—I pluck the rose
　　And love it more than tongue can speak—
Then the good minute goes.

Already how am I so far
　　Out of that minute? Must I go
Still like the thistle-ball, no bar,
　　Onward, whenever light winds blow,
Fixed by no friendly star?

Just when I seemed about to learn!
    Where is the thread now? Off again!
The old trick! Only I discern—
    Infinite passion, and the pain
Of finite hearts that yearn.

UP AT A VILLA—DOWN IN THE CITY

As distinguished by an Italian Person of Quality

Had I but plenty of money, money enough and to spare,
The house for me, no doubt, were a house in the city-square;
Ah, such a life, such a life, as one leads at the window there!

Something to see, by Bacchus, something to hear, at least!
There, the whole day long, one's life is a perfect feast;
While up at a villa one lives, I maintain it, no more than a beast.

Well now, look at our villa! stuck like the horn of a bull
Just on a mountain-edge as bare as the creature's skull,
Save a mere shag of a bush with hardly a leaf to pull!
—I scratch my own, sometimes, to see if the hair's turned wool.

But the city, oh the city—the square with the houses! Why?
They are stone-faced, white as a curd, there's something to take
    the eye!
Houses in four straight lines, not a single front awry;
You watch who crosses and gossips, who saunters, who hurries
    by;
Green blinds, as a matter of course, to draw when the sun gets
    high;
And the shops with fanciful signs which are painted properly.

What of a villa? Though winter be over in March by rights,
'Tis May perhaps ere the snow shall have withered well off the
    heights:

You've the brown ploughed land before, where the oxen steam
     and wheeze,
And the hills over-smoked behind by the faint grey olive-trees.

Is it better in May, I ask you? You've summer all at once;
In a day he leaps complete with a few strong April suns.
'Mid the sharp short emerald wheat, scarce risen three fingers
     well,
The wild tulip, at end of its tube, blows out its great red bell
Like a thin clear bubble of blood, for the children to pick and
     sell.

Is it ever hot in the square? There's a fountain to spout and
     splash!
In the shade it sings and springs; in the shine such foam-bows
     flash
On the horses with curling fish-tails, that prance and paddle and
     pash
Round the lady atop in her conch—fifty gazers do not abash,
Though all that she wears is some weeds round her waist in a
     sort of sash.

All the year long at the villa, nothing to see though you linger,
Except yon cypress that points like death's lean lifted forefinger.
Some think fireflies pretty, when they mix i' the corn and mingle,
Or thrid the stinking hemp till the stalks of it seem a-tingle.
Late August or early September, the stunning cicala is shrill,
And the bees keep their tiresome whine round the resinous firs
     on the hill.
Enough of the seasons,—I spare you the months of the fever and
     chill.

Ere you open your eyes in the city, the blessed church-bells begin
No sooner the bells leave off than the diligence rattles in:
You get the pick of the news, and it costs you never a pin.
By-and-by there's the travelling doctor gives pills, lets blood,
     draws teeth;

Or the Pulcinello-trumpet breaks up the market beneath.
At the post-office such a scene-picture—the new play, piping hot!
And a notice how, only this morning, three liberal thieves were
 shot.
Above it, behold the Archbishop's most fatherly of rebukes,
And beneath, with his crown and his lion, some little new law of
 the Duke's!
Or a sonnet with flowery marge, to the Reverend Don So-and-so
Who is Dante, Boccaccio, Petrarca, Saint Jerome and Cicero,
'And moreover,' (the sonnet goes rhyming,) 'the skirts of Saint
 Paul has reached,
'Having preached us those six Lent-lectures more unctuous than
 ever he preached.'
Noon strikes,—here sweeps the procession! our Lady borne
 smiling and smart
With a pink gauze gown all spangles, and seven swords stuck in
 her heart!
Bang-whang-whang goes the drum, *tootle-te-tootle* the fife;
No keeping one's haunches still: it's the greatest pleasure in life.

But bless you, it's dear—it's dear! fowls, wine, at double the rate.
They have clapped a new tax upon salt, and what oil pays passing
 the gate
It's a horror to think of. And so, the villa for me, not the city!
Beggars can scarcely be choosers: but still—ah, the pity, the pity!
Look, two and two go the priests, then the monks with cowls and
 sandals,
And the penitents dressed in white shirts, a-holding the yellow
 candles;
One, he carries a flag up straight, and another a cross with
 handles,
And the Duke's guard brings up the rear, for the better
 prevention of scandals:
Bang-whang-whang goes the drum, *tootle-te-tootle* the fife.
Oh, a day in the city-square, there is no such pleasure in life!

Edward FitzGerald (1809-1883)

Edward FitzGerald, 'Old Fitz' as Tennyson called him, was a recluse and a vegetarian. After Tennyson had stayed with him for some time he came away and remarked that a steak had never tasted so good before! FitzGerald is famous for his version of *The Rubaiyat of Omar Khayyam*. This great poem was virtually 'discovered' by Rossetti and Swinburne and made FitzGerald's name. Scholars object that it is not much like the original Omar—if you can read Persian. But to read it in English (not knowing Persian) is a delight. All great translations must, to a certain extent, recreate the original.

OLD SONG

'Tis a dull sight
    To see the year dying,
When winter winds
    Set the yellow wood sighing:
        Sighing, O sighing!

When such a time cometh
    I do retire
Into an old room
    Beside a bright fire:
        O, pile a bright fire!

And there I sit
    Reading old things,
Of knights and lorn damsels,
    While the wind sings—
        O, drearily sings!

I never look out
    Nor attend to the blast;
For all to be seen
    Is the leaves falling fast:
        Falling, falling!

But close at the hearth,
  Like a cricket, sit I,
Reading of summer
  And chivalry—
    Gallant chivalry!

Then with an old friend
  I talk of our youth—
How 'twas gladsome, but often
  Foolish, forsooth:
    But gladsome, gladsome!

Or, to get merry,
  We sing some old rhyme
That made the wood ring again
  In summer time—
    Sweet summer time!

Then go we smoking,
  Silent and snug:
Naught passes between us,
  Save a brown jug—
    Sometimes!

And sometimes a tear
  Will rise in each eye,
Seeing the two old friends
  So merrily—
    So merrily!

And ere to bed
  Go we, go we,
Down on the ashes
  We kneel on the knee,
    Praying together!

Thus, then, live I
Till, 'mid all the gloom,
By Heaven! the bold sun
Is with me in the room
Shining, shining!

Then the clouds part,
Swallows soaring between;
The spring is alive,
And the meadows are green!

I jump up like mad,
Break the old pipe in twain,
And away to the meadows,
The meadows again!

Arthur Hugh Clough (1819-1861)

THE LATEST DECALOGUE

Arthur Clough was forced by his own conscience to give up his
Fellowship at Oxford, since every Fellow was expected to take Holy
Orders, and therefore had to subscribe to the Thirty-Nine Articles,
which set out what a clergyman must believe. Argument about the
Thirty-Nine Articles still goes on, and continues to cause disquiet
among Churchmen even today.

Thou shalt have one God only; who
Would be at the expense of two?
No graven images may be
Worshipped, except the currency:
Swear not at all; for for thy curse
Thine enemy is none the worse:
At church on Sunday to attend
Will serve to keep the world thy friend:

Honour thy parents; that is, all
From whom advancement may befall:
Thou shalt not kill; but needst not strive
Officiously to keep alive:
Do not adultery commit;
Advantage rarely comes of it:
Thou shalt not steal; an empty feat,
When it's so lucrative to cheat:
Bear not false witness; let the lie
Have time on its own wings to fly:
Thou shalt not covet; but tradition
Approves all forms of competition.

The sum of all is, thou shalt love,
If any body, God above:
At any rate shall never labour
More than thyself to love thy neighbour.

WHERE LIES THE LAND

Where lies the land to which the ship would go?
Far, far ahead, is all her seamen know.
And where the land she travels from? Away,
Far, far behind, is all that they can say.

On sunny noons upon the deck's smooth face,
Linked arm in arm, how pleasant here to pace;
Or, o'er the stern reclining, watch below
The foaming wake far widening as we go.

On stormy nights when wild north-westers rave,
How proud a thing to fight with wind and wave!
The dripping sailor on the reeling mast
Exults to bear, and scorns to wish it past.

Where lies the land to which the ship would go?
Far, far ahead, is all her seamen know.
And where the land she travels from? Away,
Far, far behind, is all that they can say.

From DIPSYCHUS

'There is no God,' the wicked saith,
    'And truly it's a blessing,
For what he might have done with us
    It's better only guessing.'

'There is no God,' a youngster thinks,
    'Or really, if there may be,
He surely didn't mean a man
    Always to be a baby.'

'There is no God, or if there is,'
    The tradesman thinks, ' 'twere funny
If he should take it ill in me
    To make a little money.'

'Whether there be,' the rich man says,
    'It matters very little,
For I and mine, thank somebody,
    Are not in want of victual.'

Some others, also, to themselves
    Who scarce so much as doubt it,
Think there is none, when they are well
    And do not think about it.

But country folks who live beneath
    The shadow of the steeple;
The parson and the parson's wife,
    And mostly married people;

Youths green and happy in first love,
    So thankful for illusion;
And men caught out in what the world
    Calls guilt, in first confusion;

And almost every one when age,
    Disease, or sorrows strike him,
Inclines to think there is a God,
    Or something very like Him.

From AMOURS DE VOYAGE

Clough, like the poets of the Romantic Revival, was a passionate believer in freedom. In 1848 and 1849, new revolutionary movements broke out in Europe. In the *Amours de Voyage,* Clough describes the siege of Rome by the French (compare Wordsworth in *The Prelude,* p. 156). The poem is written in hexameters, which is really a Latin metre; and Clough has used it in English better than anyone before or since. You may find Day Lewis consciously imitating Clough in his poem, *An Italian Visit* (1953).

Letters from Claude to Eustace

I

Rome disappoints me still; but I shrink and adapt myself to it.
Somehow a tyrannous sense of a superincumbent oppression
Still, wherever I go, accompanies ever, and makes me
Feel like a tree (shall I say?) buried under a ruin of brickwork.
Rome, believe me, my friend, is like its own Monte Testaceo,
Merely a marvellous mass of broken and castaway wine-pots.
Ye gods! what do I want with this rubbish of ages departed,
Things that nature abhors, the experiments that she has failed in?
What do I find in the Forum? An archway and two or three
       pillars.
Well, but St. Peter's? Alas, Bernini has filled it with sculpture!
No one can cavil, I grant, at the size of the great Coliseum.
Doubtless the notion of grand and capacious and massive
       amusement,
This the old Romans had; but tell me, is this an idea?

Yet of solidity much, but of splendour little is extant:
'Brickwork I found thee, and marble I left thee!' their Emperor
    vaunted;
'Marble I thought thee, and brickwork I find thee!' the Tourist
    may answer . . .

II

What do the people say, and what does the government do?—you
Ask, and I know not at all. Yet fortune will favour your hopes;
    and
I, who avoided it all, am fated, it seems, to describe it.
I, who nor meddle nor make in politics,—I who sincerely
Put not my trust in leagues nor any suffrage by ballot,
Never predicted Parisian millenniums, never beheld a
New Jerusalem coming down dressed like a bride out of heaven
Right on the Place de la Concorde,—I, nevertheless, let me say it,
Could in my soul of souls, this day, with the Gaul at the gates,
    shed
One true tear for thee, thou poor little Roman Republic!
What, with the German restored, with Sicily safe to the Bourbon,
Not leave one poor corner for native Italian exertion?
France, it is foully done! and you, poor foolish England,—
You, who a twelvemonth ago said nations must choose for
    themselves, you
Could not, of course, interfere,—you, now, when a nation has
    chosen—
Pardon this folly! *The Times* will, of course, have announced the
    occasion,
Told you the news of to-day; and although it was slightly in
    error
When it proclaimed as a fact the Apollo was sold to a Yankee,
You may believe when it tells you the French are at Civita
    Vecchia . . .

III

Dulce it is, and *decorum*, no doubt, for the country to fall,—to
Offer one's blood an oblation to Freedom, and die for the Cause;
     yet
Still, individual culture is also something, and no man
Finds quite distinct the assurance that he of all others is called on,
Or would be justified, even, in taking away from the world that
Precious creature, himself. Nature sent him here to abide here,
Else why sent him at all? Nature wants him still, it is likely.
On the whole, we are meant to look after ourselves; it is certain
Each has to eat for himself, digest for himself, and in general
Care for his own dear life, and see to his own preservation;
Nature's intentions, in most things uncertain, in this are decisive;
Which, on the whole, I conjecture the Romans will follow, and
     I shall.

    So we cling to our rocks like limpets; Ocean may bluster,
Over and under and round us; we open our shells to imbibe our
Nourishment, close them again, and are safe, fulfilling the purpose
Nature intended,—a wise one, of course, and a noble, we doubt
     not.
Sweet it may be and decorous, perhaps, for the country to die; but,
On the whole, we conclude the Romans won't do it, and I shan't.

Matthew Arnold (1822-1888)

From SOHRAB AND RUSTUM

In the folk-lore of almost every country there is a story of a father killing his son without knowing it. Arnold took this oriental one, out of many, to write about. You will find W. B. Yeats doing the same thing in his many poems about the mythical Irish king Cuchulain.

The Death of Sohrab

And, with a grave mild voice, Sohrab replied:—
'Desire not that, my father; thou must live.
For some are born to do great deeds, and live,
As some are born to be obscured, and die.
Do thou the deeds I die too young to do,
And reap a second glory in thine age.
Thou art my father, and thy gain is mine.
But come: thou seest this great host of men
Which follow me; I pray thee, slay not these:
Let me entreat for them: what have they done?
They followed me, my hope, my fame, my star.
Let them all cross the Oxus back in peace.
But me thou must bear hence, not send with them,
But carry me with thee to Seistan,
And place me on a bed, and mourn for me,
Thou, and the snow-haired Zal, and all thy friends.
And thou must lay me in that lovely earth,
And heap a stately mound above my bones,
And plant a far-seen pillar over all:
That so the passing horseman on the waste
May see my tomb a great way off, and say—
Sohrab, the mighty Rustum's son, lies there,
Whom his great father did in ignorance kill—
And I be not forgotten in my grave.'
          And, with a mournful voice, Rustum replied:—
'Fear not; as thou hast said, Sohrab, my son,
So shall it be: for I will burn my tents,
And quit the host, and bear thee hence with me,
And carry thee away to Seistan,

And place thee on a bed, and mourn for thee,
With the snow-headed Zal, and all my friends.
And I will lay thee in that lovely earth,
And heap a stately mound above thy bones,
And plant a far-seen pillar over all:
And men shall not forget thee in thy grave.
And I will spare thy host: yea, let them go:
Let them all cross the Oxus back in peace.
What should I do with slaying any more?
For would that all whom I have ever slain
Might be once more alive; my bitterest foes,
And they who were called champions in their time,
And through whose death I won that fame I have;
And I were nothing but a common man,
A poor, mean soldier, and without renown,
So thou mightest live too, my Son, my Son!
Or rather would that I, even I myself,
Might now be lying on this bloody sand,
Near death, and by an ignorant stroke of thine,
Not thou of mine; and I might die, not thou;
And I, not thou, be borne to Seistan;
And Zal might weep above my grave, not thine;
And say—*O son, I weep thee not too sore,*
For willingly, I know, thou met'st thine end.—
But now in blood and battles was my youth,
And full of blood and battles is my age;
And I shall never end this life of blood.'
    Then, at the point of death, Sohrab replied:—
'A life of blood indeed, thou dreadful Man!
But thou shalt yet have peace; only not now:
Not yet: but thou shalt have it on that day,
When thou shalt sail in a high-masted Ship,
Thou and the other peers of Kai-Khosroo,
Returning home over the salt blue sea,
From laying thy dear Master in his grave.'
    And Rustum gazed on Sohrab's face, and said:—
'Soon be that day, my Son, and deep that sea!
Till then, if Fate so wills, let me endure.'

He spoke; and Sohrab smiled on him, and took
The spear, and drew it from his side, and eased
His wound's imperious anguish: but the blood
Came welling from the open gash, and life
Flowed with the stream: all down his cold white side
The crimson torrent ran, dim now, and soiled,
Like the soiled tissue of white violets
Left, freshly gathered, on their native bank,
By romping children, whom their nurses call
From the hot fields at noon: his head drooped low,
His limbs grew slack; motionless, white, he lay—
White, with eyes closed; only when heavy gasps,
Deep, heavy gasps, quivering through all his frame,
Convulsed him back to life, he opened them,
And fixed them feebly on his father's face:
Till now all strength was ebbed, and from his limbs
Unwillingly the spirit fled away,
Regretting the warm mansion which it left,
And youth and bloom, and this delightful world.
    So, on the bloody sand, Sohrab lay dead.
And the great Rustum drew his horseman's cloak
Down o'er his face, and sat by his dead son.
As those black granite pillars, once high-reared
By Jemshid in Persepolis, to bear
His house, now, mid their broken flights of steps,
Lie prone, enormous, down the mountain side—
So in the sand lay Rustum by his son.
    And night came down over the solemn waste,
And the two gazing hosts, and that sole pair,
And darkened all; and a cold fog, with night,
Crept from the Oxus. Soon a hum arose,
As of a great assembly loosed, and fires
Began to twinkle through the fog: for now
Both armies moved to camp, and took their meal:
The Persians took it on the open sands
Southward; the Tartars by the river marge:
And Rustum and his son were left alone.

But the majestic River floated on,
Out of the mist and hum of that low land,
Into the frosty starlight, and there moved,
Rejoicing, through the hushed Chorasmian waste,
Under the solitary moon: he flowed
Right for the Polar Star, past Orgunjè,
Brimming, and bright, and large: then sands begin
To hem his watery march, and dam his streams,
And split his currents; that for many a league
The shorn and parcelled Oxus strains along
Through beds of sand and matted rushy isles—
Oxus, forgetting the bright speed he had
In his high mountain cradle in Pamere,
A foiled circuitous wanderer:—till at last
The longed-for dash of waves is heard, and wide
His luminous home of waters opens, bright
And tranquil, from whose floor the new-bathed stars
Emerge, and shine upon the Aral Sea.

PIS-ALLER

This poem and the next, both in their pessimism and rhythm, fore-
shadow much of the work of A. E. Housman (p. 339). *Pis-aller* in
particular is an expression of the Victorian faced with the choice
between Christian morality and the new ideas about Man, arising out
of the discoveries of the early geologists and Charles Darwin.

'Man is blind because of sin;
Revelation makes him sure.
Without that, who looks within,
Looks in vain, for all's obscure.'

Nay, look closer into man!
Tell me, can you find indeed
Nothing sure, no moral plan
Clear prescribed, without your creed?

'No, I nothing can perceive;
Without that, all's dark for men.
That, or nothing, I believe.'—
For God's sake, believe it then!

THE LAST WORD

Creep into thy narrow bed,
Creep, and let no more be said!
Vain thy onset! all stands fast;
Thou thyself must break at last.

Let the long contention cease!
Geese are swans, and swans are geese.
Let them have it how they will!
Thou art tired; best be still!

They out-talk'd thee, hiss'd thee, tore thee.
Better men fared thus before thee;
Fired their ringing shot and pass'd,
Hotly charged—and broke at last.

Charge once more, then, and be dumb!
Let the victors, when they come,
When the forts of folly fall,
Find thy body by the wall.

From THE SCHOLAR GIPSY

The Scholar Gipsy is based on a real story. It is an 'escape-poem'—a piece of longing to get away from civilisation and back to a more simple and primitive world. Many people look back on mid-Victorian England (this poem was published in 1853) as in many ways a secure and happy world; yet Arnold wrote of this 'strange disease of modern life'.

Thou waitest for the spark from Heaven: and we,
   Vague half-believers of our casual creeds,
      Who never deeply felt, nor clearly willed,
   Whose insight never has borne fruit in deeds,
      Whose weak resolves never have been fulfilled;
         For whom each year we see
   Breeds new beginnings, disappointments new;
      Who hesitate and falter life away,
      And lose to-morrow the ground won to-day—
        Ah, do not we, Wanderer, await it too?

Yes, we await it, but it still delays,
   And then we suffer; and amongst us One,
      Who most has suffered, takes dejectedly
   His seat upon the intellectual throne;
      And all his store of sad experience he
         Lays bare of wretched days;
   Tells us his misery's birth and growth and signs,
      And how the dying spark of hope was fed,
      And how the breast was soothed, and how the head,
        And all his hourly varied anodynes.

This for our wisest: and we others pine,
   And wish the long unhappy dream would end,
      And waive all claim to bliss, and try to bear,
   With close-lipped Patience for our only friend,
      Sad Patience, too near neighbour to Despair:
        But none has hope like thine

Thou through the fields and through the woods dost stray,
   Roaming the country side, a truant boy,
   Nursing thy project in unclouded joy,
     And every doubt long blown by time away.

O born in days when wits were fresh and clear,
   And life ran gaily as the sparkling Thames;
     Before this strange disease of modern life,
   With its sick hurry, its divided aims,
     Its heads o'ertaxed, its palsied hearts, was rife—
      Fly hence, our contact fear!
   Still fly, plunge deeper in the bowering wood!
     Averse, as Dido did with gesture stern
     From her false friend's approach in Hades turn,
      Wave us away, and keep thy solitude.

Still nursing the unconquerable hope,
   Still clutching the inviolable shade,
     With a free onward impulse brushing through,
   By night, the silvered branches of the glade—
     Far on the forest skirts, where none pursue,
      On some mild pastoral slope
   Emerge, and resting on the moonlit pales,
     Freshen thy flowers, as in former years,
     With dew, or listen with enchanted ears,
      From the dark dingles, to the nightingales.

But fly our paths, our feverish contact fly!
   For strong the infection of our mental strife,
     Which, though it gives no bliss, yet spoils for rest;
   And we should win thee from thy own fair life,
     Like us distracted, and like us unblest.
      Soon, soon thy cheer would die,
   Thy hopes grow timorous, and unfixed thy powers,
     And thy clear aims be cross and shifting made:
     And then thy glad perennial youth would fade,
      Fade, and grow old at last, and die like ours.

Then fly our greetings, fly our speech and smiles!
　　—As some grave Tyrian trader, from the sea,
　　　　Descried at sunrise an emerging prow
　　Lifting the cool-haired creepers stealthily,
　　　　The fringes of a southward-facing brow
　　　　　　Among the Aegean isles;
　　And saw the merry Grecian coaster come,
　　　　Freighted with amber grapes, and Chian wine,
　　　　Green bursting figs, and tunnies steeped in brine;
　　　　　　And knew the intruders on his ancient home,

The young light-hearted Masters of the waves;
　　And snatched his rudder, and shook out more sail,
　　　　And day and night held on indignantly
　　O'er the blue Midland waters with the gale,
　　　　Betwixt the Syrtes and soft Sicily,
　　　　　　To where the Atlantic raves
　　Outside the Western Straits, and unbent sails
　　　　There, where down cloudy cliffs, through sheets of foam,
　　　　Shy traffickers, the dark Iberians come;
　　　　　　And on the beach undid his corded bales.

WEST LONDON

Compare this with Johnson, Blake and Hood. Arnold merely com-
ments where they wanted actively to alleviate the lot of the poor.

Crouched on the pavement close by Belgrave Square
A tramp I saw, ill, moody, and tongue-tied;
A babe was in her arms, and at her side
A girl; their clothes were rags, their feet were bare.

Some labouring men, whose work lay somewhere there,
Passed opposite, she touch'd her girl, who hied
Across, and begged, and came back satisfied.
The rich she had let pass with frozen stare.

Thought I: Above her state this spirit towers;
She will not ask of aliens, but of friends,
Of sharers in a common human fate.

She turns from that cold succour, which attends
The unknown little from the unknowing great,
And points us to a better time than ours.

DOVER BEACH

The sea is calm to-night,
The tide is full, the moon lies fair
Upon the Straits;—on the French coast, the light
Gleams, and is gone; the cliffs of England stand,
Glimmering and vast, out in the tranquil bay.
Come to the window, sweet is the night air!
Only, from the long line of spray
Where the ebb meets the moon-blanch'd sand,
Listen! you hear the grating roar
Of pebbles which the waves suck back, and fling,
At their return, up the high strand,
Begin, and cease, and then again begin,
With tremulous cadence slow, and bring
The eternal note of sadness in.

Sophocles long ago
Heard it on the Aegean, and it brought
Into his mind the turbid ebb and flow
Of human misery; we
Find also in the sound a thought,
Hearing it by this distant northern sea.

The sea of faith
Was once, too, at the full, and round earth's shore
Lay like the folds of a bright girdle furl'd;

But now I only hear
Its melancholy, long, withdrawing roar,
Retreating to the breath
Of the night-wind down the vast edges drear
And naked shingles of the world.

Ah, love, let us be true
To one another! for the world, which seems
To lie before us like a land of dreams,
So various, so beautiful, so new,
Hath really neither joy, nor love, nor light,
Nor certitude, nor peace, nor help for pain;
And we are here as on a darkling plain
Swept with confused alarms of struggle and flight,
Where ignorant armies clash by night.

Coventry Patmore (1823-1896)

THE BARREN SHORE

Full many sing to me and thee
Their riches gather'd by the sea;
    But I will sing, for I'm footsore,
    The burthen of the barren shore.

The hue of love how lively shown
In this sole found cerulean stone
    By twenty leagues of ocean roar.
    O, burthen of the barren shore!

And these few crystal fragments bright,
As clear as truth, as strong as right,
    I found in footing twenty more.
    O, burthen of the barren shore!

And how far did I go for this
Small, precious piece of ambergris?
    Of weary leagues I went threescore.
    O, burthen of the barren shore!

The sand is poor, the sea is rich,
And I, I am I know not which;
    And well it were to know no more
    The burthen of the barren shore!

Emily Dickinson (1830-1886)

Emily Dickinson was an American. Unlike most poets, she made no attempt to publish her poems. She lived almost all her life in one place, one house, even one room. Perhaps this gave her her peculiarly original power. She is quite unlike any other poet. Her use of words and her turns of phrase are continually unexpected, but always just right. Many people think her the greatest woman poet.

PAPA ABOVE!

Papa above!
            Regard a Mouse
O'erpowered by the Cat;
Reserve within thy Kingdom
A 'mansion' for the Rat!
Snug in seraphic cupboards
To nibble all the day,
While unsuspecting cycles
Wheel pompously away.

TO MAKE A PRAIRIE

To make a prairie it takes a clover and one bee,—
And revery.
The revery alone will do
If bees are few.

TO FIGHT ALOUD

To fight aloud is very brave,
But gallanter, I know,
Who charge within the bosom,
The cavalry of woe.

Who win, and nations do not see,
Who fall, and none observe,
Whose dying eyes no country
Regards with patriot love.

We trust, in plumed procession,
For such the angels go,
Rank after rank, with even feet
And uniforms of snow.

THERE'S A CERTAIN SLANT OF LIGHT

There's a certain slant of light,
On winter afternoons,
That oppresses, like the weight
Of cathedral tunes.

Heavenly hurt it gives us;
We can find no scar,
But internal difference
Where the meanings are.

None may teach it anything,
'Tis the seal, despair,—
An imperial affliction
Sent us of the air.

When it comes, the landscape listens,
Shadows hold their breath;
When it goes, 'tis like the distance
On the look of death.

James Thomson (1834-1882)

From THE CITY OF DREADFUL NIGHT

The City of Dreadful Night is James Thomson's one great poem. It is
based upon London, upon the sense of loneliness a great city breeds.
It is the first poem fully to portray the soullessness of great cities,
to express what Wordsworth foretold in the famous preface to the
1802 edition of *Lyrical Ballads* (see note p. 166). Thomson's poem
had a profound effect on T. S. Eliot when he was young and his
attitude to cities derives much from Thomson.

A void Abyss

How the moon triumphs through the endless nights!
    How the stars throb and glitter as they wheel
Their thick processions of supernal lights
    Around the blue vault obdurate as steel!
And men regard with passionate awe and yearning
The mighty marching and the golden burning,
    And think the heavens respond to what they feel.

Boats gliding like dark shadows of a dream,
    Are glorified from vision as they pass
The quivering moonbridge on the deep black stream;
    Cold windows kindle their dead glooms of glass
To restless crystals; cornice, dome, and column
Emerge from chaos in the splendour solemn;
    Like faery lakes gleam lawns of dewy grass.

With such a living light these dead eyes shine,
    These eyes of sightless heaven, that as we gaze
We read a pity, tremulous, divine,
    Or cold majestic scorn in their pure rays:
Fond man! they are not haughty, are not tender;
There is no heart or mind in all their splendour,
    They thread mere puppets all their marvellous maze.

If we could near them with the flight unflown,
    We should but find them worlds as sad as this,
Or suns all self-consuming like our own
    Enringed by planet worlds as much amiss:
They wax and wane through fusion and confusion;
The spheres eternal are a grand illusion,
    The empyrean is a void abyss.

A vision

I sat me weary on a pillar's base,
    And leaned against the shaft; for broad moonlight
O'er flowed the peacefulness of cloistered space,
    A shore of shadow slanting from the right:
The great cathedral's western front stood there,
A wave-worn rock in that calm sea of air.

Before it, opposite my place of rest,
    Two figures faced each other, large, austere;
A couchant sphinx in shadow to the breast,
    An angel standing in the moonlight clear;
So mighty by magnificence of form,
They were not dwarfed beneath that mass enorm.

Upon the cross-hilt of a naked sword
    The angel's hands, as prompt to smite, were held;
His vigilant intense regard was poured
    Upon the creature placidly unquelled,
Whose front was set at level gaze which took
No heed of aught, a solemn trance-like look.

And as I pondered these opposed shapes
    My eyelids sank in stupor, that dull swoon
Which drugs and with a leaden mantle drapes
    The outworn to worse weariness. But soon
A sharp and clashing noise the stillness broke,
And from the evil lethargy I woke.

The angel's wings had fallen, stone on stone,
    And lay there shattered; hence the sudden sound:
A warrior leaning on his sword alone
    Now watched the sphinx with that regard profound;
The sphinx unchanged looked forthright, as aware
Of nothing in the vast abyss of air.

Again I sank in that repose unsweet,
    Again a clashing noise my slumber rent;
The warrior's sword lay broken at his feet:
    An unarmed man with raised hands impotent
Now stood before the sphinx, which ever kept
Such mien as if with open eyes it slept.

My eyelids sank in spite of wonder grown;
    A louder crash upstartled me in dread:
The man had fallen forward, stone on stone,
    And lay there shattered, with his trunkless head
Between the monster's large quiescent paws,
Beneath its grand front changeless as life's laws.

The moon had circled westward full and bright,
    And made the temple-front a mystic dream,
And bathed the whole enclosure with its light,
    The sworded angel's wrecks, the sphinx supreme:
I pondered long that cold majestic face
Whose vision seemed of infinite void space.

Jean Ingelow (1820-1897)

From BROTHERS AND A SERMON

It was a village built in a green rent,
Between two cliffs that skirt the dangerous bay.
A reef of level rock runs out to sea,
And you may lie on it and look sheer down,
Just where the 'Grace of Sunderland' was lost,
And see the elastic banners of the dulse
Rock softly, and the orange star-fish creep
Across the laver, and the mackerel shoot
Over and under it, like silver boats
Turning at will and plying under water.

There on that reef we lay upon our breasts,
My brother and I, and half the village lads,
For an old fisherman had called to us
With 'Sirs, the syle be come'. 'And what are they?'
My brother said. 'Good lack!' the old man cried,
And shook his head; 'to think you gentlefolk
Should ask what syle be! Look you; I can't say
What syle be called in your fine dictionaries,
Nor what name God Almighty calls them by
When their food's ready and He sends them south;
But our folk call them syle, and nought but syle,
And when they're grown, why then we call them herring.
I tell you Sir, the water is as full
Of them as pastures be of blades of grass;
You'll draw a score out in a landing net,
And none of them be longer than a pin.

'Syle! aye, indeed, we should be badly off,
I reckon, and so would God Almighty's gulls,'
He grumbled on in his quaint picty,
'And all His other birds, if He should say
I will not drive My syle into the south;
The fisher folk may do without my syle,
And do without the shoals of fish it draws

To follow and feed on it.'
        This said, we made
Our peace with him by means of two small coins,
And down we ran and lay upon the reef,
And saw the swimming infants, emerald green,
In separate shoals, the scarcely turning ebb
Bringing them in; while sleek, and not intent
On chase, but taking that which came to hand,
The full-fed mackerel and the gurnet swam
Between; and settling on the polished sea,
A thousand snow-white gulls sat lovingly
In social rings, and twittered while they fed.
The village dogs and ours, elate and brave,
Lay looking over, barking at the fish;
Fast, fast the silvery creatures took the bait,
And when they heaved and floundered on the rock,
In beauteous misery, a sudden pat
Some shaggy pup would deal, then back away,
At distance eye them with sagacious doubt,
And shrink half frightened from the slippery things.

Sydney Dobell (1824-1874)

DESOLATE

From the sad eaves the drip-drop of the rain!
The water washing at the latchet door;
A slow step plashing by upon the moor;
A single bleat far from the famished fold;
The clicking of an embered hearth and cold;
The rainy Robin tic-tac at the pane.

So as it is with thee
Is it with me,
So as it is and it used not to be,
With thee used not to be,
Nor me.
So singeth Robin on the willow tree,
The rainy Robin tic-tac at the pane.

Here in this breast all day
The fire is dim and low,
Within I care not to stay,
Without I care not to go.

A sadness ever sings
Of unforgotten things,
And the bird of love is patting at the pane;
But the wintry water deepens at the door,
And a step is plashing by upon the moor
Into the dark upon the darkening moor,
And alas, alas, the drip-drop of the rain!

Walter C. Smith (1824-1908)

GLENARADALE

In the nineteenth century the Scottish peasant-farmers, or crofters, suffered great distress when their traditionally 'common' lands began to be enclosed by the rich to make large sporting estates for deer-stalking and salmon-fishing. Many were forced to emigrate to America, Australia or other parts of the world in order to earn a living. This poem expresses the bitterness they felt, more powerfully and with more economy than it could be expressed in any other way. Compare Goldsmith's *Deserted Village* p. 129.

There is no fire of the crackling boughs
    On the hearth of our fathers,
There is no lowing of brown-eyed cows
    On the green meadows,
Nor do the maidens whisper vows
    In the still gloaming,
        Glenaradale.

There is no bleating of sheep on the hill
    Where the mists linger,
There is no sound of the low hand-mill
    Ground by the women,
And the smith's hammer is lying still
    By the brown anvil,
        Glenaradale.

Ah! we must leave thee and go away
    Far from Ben Luibh,
Far from the graves where we hoped to lay
    Our bones with our fathers',
Far from the kirk where we used to pray
    Lowly together,
        Glenaradale.

We are not going for hunger of wealth,
 For the gold and silver,
We are not going to seek for health
 On the flat prairies,
Nor yet for the lack of fruitful tilth
 On thy green pastures,
  Glenaradale.

Content with the croft and the hill were we,
 As all our fathers,
Content with the fish in the lake to be
 Carefully netted,
And garments spun of the wool from thee,
 O black-faced wether
  Of Glenaradale!

No father here but would give a son
 For the old country,
And his mother the sword would have girded on
 To fight her battles:
Many's the battle that has been won
 By the brave tartans,
  Glenaradale.

But the big-horned stag and his hinds, we know,
 In the high corries,
And the salmon that swirls in the pool below
 Where the stream rushes
Are more than the hearts of men, and so
 We leave thy green valley,
  Glenaradale.

Edward Robert Bulwer Lytton (1831-1891)

THE CHESS-BOARD

Irene, do you yet remember
Ere we were grown so sadly wise,
Those evenings in the bleak December,
Curtained warm from the snowy weather,
When you and I played chess together,
    Checkmated by each other's eyes?
    Ah, still I see your soft white hand
Hovering warm o'er Queen and Knight,
    Brave Pawns in valiant battle stand:
The double Castles guard the wings:
The Bishop, bent on distant things,
Moves, sidling, through the fight,
    Our fingers touch; our glances meet,
    And falter; falls your golden hair
    Against my cheek; your bosom sweet
Is heaving. Down the field, your Queen
Rides slow her soldiery all between,
    And checks me unaware.
    Ah me! the little battle's done,
Disperst is all its chivalry;
Full many a move, since then, have we
'Mid Life's perplexing chequers made,
And many a game with Fortune play'd,—
    What is it we have won?
    This, this at least—if this alone;—
That never, never, never more,
As in those old still nights of yore,
    (Ere we were grown so sadly wise)
    Can you and I shut out the skies,
Shut out the world, and wintry weather,
And, eyes exchanging warmth with eyes,
Play chess, as then we played, together!

THE FAIR CIRCASSIAN

Forty Viziers saw I go
Up to the Seraglio,
Burning, each and every man,
For the fair Circassian.

Ere the morn had disappeared,
Every Vizier wore a beard;
Ere the afternoon was born,
Every Vizier came back shorn.

'Let the man that woos to win
Woo with an unhairy chin:'
Thus she said, and as she bid
Each devoted Vizier did.

From the beards a cord she made,
Looped it to the balustrade,
Glided down and went away
To her own Circassia.

When the Sultan heard, waxed he
Somewhat wroth, and presently
In the noose themselves did lend
      Every Vizier did suspend.

Sages all, this rhyme who read,
Of your beards take prudent heed,
And beware the wily plans
Of the fair Circassians.

Robert Louis Stevenson (1850-1894)

THE HOUSE BEAUTIFUL

A naked house, a naked moor,
A shivering pool before the door,
A garden bare of flowers and fruit
And poplars at the garden foot:
Such is the place that I live in,
Bleak without and bare within.

Yet shall your ragged moor receive
The incomparable pomp of eve,
And the cold glories of the dawn
Behind your shivering trees be drawn;
And when the wind from place to place
Doth the unmoored cloud-galleons chase,
Your garden gloom and gleam again,
With leaping sun, with glancing rain.
Here shall the wizard moon ascend
The heavens, in the crimson end
Of day's declining splendour; here
The army of the stars appear.
The neighbour hollows dry or wet,
Spring shall with tender flowers beset;
And oft the morning muser see
Larks rising from the broomy lea,
And every fairy wheel and thread
Of cobweb dew-bediamonded.
When daisies go, shall winter time
Silver the simple grass with rime;
Autumnal frosts enchant the pool
And make the cart-ruts beautiful;
And when snow-bright the moor expands,
How shall your children clap their hands!
To make this earth our hermitage,
A cheerful and a changeful page,
God's bright and intricate device
Of days and seasons doth suffice.

VISIT FROM THE SEA

Far from the loud sea beaches
    Where he goes fishing and crying,
Here in the inland garden
    Why is the sea-gull flying?

Here are no fish to dive for;
    Here is the corn and lea;
Here are the green trees rustling.
    Hie away home to sea!

Fresh is the river water
    And quiet among the rushes;
This is no home for the sea-gull
    But for the rooks and thrushes.

Pity the bird that has wandered!
    Pity the sailor ashore!
Hurry him home to the ocean,
    Let him come here no more!

High on the sea-cliff ledges
    The white gulls are trooping and crying,
Here among rooks and roses,
    Why is the sea-gull flying?

Ernest Dowson (1867-1900)

NON SUM QUALIS ERAM BONAE SUB REGNO CYNARAE

Ernest Dowson took the title of his poem from the Roman p[?]
Horace. For the rhythm of this poem you must pronounce Cyna[?]
with the accent on the first syllable as in a name like Barbara. In t[?]
1890's it was fashionable to pretend to be 'decadent'—to have l[?]
a wicked and self-indulgent life. This poem survives for its rhyth[?]
and for its perfect expression of a pose. In fact, you don't take it[?]
factual truth, but as an expression of the feeling of the time.

Last night, ah, yesternight, betwixt her lips and mine
There fell thy shadow, Cynara! thy breath was shed
Upon my soul between the kisses and the wine;
And I was desolate and sick of an old passion,
  Yea, I was desolate and bowed my head:
I have been faithful to thee, Cynara! in my fashion.

All night upon mine heart I felt her warm heart beat,
Night-long within mine arms in love and sleep she lay;
Surely the kisses of her bought red mouth were sweet;
But I was desolate and sick of an old passion,
  When I awoke and found the dawn was gray:
I have been faithful to thee, Cynara! in my fashion.

I have forgot much, Cynara! gone with the wind,
Flung roses, roses riotously with the throng,
Dancing, to put thy pale, lost lilies out of mind;
But I was desolate and sick of an old passion,
  Yea, all the time, because the dance was long:
I have been faithful to thee, Cynara! in my fashion.

I cried for madder music and for stronger wine,
But when the feast is finished and the lamps expire,
Then falls thy shadow, Cynara! the night is thine;
And I am desolate and sick of an old passion,
  Yea, hungry for the lips of my desire:
I have been faithful to thee, Cynara! in my fashion.

VILLANELLE OF THE POET'S ROAD

Wine and woman and song,
  Three things garnish our way:
Yet is day over long.

Lest we do our youth wrong,
  Gather them while we may:
Wine and woman and song.

Three things render us strong,
  Vine leaves, kisses and bay;
Yet is day over long.

Unto us they belong,
  Us the bitter and gay,
Wine and woman and song.

We, as we pass along,
  Are sad that they will not stay;
Yet is day over long.

Fruits and flowers among,
  What is better than they:
Wine and woman and song?
  Yet is day over long.

MULOS LUNAE

I would not alter thy cold eyes,
Nor trouble the calm fount of speech
With aught of passion or surprise.
The heart of thee I cannot reach:
I would not alter thy cold eyes!

I would not alter thy cold eyes;
Nor have thee smile, nor make thee weep:
Though all my life droops down and dies,
Desiring thee, desiring sleep,
I would not alter thy cold eyes.

I would not alter thy cold eyes;
I would not change thee if I might,
To whom my prayers for incense rise,
Daughter of dreams! my moon of night!
I would not alter thy cold eyes.

I would not alter thy cold eyes,
With trouble of the human heart:
Within their glance my spirit lies,
A frozen thing, alone, apart;
I would not alter thy cold eyes.

Lionel Johnson (1867-1902)

BY THE STATUE OF KING CHARLES AT CHARING CROSS

Sombre and rich, the skies;
Great glooms, and starry plains.
Gently the night wind sighs;
Else a vast silence reigns.

The splendid silence clings
Around me: and around
The saddest of all kings
Crowned, and again discrowned.

Comely and calm, he rides
Hard by his own Whitehall:
Only the night wind glides:
No crowds, nor rebels, brawl.

Gone, too, his Court: and yet,
The stars his courtiers are:
Stars in their stations set;
And every wandering star.

Alone he rides, alone,
The fair and fatal king:
Dark night is all his own,
That strange and solemn thing.

Which are more full of fate:
The stars; or those sad eyes?
Which are more still and great:
Those brows; or the dark skies?

Although his whole heart yearn
In passionate tragedy:
Never was face so stern
With sweet austerity.

Vanquished in life, his death
By beauty made amends:
The passing of his breath
Won his defeated ends.

Brief life, and hapless? Nay:
Through death, life grew sublime.
Speak after sentence? Yea:
And to the end of time.

Armoured he rides, his head
Bare to the stars of doom:
He triumphs now, the dead,
Beholding London's gloom.

Our wearier spirit faints,
Vexed in the world's employ:
His soul was of the saints:
And art to him was joy.

King, tried in fires of woe!
Men hunger for thy grace:
And through the night I go,
Loving thy mournful face.

Yet, when the city sleeps;
When all the cries are still:
The stars and heavenly deeps
Work out a perfect will.

John Davidson (1857-1909)

THIRTY BOB A WEEK[1]

I couldn't touch a stop and turn a screw,
    And set the blooming world a-work for me,
Like such as cut their teeth—I hope, like you—
    On the handle of a skeleton gold key;
I cut mine on a leek, which I eat it every week:
    I'm a clerk at thirty bob as you can see.

But I don't allow it's luck and all a toss;
    There's no such thing as being starred and crossed;
It's just the power of some to be a boss,
    And the bally power of others to be bossed:
I face the music, sir; you bet I ain't a cur;
    Strike me lucky if I don't believe I'm lost!

---

[1] Compare Hood's *Song of the Shirt*, p. 240.

For like a mole I journey in the dark,
   A-travelling along the underground
From my Pillar'd Halls and broad Suburbean Park,
   To come the daily dull official round;
And home again at night with my pipe all alight,
   A-scheming how to count ten bob a pound.

And it's often very cold and very wet,
   And my missis stitches towels for a hunks;
And the Pillar'd Halls is half of it to let—
   Three rooms about the size of travelling trunks.
And we cough, my wife and I, to dislocate a sigh,
   When the noisy little kids are in their bunks.

But you never hear her do a growl or whine,
   For she's made of flint and roses, very odd;
And I've got to cut my meaning rather fine,
   Or I'd blubber, for I'm made of greens and sod:
So p'r'aps we are in Hell for all that I can tell,
   And lost and damn'd and served up hot to God.

I ain't blaspheming, Mr. Silver-tongue;
   I'm saying things a bit beyond your art:
Of all the rummy starts you ever sprung,
   Thirty bob a week's the rummiest start!
With your science and your books and your the'ries about spooks,
   Did you ever hear of looking in your heart?

I didn't mean your pocket, Mr., no:
   I mean that having children and a wife,
With thirty bob on which to come and go,
   Isn't dancing to the tabor and the fife:
When it doesn't make you drink, by Heaven! it makes you think,
   And notice curious items about life.

I step into my heart and there I meet
    A god-almighty devil singing small,
Who would like to shout and whistle in the street,
    And squelch the passers flat against the wall;
If the whole world was a cake he had the power to take,
    He would take it, ask for more, and eat it all.

And I meet a sort of simpleton beside,
    The kind that life is always giving beans;
With thirty bob a week to keep a bride
    He fell in love and married in his teens:
At thirty bob he stuck; but he knows it isn't luck:
    He knows the seas are deeper than tureens.

And the god-almighty devil and the fool
    That meet me in the High Street on the strike,
When I walk about my heart a-gathering wool,
    Are my good and evil angels if you like.
And both of them together in every kind of weather
    Ride me like a double-seated bike.

That's rough a bit and needs its meaning curled.
    But I have a high old hot 'un in my mind—
A most engrugious notion of the world,
    That leaves your lightning 'rithmetic behind
I give it at a glance when I say 'There ain't no chance,
    Nor nothing of the lucky-lottery kind.'

And it's this way that I make it out to be:
    No fathers, mothers, countries, climates—none;
Not Adam was responsible for me,
    Nor society, nor systems, nary one:
A little sleeping seed, I woke—I did, indeed—
    A million years before the blooming sun.

I woke because I thought the time had come;
  Beyond my will there was no other cause;
And everywhere I found myself at home,
  Because I chose to be the thing I was;
And in whatever shape of mollusc or of ape
  I always went according to the laws.

I was the love that chose my mother out;
  I joined two lives and from the union burst;
My weakness and my strength without a doubt
  Are mine alone for ever from the first:
It's just the very same with a difference in the name
  As 'Thy will be done.' You say it if you durst!

They say it daily up and down the land
  As easy as you take a drink, it's true;
But the difficultest go to understand,
  And the difficultest job a man can do,
Is to come it brave and meek with thirty bob a week,
  And feel that that's the proper thing for you.

It's a naked child against a hungry wolf;
  It's playing bowls upon a splitting wreck;
It's walking on a string across a gulf
  With millstones fore-and-aft about your neck;
But the thing is daily done by many and many a one;
  And we fall, face forward, fighting, on the deck.

Rudyard Kipling (1865-1936)

McANDREW'S HYMN
1893

> If you read Kipling's stories or poems, in whatever age they are set
> one thing is sure: you will recognise his knowledge of how things
> *work*. Poets have usually wanted to know accurately the mechanics
> of man's tools, though Tennyson coined a magnificent phrase—'the
> ringing grooves of change'—after his first railway journey, under
> the mistaken impression that the wheels were grooved and fitted over
> both sides of each rail. Kipling is the master of expertise; and, as it
> were in rivalry to the doubts of the laity in religion, sets up engineers
> —men like McAndrew—almost as if they were priests, who see the
> manifestation of the Divine in the new machines.

Lord, Thou hast made this world below the shadow of a dream,
An', taught by time, I tak' it so—expectin' always Steam.
From coupler-flange to spindle-guide I see Thy Hand, O God—
Predestination in the stride o' yon connectin'-rod.
John Calvin might ha' forged the same—enorrmous, certain,
    slow—
Ay, wrought it in the furnace-flame—*my* 'Institutio.'
I cannot get my sleep to-night; old bones are hard to please;
I'll stand the middle watch up here—alone wi' God an' these
My engines, after ninety days o' race an' rack an' strain
Through all the seas of all Thy world, slam-bangin' home again.
Slam-bang too much—they knock a wee—the crosshead-gibs are
    loose,
But thirty thousand mile o' sea has gied them fair excuse. . . .
Fine, clear an' dark—a full-draught breeze, wi' Ushant out o'
    sight,
An' Ferguson relievin' Hay. Old girl, ye'll walk to-night!
His wife's at Plymouth. . . . Seventy—One—Two—Three since he
    began—
Three turns for Mistress Ferguson . . . and who's to blame the
    man?
There's none at any port for me, by drivin' fast or slow,
Since Elsie Campbell went to Thee, Lord, thirty years ago.
(The year the *Sarah Sands* was burned. Oh, roads we used to
    tread,
Fra' Maryhill to Pollokshaws—fra' Govan to Parkhead!)

Not but they're ceevil on the Board. Ye'll hear Sir Kenneth say:
'Good morrn, McAndrew! Back again? An' how's your bilge
    to-day?'
Miscallin' technicalities but handin' me my chair
To drink Madeira wi' three Earls—the auld Fleet Engineer
That started as a boiler-whelp—when steam and he were low.
I mind the time we used to serve a broken pipe wi' tow!
Ten pound was all the pressure then—Eh! Eh!—a man wad drive;
An' here, our workin' gauges give one hunder sixty-five!
We're creepin' on wi' each new rig—less weight an' larger power;
There'll be the loco-boiler next an' thirty mile an hour!
Thirty an' more. What I ha' seen since ocean-steam began
Leaves me na doot for the machine: but what about the man?
The man that counts, wi' all his runs, one million mile o' sea:
Four time the span from earth to moon. . . . How far, O Lord,
    from Thee
That wast beside him night an' day? Ye mind my first typhoon?
It scoughed the skipper on his way to jock wi' the saloon.
Three feet were on the stokehold-floor—just slappin' to and fro—
An' cast me on a furnace-door. I have the marks to show.
Marks! I ha' marks o' more than burns—deep in my soul an'
    black,
An' times like this, when things go smooth, my wickudness comes
    back.
The sins o' four an' forty years, all up an' down the seas,
Clack an' repeat like valves half-fed. . . . Forgie's our trespasses!
Nights when I'd come on deck to mark, wi' envy in my gaze,
The couples kittlin' in the dark between the funnel-stays;
Years when I raked the Ports wi' pride to fill my cup o' wrong—
Judge not, O Lord, my steps aside at Gay Street in Hong-Kong!
Blot out the wastrel hours of mine in sin when I abode—
Jane Harrigan's an' Number Nine, The Reddick an' Grant Road!
An' waur than all—my crownin' sin—rank blasphemy an' wild.
I was not four and twenty then—Ye wadna judge a child?
I'd seen the Tropics first that run—new fruit, new smells, new
    air—
How could I tell—blind-fou wi' sun—the Deil was lurkin' there?
By day like playhouse-scenes the shore slid past our sleepy eyes;
By night those soft, lasceevious stars leered from those velvet
    skies,

In port (we used no cargo-steam) I'd daunder down the streets—
An ijjit grinnin' in a dream—for shells an' parrakeets,
An' walkin'-sticks o' carved bamboo an' blowfish stuffed an'
    dried—
Fillin' my bunk wi' rubbishry the Chief put overside.
Till, off Sambawa Head, Ye mind, I heard a land-breeze ca',
Milk-warm wi' breath o' spice an' bloom: "McAndrew, come
    awa'!"
Firm, clear an' low—no haste, no hate—the ghostly whisper went
Just statin' eevidential facts beyon' all argument:
'Your mither's God's a graspin' deil, the shadow o' yoursel',
'Got out o' books by meenisters clean daft on Heaven an' Hell.
'They mak' him in the Broomielaw, o' Glasgie cold an' dirt,
'A jealous, pridefu' fetich, lad, that's only strong to hurt.
'Ye'll not go back to Him again an' kiss His red-hot rod,
'But come wi' Us' (Now, who were *They?*) 'an' know the Leevin'
    God,
'That does not kipper souls for sport or break a life in jest,
'But swells the ripenin' cocoanuts an' ripes the woman's breast.'
An' there it stopped—cut off—no more—that quiet, certain
    voice—
For me, six months o' twenty-four, to leave or take at choice.
'Twas on me like a thunderclap—it racked me through an'
    through—
Temptation past the show o' speech, unnameable an' new—
The Sin against the Holy Ghost? . . . An' under all, our screw.

That storm blew by but left behind her anchor-shiftin' swell.
Thou knowest all my heart an' mind, Thou knowest, Lord, I
    fell—
Third on the *Mary Gloster* then, and first that night in Hell!
Yet was Thy Hand beneath my head, about my feet Thy Care—
Fra' Deli clear to Torres Strait, the trial o' despair,
But when we touched the Barrier Reef Thy answer to my
    prayer! . . .
We dared na run that sea by night but lay an' held our fire,
An' I was drowsin' on the hatch—sick—sick wi' doubt an' tire:
'Better the sight of eyes that see than wanderin' o' desire!'

Ye mind that word? Clear as our gongs—again, an' once again,
When rippin' down through coral-trash ran out our moorin'-
    chain:
An', by Thy Grace, I had the Light to see my duty plain.
Light on the engine-room—no more—bright as our carbons burn.
I've lost it since a thousand times, but never past return!

Obsairve! Per annum we'll have here two thousand souls aboard—
Think not I dare to justify myself before the Lord,
But—average fifteen hunder souls safe-borne fra' port to port—
I *am* o' service to my kind. Ye wadna blame the thought?
Maybe they steam from Grace to Wrath—to sin by folly led—
It isna mine to judge their path—their lives are on my head.
Mine at the last—when all is done it all comes back to me,
The fault that leaves six thousand ton a log upon the sea.
We'll tak' one stretch—three weeks an' odd by ony road ye steer—
Fra' Cape Town east to Wellington—ye need an engineer.
Fail there—ye've time to weld your shaft—ay, eat it, ere ye're
    spoke;
Or make Kerguelen under sail—three jiggers burned wi' smoke!
An' home again—the Rio run: it's no child's play to go
Steamin' to bell for fourteen days o' snow an' floe an' blow.
The bergs like kelpies overside that girn an' turn an' shift
Whaur, grindin' like the Mills o' God, goes by the big South drift.
(Hail, Snow and Ice that praise the Lord. I've met them at their
    work.
An' wished we had anither route or they anither kirk.)
Yon's strain, hard strain, o' head an' hand, for though Thy Power
    brings
All skill to naught, Ye'll understand a man must think o' things.
Then, at the last, we'll get to port an' hoist their baggage clear—
The passengers, wi' gloves an' canes—an' this is what I'll hear:
'Well, thank ye for a pleasant voyage. The tender's comin' now.'
While I go testin' follower-bolts an' watch the skipper bow.
They've words for every one but me—shake hands wi' half the
    crew,
Except the dour Scots engineer, the man they never knew.
An' yet I like the wark for all we've dam'-few pickin's here—
No pension, an' the most we'll earn's four hunder pound a year.

Better myself abroad? Maybe. *I'd* sooner starve than sail
Wi' such as call a snifter-rod *ross* . . . French for nightingale.
Commeesion on my stores? Some do; but I cannot afford
To lie like stewards wi' patty-pans. I'm older than the Board.
A bonus on the coal I save? Ou ay, the Scots are close,
But when I grudge the strength Ye gave I'll grudge their food to
    those.
(There's bricks that I might recommend—an' clink the firebars
    cruel.
No! Welsh—Wangarti at the worst—an' damn all patent fuel!)
Inventions? Ye must stay in port to mak' a patent pay.
My Deeferential Valve-Gear taught me how that business lay.
I blame no chaps wi' clearer heads for aught they make or sell.
I found that I could not invent an' look to these as well.
So, wrestled wi' Apollyon—Nah!—fretted like a bairn—
But burned the workin'-plans last run, wi' all I hoped to earn.
Ye know how hard an Idol dies, an' what that meant to me—
E'en tak' it for a sacrifice acceptable to Thee. . . .
Below there! Oiler! What's your wark? Ye find it runnin' hard?
Ye needn't swill the cup wi' oil—this isn't the Cunard!
Ye thought? Ye are not paid to think. Go, sweat that off again!
Tck! Tck! It's deeficult to sweer nor tak' The Name in vain!
Men, ay, an' women, call me stern. Wi' these to oversee
Ye'll note I've little time to burn on social repartee.
The bairns see what their elders miss; they'll hunt me to an' fro,
Till for the sake of—well, a kiss—I tak' 'em down below.
That minds me of our Viscount loon—Sir Kenneth's kin—the
    chap
Wi' Russia-leather tennis-shoon an' spar-decked yachtin'-cap.
I showed him round last week, o'er all—an' at the last says he:
'Mister McAndrew, don't you think steam spoils romance at sea?'
Damned ijjit! I'd been doon that morn to see what ailed the
    throws,
Manholin', on my back—the cranks three inches off my nose.
Romance! Those first-class passengers they like it very well,
Printed an' bound in little books; but why don't poets tell?

I'm sick of all their quirks an' turns—the loves an' doves they
dream—
Lord, send a man like Robbie Burns to sing the Song o' Steam!
To match wi' Scotia's noblest speech yon orchestra sublime
Whaurto—uplifted like the Just—the tail-rods mark the time.
The crank-throws give the double-bass, the feed-pump sobs an'
heaves,
An' now the main eccentrics start their quarrel on the sheaves:
Her time, her own appointed time, the rocking link-head bides,
Till—hear that note?—the rod's return whings glimmerin'
through the guides.
They're all awa'! True beat, full power, the clangin' chorus goes
Clear to the tunnel where they sit, my purrin' dynamoes.
Interdependence absolute, foreseen, ordained, decreed,
To work, Ye'll note, at ony tilt an' every rate o' speed.
Fra' skylight-lift to furnace-bars, backed, bolted, braced an'
stayed,
An' singin' like the Mornin' Stars for joy that they are made;
While, out o' touch o' vanity, the sweatin' thrust-block says:
'Not unto us the praise, or man—not unto us the praise!'
Now, a' together, hear them lift their lesson—theirs an' mine:
'Law, Orrder, Duty an' Restraint, Obedience, Discipline!'
Mill, forge an' try-pit taught them that when roarin' they arose,
An' whiles I wonder if a soul was gied them wi' the blows.
Oh for a man to weld it then, in one trip-hammer strain,
Till even first-class passengers could tell the meanin' plain!
But no one cares except mysel' that serve an' understand
My seven thousand horse-power here. Eh, Lord! They're grand—
they're grand!
Uplift am I? When first in store the new-made beasties stood,
Were Ye cast down that breathed the Word declarin' all things
good?
Not so! O' that warld-liftin' joy no after-fall could vex,
Ye've left a glimmer still to cheer the Man—the Arrtifex!
That holds, in spite o' knock and scale, o' friction, waste an' slip,
An' by that light—now, mark my word—we'll build the Perfect
Ship.
I'll never last to judge her lines or take her curve—not I.
But I ha' lived an' I ha' worked. Be thanks to Thee, Most High!

An' I ha' done what I ha' done—judge Thou if ill or well—
Always Thy Grace preventin' me. . . .

> Losh! Yon's the 'Stand-by' bell.

Pilot so soon? His flare it is. The mornin'-watch is set.
Well, God be thanked, as I was sayin', I'm no Pelagian yet.
Now I'll tak' on. . . .

> *'Morrn, Ferguson. Man, have ye ever thought*
> *What your good leddy costs in coal? . . . I'll burn 'em down to port.*

HARP SONG OF THE DANE WOMEN

What is a woman that you forsake her,
And the hearth-fire and the home-acre,
To go with the old grey Widow-maker?[1]

She has no house to lay a guest in—
But one chill bed for all to rest in,
That the pale suns and the stray bergs[2] nest in.

She has no strong white arms to fold you,
But the ten-times-fingering weed to hold you—
Out on the rocks where the tide has rolled you.

Yet, when the signs of summer thicken,
And the ice breaks, and the birch-buds quicken,
Yearly you turn from our side, and sicken—

Sicken again for the shouts and the slaughters.
You steal away to the lapping waters,
And look at your ship in her winter-quarters.

---

[1] the sea.
[2] icebergs.

You forget our mirth, and talk at the tables,
The kine in the shed and the horse in the stables—
To pitch her sides and go over her cables.

Then you drive out where the storm-clouds swallow,
And the sound of your oar-blades, falling hollow,
Is all we have left through the months to follow.

Ah, what is Woman that you forsake her,
And the hearth-fire and the home-acre,
To go with the old grey Widow-maker?

Mary Coleridge (1861-1907)

Mary Coleridge was a descendant of Samuel Taylor Coleridge, her
father being his great-nephew. She was much encouraged by two
other poets, Robert Bridges and Sir Henry Newbolt. As was still the
case in her day, she was given almost no education, being a woman.
When she was grown up she had herself taught Greek and Latin.
She also wrote romantic novels, one of which, *The King with Two
Faces,* was a great success and is still well worth reading.

OUR LADY

Mother of God! no lady thou:
    Common woman of common earth!
'Our Lady' ladies call thee now,
    But Christ was never of gentle birth;
    A common man of the common earth.

For God's ways are not as our ways.
    The noblest lady in the land
Would have given up half her days,
        Would have cut off her right hand,
        To bear the Child that was God of the land.

Never a lady did He choose,
    Only a maid of low degree,
So humble she might not refuse
        The carpenter of Galilee.
        A daughter of the people, she.

Out she sang the song of her heart.
    Never a lady so had sung.
She knew no letters, had no art;
        To all mankind, in woman's tongue,
        Hath Israelitish Mary sung.

And still for men to come she sings,
    Nor shall her singing pass away.
'He hath filled the hungry with good things'—
        Oh, listen, lords and ladies gay!—
        'And the rich He hath sent empty away.'

IN ONE ESTATE

In one estate not for one moment resting
    The rooted trees throughout the forest range.
The everlasting hills are everlasting
        Only in change.

The quick stars with quenchless fire are burning,
    Not for an instant may their motions cease.
And man, to break the laws of Nature yearning
        Still dreams of peace.

I SAW A STABLE

I saw a stable, low and very bare,
    A little child in a manger.
The oxen knew Him, had Him in their care,
    To men He was a stranger.
The safety of the world was lying there,
    And the world's danger.

Henry Newbolt (1862-1938)

THE MIDDLE WATCH

In a blue dusk the ship astern
    Uplifts her slender spars,
With golden lights that seem to burn
    Among the silver stars.
Like fleets along a cloudy shore
    The constellations creep,
Like planets on the ocean floor
    Our silent course we keep.

    And over the endless plain,
        Out of the night forlorn
    Rises a faint refrain,
        A song of the day to be born—
    Watch, oh watch till ye find again
        Life and the land of morn.

From a dim West to a dark East
    Our lines unwavering head,
As if their motion long had ceased
    And Time itself were dead.
Vainly we watch the deep below,
    Vainly the void above,
They died a thousand years ago—
    Life and the land we love.

> *But over the endless plain,*
> *Out of the night forlorn*
> *Rises a faint refrain,*
> *A song of the day to be born—*
> *Watch, oh watch till ye find again*
> *Life and the land of morn.*

CRAVEN

Mobile Bay, 1864

Over the turret, shut in his iron-clad tower,
    Craven was conning his ship through smoke and flame;
Gun to gun he had battered the fort for an hour,
    Now was the time for a charge to end the game.

There lay the narrowing channel, smooth and grim,
    A hundred deaths beneath it, and never a sign;
There lay the enemy's ships, and sink or swim
    The flag was flying, and he was head of the line.

The fleet behind was jamming; the monitor hung
    Beating the stream; the roar for a moment hushed.
Craven spoke to the pilot; slow she swung;
    Again he spoke, and right for the foe she rushed.

Into the narrowing channel, between the shore
    And the sunk torpedoes lying in treacherous rank;
She turned but a yard too short; a muffled roar,
    A mountainous wave, and she rolled, righted, and sank.

Over the manhole, up in the iron-clad tower,
    Pilot and Captain met as they turned to fly:
The hundredth part of a moment seemed an hour,
    For one could pass to be saved, and one must die.

They stood like men in a dream: Craven spoke,
>Spoke as he lived and fought, with a Captain's pride,
'After you, Pilot:' the pilot woke,
>Down the ladder he went, and Craven died.

All men praise the deed and the manner, but we—
>*We set it apart from the pride that stoops to the proud,*
The strength that is supple to serve the strong and free,
>*The grace of the empty hands and promises loud:*

Sidney thirsting a humbler need to slake,
>*Nelson waiting his turn for the surgeon's hand,*
Lucas crushed with chains for a comrade's sake,
>*Outram coveting right before command,*

These were paladins, these were Craven's peers,
>*These with him shall be crowned in story and song,*
Crowned with the glitter of steel and the glimmer of tears,
>*Princes of courtesy, merciful, proud and strong.*

THE VOLUNTEER[1]

'He leapt to arms unbidden,
>Unneeded, over-bold;
His face by earth is hidden,
>His heart in earth is cold.

'Curse on the reckless daring
>That could not wait the call,
The proud fantastic bearing
>That would be first to fall!'

O tears of human passion,
>Blur not the image true;
This was not folly's fashion,
>This was the man we knew.

---

[1] Compare Housman's *Epitaph on an Army of Mercenaries*, p. 339.

V

Our own age

The word *modern* is not a monopoly of the present century. Ben Jonson was as modern in his day as Auden is in ours. Today, 'modern' is used to define poetry which, in fact, differs in style and form as widely as Victorian poetry does. But very many people seem to imagine that there are two quite separate sorts of poetry: 'poetry', which is sometimes called 'traditional poetry', and something different, which is called 'modern poetry'. The elderly are apt to say impatiently (and often without having read any): 'I can't understand this modern poetry.' The younger are apt to dismiss anything that is traditional as worthless. Sometimes, indeed, they are taught to do so.

It was not the turn of the century but the First World War (1914–1918) which really marked the beginning of a new age. The whole fabric of European society was desperately damaged or destroyed. This destruction and dis-integration is reflected in the first famous 'modern' poem of the twentieth century—*The Waste Land* by T. S. Eliot, published in 1922. As far back as 1912, the poems of another American, Robert Frost, had been called 'revolutionary'. No two poets could be more different, for Eliot represents the urban while Frost is wholly of the country; yet both poets return from written language to speech: Frost, to the slow rhythm of country speech, Eliot, to the quick jerky rhythms of city speech. Eliot in particular caught the speech rhythms of the age. This poetic revolution, just like Wordsworth's, was based on the overthrow of formal artificial language and the setting-up of natural colloquial language. It was literally a bringing-back of poetry to life. This, of course, is a simplification but it indicates the basis of most of the misunderstanding about modern and traditional poetry.

The end of the war saw also the first publication of a highly original poet, Gerard Manley Hopkins, who had been dead since 1889. It will always be argued whether Robert Bridges was right to withhold his friend's MSS. from publication for so long. But certainly its impact in 1918 was as startling as Eliot's, and behind Hopkins's often complex and tortuous use of language and rhythm was the same intense desire to speak. In the 1920's the Irish poet W. B. Yeats—born as long ago as 1865—rose to his full stature; and here, again, is a poet whose style throughout his life is a movement away from artificiality towards natural speech. To put 'the natural words in the natural order' was Yeats's declared aim. This is an end intensely difficult to achieve. Look at Yeats's *Easter 1916* or Philip Larkin's *Church-going* as examples, or at Louis MacNeice's *Meeting Point* or W. H. Auden's *Lay Your Sleeping Head*.

People quickly become used to some particular convention in any art. There are still those who will not admit a play to be in verse if it is not in *blank* verse: 'modern' music cannot be music because it does not use the harmonics of Beethoven;

> Greatly his opera's strains intend,
>
> But in music we know how fashions end!

as Browning wrote. What is merely fashionable will not remain 'modern' for very long, as everyone knows who looks at the clothes worn five years ago. 'Modern Poetry' is nearly fifty years old; but the poetry being written now is not the same sort of poetry as the moderns of 1915 were writing. Poetry is never at a standstill:

> ... every attempt
>
> Is a wholly new start, and a different kind of failure
>
> Because one has only learnt to get the better of words
>
> For the thing one no longer has to say, or the way in which
>
> One is no longer disposed to say it. And so each venture
>
> Is a new beginning, a raid on the inarticulate ...

Eliot's words exactly describe what has *always* been 'modern' in poetry and always will be.

As to the success or failure of poets' raids, time has a way of telling, which is often very different from the contemporary critic's.

Because it uses words—our means of usual, casual, daily and serious communication—poetry is a more vulnerable art than painting or music, yet:

> Words move, music moves
>
> Only in time; but that which is only living
>
> Can only die. Words, after speech, reach
>
> Into the silence. Only by the form, the pattern,
>
> Can words or music reach
>
> The stillness ...

It is only the forms and patterns that change. 'For God's sake, hold your tongue, and let me love'—said a poet speaking in the reigns of Queen Elizabeth I. and King James I. You can *say* it now, but you cannot successfully imitate the forms and patterns of John Donne. We make each for our own time our own patterns. 'Art is art because it is not nature.' So as a young man thought W. B. Yeats. At its greatest it is both: art and nature. Keep an open mind, and much of your own time will come in; shut your mind, and you shut out not only the present but also the past. Shut out Tennyson, and you shut out Eliot; shut out Eliot, and you shut out Donne and Shakespeare; shut out Shakespeare, and you bar Dryden who looked to Chaucer for 'the well of English undefil'd'. For Chaucer, a 'modern' in his own day, though owing much to the traditions of Italy and France, was yet the first poet to use the English language for serious poetry and to use it as colloquially for his own time as Auden for ours. Poetry is a human activity. Critics like it to stop and wait so that they can catch up with it and analyse it and label it and evaluate it and give you marks for knowing what is their particular what. Poets like to get on with it, communicating with you, delighting, annoying, exciting, puzzling you, telling you you are alive and what it is like to be alive: read Helen Spalding's *Prime Numbers* or Stevie Smith's *Six Romans*—or any of these poems. Poetry is never the worse for wear; think of Robert Frost's lines:

I never dared be radical when young

For fear it would make me conservative when old.

It's a philosophy worth attention: a poet's philosophy, a way of saying what never will be said or can be said, a way of saying what poetry *is*.

Heavenly hurt it gives us;

We can find no scar,

But internal difference

Where the meanings are.

A. E. Housman (1859-1936)

EPITAPH ON AN ARMY OF MERCENARIES

Compare Newbolt's *The Volunteer,* p. 333. Housman's poem was written as a direct answer to the German Kaiser's jibe at the regulars of the British Army in 1914—a 'contemptible little army'. The phrase, 'the old contemptibles', became a source of pride in England.

These, in the day when heaven was falling,
 The hour when earth's foundations fled,
Followed their mercenary calling
 And took their wages and are dead.

Their shoulders held the sky suspended;
 They stood, and earth's foundations stay;
What God abandoned, these defended,
 And saved the sum of things for pay.

IN VALLEYS GREEN AND STILL[1]

In valleys green and still
 Where lovers wander maying
They hear from over hill
 A music playing.

Behind the drum and fife,
 Past hawthornwood and hollow,
Through earth and out of life
 The soldiers follow.

The soldier's is the trade:
 In any wind or weather
He steals the heart of maid
 And man together.

---

[1] Compare John Clare's *Married to a Soldier,* p. 224.

The lover and his lass
    Beneath the hawthorn lying
Have heard the soldiers pass,
    And both are sighing.

And down the distance they
    With dying note and swelling
Walk the resounding way
    To the still dwelling.

THE STREET SOUNDS TO THE SOLDIERS' TREAD

The street sounds to the soldiers' tread,
    And out we troop to see:
A single redcoat turns his head,
    He turns and looks at me.

My man, from sky to sky's so far,
    We never crossed before;
Such leagues apart the world's ends are,
    We're like to meet no more;

What thoughts at heart have you and I
    We cannot stop to tell;
But dead or living, drunk or dry,
    Soldier, I wish you well.

FAR IN A WESTERN BROOKLAND

Far in a western brookland
    That bred me long ago
The poplars stand and tremble
    By pools I used to know.

There, in the windless night-time,
    The wanderer, marvelling why,
Halts on the bridge to hearken
    How soft the poplars sigh.

He hears: no more remembered
    In fields where I was known,
Here I lie down in London
    And turn to rest alone.

There, by the starlit fences,
    The wanderer halts and hears
My soul that lingers sighing
    About the glimmering weirs.

Gerard Manley Hopkins (1844-1889)

INVERSNAID [1]

This darksome burn, horseback brown,
His rollrock highroad roaring down,
In coop and in comb the fleece of his foam
Flutes and low to the lake falls home.

A windpuff-bonnet of fáwn-fróth
Turns and twindles over the broth
Of a pool so pitchblack, féll-fpówning,
It rounds and rounds Despair to drowning.

Degged with dew, dappled with dew
Are the groins of the braes that the brook treads through,
Wiry heathpacks, flitches of fern,
And the beadbonny ash that sits over the burn.

What would the world be, once bereft
Of wet and of wildness? Let them be left,
O let them be left, wildness and wet;
Long live the weeds and the wilderness yet.

---

[1] See Introduction, p. 335.

Gerard Manley Hopkins

I WAKE AND FEEL

I wake and feel the fell of dark, not day.
What hours, O what black hours we have spent
This night! what sights you, heart, saw; ways you went!
And more must, in yet longer light's delay.

    With witness I speak this. But where I say
Hours I mean years, mean life. And my lament
Is cries countless, cries like dead letters sent
To dearest him that lives alas! away.

    I am gall, I am heartburn. God's most deep decree
Bitter would have me taste: my taste was me;
Bones built in me, flesh filled, blood brimmed the curse.
    Selfyeast of spirit a dull dough sours. I see
The lost are like this, and their scourge to be
As I am mine, their sweating selves; but worse.

Robert Bridges (1844-1930)

WHO HAS NOT WALKED UPON THE SHORE

Who has not walked upon the shore,
And who does not the morning know,
The day the angry gale is o'er,
The hour the wind has ceased to blow?

The horses of the strong south-west
Are pastured round his tropic tent,
Careless how long the ocean's breast
Sob on and sigh for passion spent.

The frightened birds, that fled inland
To house in rock and tower and tree,
Are gathering on the peaceful strand,
To tempt again the sunny sea;

Whereon the timid ships steal out
And laugh to find their foe asleep,
That lately scattered them about,
And drave them to the fold like sheep.

The snow-white clouds he northward chased
Break into phalanx, line, and band:
All one way to the south they haste,
The south, their pleasant fatherland.

From distant hills their shadows creep,
Arrive in turn and mount the lea,
And flit across the downs, and leap
Sheer off the cliff upon the sea;

And sail and sail far out of sight.
But still I watch their fleecy trains,
That piling all the south with light,
Dapple in France the fertile plains.

THE SNOW LIES SPRINKLED

The snow lies sprinkled on the beach,
And whitens all the marshy lea:
The sad gulls wail adown the gale,
The day is dark and black the sea.
    Shorn of their crests the blighted waves
    With driven foam the offing fleck:
The ebb is low and barely laves
The red rust of the giant wreck.

On such a stony, breaking beach
My childhood chanced and chose to be:
'Twas here I played, and musing made
My friend the melancholy sea.

He from his dim enchanted caves
With shuddering roar and onrush wild
Fell down in sacrificial waves
At feet of his exulting child.

Unto a spirit too light for fear
His wrath was mirth, his wail was glee:—
My heart is now too fixed to bow
Tho' all his tempests howl at me:

For to the gain life's summer saves,
My solemn joy's increasing store,
The tossing of his mournful waves
Makes sweetest music evermore.

ONE GRIEF OF THINE

One grief of thine
    if truth be confest
Was joy to me;
    for it drave to my breast
Thee, to my heart
    to find thy rest.

How long it was
    I never shall know:
I watcht the earth
    so stately and slow,
And the ancient things
    that waste and grow.

But now for me
      what speed devours
Our heavenly life,
      our brilliant hours!
How fast they fly,
      the stars and flowers!

POOR POLL [1]

I saw it all, Polly, how when you had called for sop
and your good friend the cook came and filled up your pan
you yerked it out deftly by beakfuls scattering it
away far as you might upon the sunny lawn
then summoned with loud cry the little garden birds
to take their feast. Quickly came they flustering around
ruddock and merle and finch squabbling among themselves
nor gave you thanks nor heed while you sat silently
watching, and I beside you in perplexity
lost in the maze of all mystery and all knowledge
felt how deep lieth the fount of man's benevolence
if a bird can share it and take pleasure in it.
    If you, my bird, I thought, had a philosophy
it might be a sounder scheme than what our moralists
propound: because thou, Poll, livest in the darkness
which human Reason searching from outside would pierce,
but, being of so feeble a candle-power, can only
show up to view the cloud that it illuminates.
Thus reasoned I: then marvelled how you can adapt
your wild bird-mood to endure your tame environment
the domesticities of English household life
and your small brass-wire cabin, who should'st live on wing
harrying the tropical branch-flowering wilderness:

---

[1] Compare Campbell and his parrot, p. 151.

Yet Nature gave you a gift of easy mimicry
whereby you have come to win uncanny sympathies
and morselled utterance of our Germanic talk
as schoolmasters in Greek will flaunt their hackneyed tags
φωνᾶντα συνετοῖσιν and κτῆμα ἐς ἀεὶ,
ἡ γλῶσσ' ὀμώμοχ', ἡ δὲ φρὴν ἀνώμοτος[1]
tho' you with a better ear copy *us* more perfectly
nor without connotation as when you call'd for sop
all with that stumpy wooden tongue and vicious beak
that dry whistling shrieking tearing cutting pincer
now eagerly subservient to your cautious claws
exploring all varieties of attitude
in irrepressible blind groping for escape
—a very figure and image of man's soul on earth
the almighty cosmic Will fidgeting in a trap—
in your quenchless unknown desire for the unknown life
of which some homely British sailor robb'd you, alas!
'Tis all that doth your silly thoughts so busy keep
the while you sit moping like Patience on a perch
—*Wie viele Tag' und Nächte bist du geblieben!*[2]
La possa delle gambe posta in tregue—[3]
the impeccable spruceness of your grey-feather'd poll
a model in hairdressing for the dandiest old Duke
enough to qualify you for the House of Lords
or the Athenaeum Club, to poke among the nobs
great intellectual nobs and literary nobs
scientific nobs and Bishops *ex officio*:
nor lack you simulation of profoundest wisdom
such as men's features oft acquire in very old age
by mere cooling of passion and decay of muscle

---

[1] words intelligible to the wise *and* a gift for all time
my tongue swore the oath, my soul stayed unbound.
[2] How many days and nights have you rested!
[3] Strength lies in balance—

by faint renunciation even of untold regrets;
who seeing themselves a picture of that which man should-be
learn almost what it were to be what they are-not.
But you can never have cherish'd a determined hope
consciously to renounce or lose it, you will live
your threescore years and ten idle and puzzle-headed
as any mumping monk in his unfurnish'd cell
in peace that, poor Polly, passeth Understanding—
merely because you lack what we men understand
by Understanding. Well! well! that's the difference
C'est la seule différence, mais c'est important.[1]
Ah! your pale sedentary life! but would you change?
exchange it for one crowded hour of glorious life,
one blind furious tussle with a madden'd monkey
who would throttle you and throw your crude fragments away
shreds unintelligible of an unmeaning act
dans la profonde horreur de l'éternelle nuit?[2]
Why ask? You cannot know. 'Twas by no choice of yours
that you mischanged for monkeys' man's society,
'twas that British sailor drove you from Paradise—
εἴθ ὤφελ' Ἀργοῦς μὴ διαπτάσθαι σκάφος[3]
I'd hold embargoes on such a ghastly traffic.

    I am writing verses to you and grieve that you should be
absolument incapable de les comprendre,[4]
Tu, Polle, nescis ista nec potes scire:—[5]
Alas! Iambic, scazon and alexandrine,
spondee or choriamb,[6] all is alike to you—
my well-continued fanciful experiment
whrein so many strange verses amalgamate
on the secure bedrock of Milton's prosody:

---

[1] It is the only difference, but it is important.
[2] In the deep horror of eternal night.
[3] I wish I'd stopped the Argo sailing.
[4] Absolutely incapable of understanding them.
[5] You, Polly, do not know this, and are incapable of knowing it.
[6] Names of different metres.

not but that when I speak you will incline an ear
in critical attention lest by *chance* I *might*
possibly say *something* that was worth repeating:
I am adding (do you think?) pages to literature
that gouty excrement of human intellect
accumulating slowly and everlastingly
depositing, like guano on the Peruvian shore,
to be perhaps exhumed in some remotest age
(*piis secunda, vate me, detur fuga*)[1]
to fertilize the scanty dwarf'd intelligence
of a new race of beings the unhallow'd offspring
of them who shall have quite dismember'd and destroy'd
our temple of Christian faith and fair Hellenic art
just as that monkey would, poor Polly, have done for you.

---

[1] Let a fair passage to me, after the blessed dead, poet as I am.

N THE BRITISH MUSEUM

Thomas Hardy was both a great novelist and poet. He lived to a great age, and what is so fascinating about him as a poet is that he wrote most of his poems when he was old: often about events, love affairs, and encounters which had taken place fifty years before. However this is communicated, it gives his poems a strange and wonderful timelessness like nobody else's—'as if stone could speak'.

'What do you see in that time-touched stone,
        When nothing is there
But ashen blankness, although you give it
        A rigid stare?

'You look not quite as if you saw,
        But as if you heard,
Parting your lips, and treading softly
        As mouse or bird.

'It is only the base of a pillar, they'll tell you,
        That came to us
From a far old hill men used to name
        Areopagus.'

—'I know no art, and I only view
        A stone from a wall,
But I am thinking that stone has echoed
        The voice of Paul,

'Paul as he stood and preached beside it
        Facing the crowd,
A small gaunt figure with wasted features,
        Calling out loud

'Words that in all their intimate accents
        Pattered upon
That marble front, and were wide reflected,
        And then were gone.

'I'm a labouring man, and know but little,
     Or nothing at all;
But I can't help thinking that stone once echoed
     The voice of Paul.'

A THUNDERSTORM IN TOWN

A Reminiscence: 1893

She wore a new 'terra-cotta' dress,
And we stayed, because of the pelting storm,
Within the hansom's[1] dry recess,
Though the horse had stopped; yea, motionless
     We sat on, snug and warm.

Then the downpour ceased, to my sharp sad pain
And the glass that had screened our forms before
Flew up, and out she sprang to her door:
I should have kissed her if the rain
     Had lasted a minute more.

---

[1] a horse-drawn cab.

A BEAUTY'S SOLILOQUY DURING HER HONEYMOON

n a London Hotel, 1892

Too late, too late! I did not know my fairness
    Would catch the world's keen eyes so!
How the men look at me! My radiant rareness
    I deemed not they would prize so!

That I was a peach for any man's possession
    Why did not some one say
Before I leased myself in an hour's obsession
    To this dull mate for aye!

His days are mine. I am one who cannot steal her
    Ahead of his plodding pace:
As he is, so am I. One doomed to feel her
    A wasted form and face!

I was so blind! It did sometimes just strike me
    All girls were not as I,
But, dwelling much alone, how few were like me
    I could not well descry;

Till, at this Grand Hotel, all looks bend on me
    In homage as I pass
To take my seat at breakfast, dinner,—con me
    As poorly spoused, alas!

I was too young. I dwelt too much on duty:
    If I had guessed my powers
Where might have sailed this cargo of choice beauty
    In its unanchored hours!

Well, husband, poor plain man; I've lost life's battle!—
    Come—let them look at me.
O damn, don't show in your looks that I'm your chattel
    Quite so emphatically!

Thomas Hardy

THE FIVE STUDENTS

The sparrow dips in his wheel-rut bath,
    The sun grows passionate-eyed,
And boils the dew to smoke by the paddock-path;
    As strenuously we stride,—
Five of us; dark He, fair He, dark She, fair She, I,
    All beating by.

The air is shaken, the high-road hot,
    Shadowless swoons the day,
The greens are sobered and cattle at rest; but not
    We on our urgent way,—
Four of us; fair She, dark She, fair He, I, are there,
    But one—elsewhere.

Autumn moulds the hard fruit mellow,
    And forward still we press
Through moors, briar-meshed plantations, clay-pits yellow
    As in the spring hours—yes,
Three of us; fair He, fair She, I, as heretofore,
    But—fallen one more.

The leaf drops: earthworms draw it in
    At night-time noiselessly,
The fingers of birch and beech are skeleton-thin,
    And yet on the beat are we,—
Two of us; fair She, I. But no more left to go
    The track we know.

Icicles tag the church-aisle leads,
    The flag-rope gibbers hoarse,
The home-bound foot-folk wrap their snow-flaked heads,
    Yet I still stalk the course—
One of us. . . . Dark and fair He, dark and fair She, gone:
    The rest—anon.

THE HAUNTER

He does not think that I haunt here nightly:
    How shall I let him know
That whither his fancy sets him wandering
    I, too, alertly go?—
Hover and hover a few feet from him
    Just as I used to do,
But cannot answer the words he lifts me—
    Only listen thereto!

When I could answer he did not say them:
    When I could let him know
How I would like to join in his journeys
    Seldom he wished to go.
Now that he goes and wants me with him
    More than he used to do,
Never he sees my faithful phantom
    Though he speaks thereto.

Yes, I companion him to places
    Only dreamers know,
Where the shy hares print long paces,
    Where the night rooks go;
Into old aisles where the past is all to him,
    Close as his shade can do,
Always lacking the power to call to him,
    Near as I reach thereto!

What a good haunter I am, O tell him!
    Quickly make him know
If he but sigh since my loss befell him
    Straight to his side I go.
Tell him a faithful one is doing
    All that love can do
Still that his path may be worth pursuing,
    And to bring peace thereto.

Hilaire Belloc (1870-1953)

EPIGRAM: ON A GENERAL ELECTION[1]

The accursèd power which stands on Privilege
(And goes with Women, and Champagne and Bridge)
Broke—and Democracy resumed her reign:
(Which goes with Bridge, and Women and Champagne).

SONNET: WOULD THAT I HAD THREE HUNDRED THOUSAND POUNDS

Would that I had £300,000
    Invested in some strong security;
A Midland Country House with formal grounds,
    A Town House, and a House beside the sea,
And one in Spain, and one in Normandy,
    And friends innumerable at my call
And youth serene—and underneath it all
    One steadfast, passionate flame to nurture me.

Then would I chuck for good my stinking trade
    Of writing tosh at 1s. 6d. a quire!
And soar like young Bellerophon arrayed
    High to the filmy Heavens of my desire. . . .
        But that's all over. Here's the world again.
        Bring me the blotter. Fill the fountain-pen.

---

[1] Compare other Epigrams, pp. 33 and 137.

John Masefield (b. 1878)

SONNET: WHAT AM I, LIFE?

What am I, Life? A thing of watery salt
Held in cohesion by unresting cells
Which work they know not why, which never halt,
Myself unwitting where their master dwells.
I do not bid them, yet they toil, they spin:
A world which uses me as I use them,
Nor do I know which end or which begin,
Nor which to praise, which pamper, which condemn.
So, like a marvel in a marvel set,
I answer to the vast, as wave by wave
The sea of air goes over, dry or wet,
Or the full moon comes swimming from her cave,
Or the great sun comes north, this myriad I
Tingles, not knowing how, yet wondering why.

SONNET: O LITTLE SELF

O little self, within whose smallness lies
All that man was, and is, and will become,
Atom unseen that comprehends the skies
And tells the tracks by which the planets roam;
That, without moving, knows the joys of wings,
The tiger's strength, the eagle's secrecy,
And in the hovel can consort with kings,
Or clothe a God with his own mystery.
O with what darkness do we cloak thy light,
What dusty folly gather thee for food,
Thou who alone art knowledge and delight,
The heavenly bread, the beautiful, the good.
O living self, O God, O morning star,
Give us thy light, forgive us what we are.

Like Hardy, Walter de la Mare was a writer with a double gift of prose and poetry; and he has often been misunderstood in both media. People say: 'he wrote poems for children' or 'he wrote ghost stories'. In a sense, he did. But he was a man of genius, and his explorations of the strange edges of human consciousness are by no means simple poems for children or ghost stories. He is a writer who has yet to be truly 'discovered'; that he will be, there is no doubt.

VOICES

Who is it calling by the darkened river
    Where the moss lies smooth and deep,
And the dark trees lean unmoving arms,
    Silent and vague in sleep,
And the bright-heeled constellations pass
    In splendour through the gloom;
Who is it calling o'er the darkened river
    In music, 'Come!'?

Who is it wandering in the summer meadows
    Where the children stoop and play
In the green faint-scented flowers, spinning
    The guileless hours away?
Who touches their bright hair? who puts
    A wind-shell to each cheek,
Whispering betwixt its breathing silences,
    'Seek! seek!'?

Who is it watching in the gathering twilight
    When the curfew bird hath flown
On eager wings, from song to silence,
    To its darkened nest alone?
Who takes for brightening eyes the stars,
    For locks the still moonbeam,
Sighs through the dews of evening peacefully
    Falling, 'Dream!'?

ALONE

The abode of the nightingale is bare,
Flowered frost congeals in the gelid air,
The fox howls from his frozen lair:
    Alas, my loved one is gone,
    I am alone:
    It is winter.

Once the pink cast a winy smell,
The wild bee hung in the hyacinth bell,
Light in effulgence of beauty fell:
    Alas, my loved one is gone,
    I am alone:
    It is winter.

My candle a silent fire doth shed,
Starry Orion hunts o'erhead;
Come moth, come shadow, the world is dead:
    Alas, my loved one is gone,
    I am alone;
    It is winter.

THE WINDOW

Sunlit, the lashes fringe the half-closed eyes
With hues no bow excels that spans the skies;
As magical the meteor's flight o'erhead,
And daybreak shimmering on a spider's thread. . . .
Thou starry Universe—whose breadth, depth, height
Contracts to such strait entry as mere sight!

AN ABANDONED CHURCH

Roofless and eyeless, weed-sodden, dank, old, cold—
Fickly the sunset glimmered through the rain,
Gilded the gravestones—faded out again;
A storm-cock shrilled its aeon-old refrain,
    Lambs bleated from their fold.

AWAY

There is no sorrow
Time heals never;
No loss, betrayal,
Beyond repair.
Balm for the soul, then,
Though grave shall sever
Lover from loved
And all they share;
See, the sweet sun shines,
The shower is over,
Flowers preen their beauty,
The day how fair!
Brood not too closely
On love, or duty;
Friends long forgotten
May wait you where
Life with death
Brings all to an issue;
None will long mourn for you,
Pray for you, miss you,
Your place left vacant,
You not there.

'OH, WHY?'

Oh, why make such ado—
This fretful care and trouble?
The sun in noonday's blue
Pours radiance on earth's bubble.
What though the heart-strings crack,
And sorrow bid thee languish,
Dew falls; the night comes back;
Sleep, and forget thine anguish.
Oh, why in shadow haunt?
Shines not the evening flower?
Hark, how the sweet birds chaunt,
The lovely light their bower.
Water her music makes,
Lulling even these to slumber;
And only dead of darkness wakes
    Stars without number.

THE EXILE

I am that Adam who, with Snake for guest,
Hid anguished eyes upon Eve's piteous breast.
I am that Adam who, with broken wings,
Fled from the Seraph's brazen trumpetings.
Betrayed and fugitive, I still must roam
A world where sin, and beauty, whisper of Home.

Oh, from wide circuit, shall at length I see
Pure daybreak lighten again on Eden's tree?
Loosed from remorse and hope and love's distress,
Enrobe me again in my lost nakedness?
No more with wordless grief a loved one grieve,
But to Heaven's nothingness re-welcome Eve?

Walter de la Mare

NAPOLEON

'What is the world, O soldiers?
        It is I:
I, this incessant snow,
        This northern sky;
Soldiers, this solitude
        Through which we go
                Is I.'

James Elroy Flecker (1884-1915

OXFORD CANAL

This poem is, for its time, very un-English; it is more like a French
Impressionist painting. Flecker was, in fact, one of the very few
English poets who knew his French contemporaries and the literature
of Europe. Free verse has never seemed to suit the rhythms of the
English language but this seems, in its clarity and discipline, to be an
excellent example of it. What most people forget when writing free
verse is just that: it needs as much discipline as the writing of a formal
stanza.

When you have wearied of the valiant spires of this County Town,
Of its wide white streets and glistening museums, and black
        monastic walls,
Of its red motors and lumbering trams, and self-sufficient people,
I will take you walking with me to a place you have not seen—
Half town and half country—the land of the Canal.
It is dearer to me than the antique town: I love it more than the
        rounded hills:
Straightest, sublimest of rivers is the long Canal.
I have observed great storms and trembled: I have wept for fear
        of the dark.
But nothing makes me so afraid as the clear water of this idle
        canal on a summer's noon.

Do you see the great telephone poles down in the water, how
  every wire is distinct?
If a body fell into the canal it would rest entangled in those wires
  for ever, between earth and air.
For the water is as deep as the stars are high.
One day I was thinking how if a man fell from that lofty pole
He would rush through the water toward me till his image was
  scattered by his splash,
When suddenly a train rushed by: the brazen dome of the engine
  flashed: the long white carriages roared;
The sun veiled himself for a moment, and the signals loomed in
  fog;
A savage woman screamed at me from a barge: little children
  began to cry:
The untidy landscape rose to life; a sawmill started;
A cart rattled down to the wharf, and workmen clanged over the
  iron footbridge;
A beautiful old man nodded from the first story window of a
  square red house,
And a pretty girl came out to hang up clothes in a small
  delightful garden.
O strange motion in the suburb of a county town: slow regular
  movement of the dance of death!
Men and not phantoms are these that move in light.
Forgotten they live, and forgotten die.

THE DYING PATRIOT

This is really the dying speech of an English Prime Minister. It comes
from Flecker's play, *Don Juan,* when Don Juan has just shot Lord
Framlingham on the Embankment, to stop him declaring war. At
the end of the speech, the Prime Minister falls backwards into the
darkness of the River Thames.

Day breaks on England down the Kentish hills,
Singing in the silence of the meadow-footing rills,
Day of my dreams, O day!

I saw them march from Dover, long ago,
With a silver cross before them, singing low,
Monks of Rome from their home where the blue seas break in
    foam,
    Augustine with his feet of snow.

Noon strikes on England, noon on Oxford town,
—Beauty she was statue cold—there's blood upon her gown:
Noon of my dreams, O noon!
    Proud and godly kings had built her, long ago,
    With her towers and tombs and statues all arow,
With her fair and floral air and the love that lingers there,
    And the streets where the great men go.

Evening on the olden, the golden sea of Wales,
When the first star shivers and the last wave pales:
O evening dreams!
    There's a house the Britons walked in, long ago,
    Where now the springs of ocean fall and flow,
And the dead robed in red and sea-lilies overhead
    Sway when the long winds blow.

Sleep not, my country: though night is here, afar
Your children of the morning are clamorous for war:
Fire in the night, O dreams!
    Though she send you as she sent you, long ago,
    South to desert, east to ocean, west to snow,
West of these out to seas colder than the Hebrides I must go
    Where the fleet of stars is anchored and the young Star-
        captains glow.

STILLNESS

When the words rustle no more,
    And the last work's done,
When the bolt lies deep in the door,
    And Fire, our Sun,
Falls on the dark-laned meadows of the floor;

When from the clock's last chime to the next chime
    Silence beats his drum,
And Space with gaunt grey eyes and her brother Time
    Wheeling and whispering come,
She with the mould of form and he with the loom of rhyme:

Then twittering out in the night my thought-birds flee,
    I am emptied of all my dreams:
I only hear Earth turning, only see
    Ether's long bankless streams,
And only know I should drown if you laid not your hand on me.

W. H. Davies (1871-1940)

THE SLEEPERS

As I walked down the waterside
  This silent morning, wet and dark;
Before the cocks in farmyards crowed,
  Before the dogs began to bark;
Before the hour of five was struck
By old Westminster's mighty clock:

As I walked down the waterside
  This morning, in the cold damp air,
I saw a hundred women and men
  Huddled in rags and sleeping there:
These people have no work, thought I,
And long before their time they die.

That moment, on the waterside,
  A lighted car[1] came at a bound;
I looked inside, and saw a score
  Of pale and weary men that frowned;
Each man sat in a huddled heap,
Carried to work while fast asleep.

Ten cars rushed down the waterside
  Like lighted coffins in the dark;
With twenty dead men in each car,
  That must be brought alive by work:
These people work too hard, thought I,
And long before their time they die.

_____

[1] Tramcar.

THE TWO HEAVENS

When, with my window opened wide at night,
To look at yonder stars with their round light,
In motion shining beautiful and clear—
As I look up, there comes this sudden fear:
That, down on earth, too dark for me to see,
Some homeless wretch looks up in misery;
And, like a man that's guilty of a sin,
I close my blinds, and draw my body in.
Still thinking of that Heaven, I dare not take
Another look, because of that man's sake;
Who in the darkness, with his mournful eyes
Has made *my* lighted home his paradise.

TO SPARROWS FIGHTING

Stop, feathered bullies!
    Peace, angry birds;
You common sparrows that,
    For a few words,
Roll fighting in wet mud,
To shed each other's blood.

Look at those linnets, they
    Like ladies sing;
See how those swallows, too,
    Play on the wing;
All other birds close by
Are gentle, clean and shy.

And yet maybe your life's
    As sweet as theirs;
The common poor that fight
    Live not for years
In one long frozen state
Of anger, like the great.

Rupert Brooke (1887-1915)

A CHANNEL PASSAGE

December 1909

This poem exactly illustrates the point made on p. 335 about 'modernity'. When first published, in 1916, it was thought to be both horrifying and offensive—and not at all the sort of thing that poetry ought to be.

The damned ship lurched and slithered. Quiet and quick
    My cold gorge rose; the long sea rolled; I knew
I must think hard of something, or be sick;
    And could think hard of only one thing—*you*!
You, you alone could hold my fancy ever!
    And with you memories come, sharp pain, and dole.
Now there's a choice—heartache or tortured liver!
    A sea-sick body, or a you-sick soul!

Do I forget you? Retchings twist and tie me,
    Old meat, good meals, brown gobbets, up I throw.
Do I remember? Acrid return and slimy,
    The sobs and slobber of a last year's woe.
And still the sick ship rolls. 'Tis hard, I tell ye,
To choose 'twixt love and nausea, heart and belly.

HEAVEN

Fish (fly-replete, in depth of June,
Dawdling away their wat'ry noon)
Ponder deep wisdom, dark or clear,
Each secret fishy hope or fear.
Fish say, they have their Stream and Pond;
But is there anything Beyond?
This life cannot be All, they swear,
For how unpleasant, if it were!
One may not doubt that, somehow, Good
Shall come of Water and of Mud;
And, sure, the reverent eye must see

A Purpose in Liquidity.
We darkly know, by Faith we cry,
The future is not Wholly Dry.
Mud unto mud!—Death eddies near—
Not here the appointed End, not here!
But somewhere, beyond Space and Time,
Is wetter water, slimier slime!
And there (they trust) there swimmeth One
Who swam ere rivers were begun,
Immense, of fishy form and mind,
Squamous, omnipotent, and kind;
And under that Almighty Fin,
The littlest fish may enter in.
Oh! never fly conceals a hook,
Fish say, in the Eternal Brook,
But more than mundane weeds are there,
And mud, celestially fair;
Fat caterpillars drift around,
And Paradisal grubs are found;
Unfading moths, immortal flies,
And the worm that never dies.
And in that Heaven of all their wish,
There shall be no more land, say fish.

THE SOLDIER

It is worth remembering that Rupert Brooke *did* die on his way to the Dardanelles in 1915. He died of blood-poisoning; and if penicillin had then been known he would not have died as he did. He would probably have been killed in action, as nearly all his friends were.

If I should die, think only this of me:
    That there's some corner of a foreign field
That is for ever England. There shall be
    In that rich earth a richer dust concealed;
A dust whom England bore, shaped, made aware,
    Gave, once, her flowers to love, her ways to roam,
A body of England's, breathing English air,
    Washed by the rivers, blest by suns of home.

And think, this heart, all evil shed away,
 A pulse in the eternal mind, no less
  Gives somewhere back the thoughts by England given;
Her sights and sounds; dreams happy as her day;
 And laughter, learnt of friends; and gentleness,
  In hearts at peace, under an English heaven.

Alice Meynell (1849-1922)

SUMMER IN ENGLAND, 1914

On London fell a clearer light;
 Caressing pencils of the sun
Defined the distances, the white
 Houses transfigured one by one,
The 'long, unlovely street' impearled.
O what a sky has walked the world!

Most happy year![1] And out of town
 The hay was prosperous, and the wheat;
The silken harvest climbed the down;
 Moon after moon was heavenly-sweet
Stroking the bread within the sheaves,
Looking twixt apples and their leaves.

And while this rose made round her cup,
 The armies died convulsed. And when
This chaste young silver sun went up
 Softly, a thousand shattered men,
One wet corruption, heaped the plain,
After a league-long throb of pain.

---

[1] War broke out on August 4th.

Flower following tender flower; and birds,
    And berries; and benignant skies
Made thrive the serried flocks and herds.—
    Yonder are men shot through the eyes.
      Love, hide thy face
From man's unpardonable race!

Charlotte Mew (1870-1928)

THE CALL

From our low seat beside the fire
    Where we have dozed and dreamed and watched the
      glow
Or raked the ashes, stopping so
We scarcely saw the sun or rain
    Above, or looked much higher
Than this same quiet red or burned-out¯fire,
    To-night we heard a call,
    A rattle on the window-pane,
    A voice on the sharp air,
And felt a breath stirring our hair,
    A flame within us: something swift and tall
Swept in and out and that was all.
Was it a bright or a dark angel? Who can know?
    It left no mark upon the snow,
    But suddenly it snapped the chain,
    Unbarred, flung wide the door
    Which will not shut again;
And so we cannot sit here any more.
    We must arise and go:
    The world is cold without
    And dark and hedged about
    With mystery and enmity and doubt,
    But we must go
    Though yet we do not know
Who called, or what marks we shall leave upon the snow.

Edward Thomas (1878-1917)

I NEVER SAW THAT LAND BEFORE

Edward Thomas was an older man than Brooke or Owen. His reasons for volunteering for the war were mixed. One bitter and cynical reason was that his army pay freed him from writing as a journalist, and all his poetry was written after his decision to join up. Very little of it is about war. He was killed in 1917.

I never saw that land before,
And now can never see it again;
Yet, as if by acquaintance hoar
Endeared, by gladness and by pain,
Great was the affection that I bore

To the valley and the river small,
The cattle, the grass, the bare ash trees,
The chickens from the farmsteads, all
Elm-hidden, and the tributaries
Descending at equal interval;

The blackthorns down along the brook
With wounds yellow as crocuses
Where yesterday the labourer's hook
Had sliced them cleanly; and the breeze
That hinted all and nothing spoke.

I neither expected anything
Nor yet remembered: but some goal
I touched then; and if I could sing
What would not even whisper my soul
As I went on my journeying,

I should use, as the trees and birds did,
A language not to be betrayed;
And what was hid should still be hid
Excepting from those like me made
Who answer when such whispers bid.

FIFTY FAGGOTS

There they stand, on their ends, the fifty faggots
That once were underwood of hazel and ash
In Jenny Pinks's Copse. Now, by the hedge
Close packed, they make a thicket fancy alone
Can creep through with the mouse and wren. Next Spring
A blackbird or a robin will nest there,
Accustomed to them, thinking they will remain
Whatever is for ever to a bird:
This Spring it is too late; the swift has come.
'Twas a hot day for carrying them up:
Better they will never warm me, though they must
Light several Winters' fires. Before they are done
The war will have ended, many other things
Have ended, maybe, that I can no more
Foresee or more control than robin and wren.

ASPENS

All day and night, save winter, every weather,
Above the inn, the smithy, and the shop,
The aspens at the cross-roads talk together
Of rain, until their last leaves fall from the top.

Out of the blacksmith's cavern comes the ringing
Of hammer, shoe, and anvil; out of the inn
The clink, the hum, the roar, the random singing—
The sounds that for these fifty years have been.

The whisper of the aspens is not drowned,
And over lightless pane and footless road,
Empty as sky, with every other sound
Not ceasing, calls their ghosts from their abode,

A silent smithy, a silent inn, nor fails
In the bare moonlight or the thick-furred gloom,
In tempest or the night of nightingales,
To turn the cross-roads to a ghostly room.

And it would be the same were no house near.
Over all sorts of weather, men, and times,
Aspens must shake their leaves and men may hear
But need not listen, more than to my rhymes.

Whatever wind blows, while they and I have leaves
We cannot other than an aspen be
That ceaselessly, unreasonably grieves,
Or so men think who like a different tree.

Siegfried Sassoon (b. 1886)

WHEN I'M ALONE

'*When I'm alone*'—the words tripped off his tongue
As though to be alone were nothing strange.
'*When I was young*,' he said; '*when I was young.* . . .'

I thought of age, and loneliness, and change.
I thought how strange we grow when we're alone,
And how unlike the selves that meet, and talk,
And blow the candles out, and say good-night.
Alone . . . The word is life endured and known.
It is the stillness where our spirits walk
And all but inmost faith is overthrown.

Wilfred Owen (1893-1918)

EXPOSURE

Written in 1916, this poem describes the conditions of trench warfare
on the Western Front. Owen was killed on November 3rd, 1918, just
a week before the Armistice.

Our brains ache, in the merciless iced east winds that knive us . . .
Wearied we keep awake because the night is silent . . .
Low, drooping flares confuse our memory of the salient . . .
Worried by silence, sentries whisper, curious, nervous,
   But nothing happens.

Watching, we hear the mad gusts tugging on the wire,
Like twitching agonies of men among its brambles.
Northward, incessantly, the flickering gunnery rumbles,
Far off, like a dull rumour of some other war.
   What are we doing here?

The poignant misery of dawn begins to grow . . .
We only know war lasts, rain soaks, and clouds sag stormy.
Dawn massing in the east her melancholy army
Attacks once more in ranks on shivering ranks of gray,
   But nothing happens.

Sudden successive flights of bullets streak the silence.
Less deadly than the air that shudders black with snow,
With sidelong flowing flakes that flock, pause, and renew,
We watch them wandering up and down the wind's nonchalance,
   But nothing happens.

Pale flakes with fingering stealth come feeling for our faces—
We cringe in holes, back on forgotten dreams, and stare, snow-
  dazed,
Deep into grassier ditches. So we drowse, sun-dozed,
Littered with blossoms trickling where the blackbird fusses.
   Is it that we are dying?

Slowly our ghosts drag home: glimpsing the sunk fires, glozed
With crusted dark-red jewels; crickets jingle there;
For hours the innocent mice rejoice: the house is theirs;
Shutters and doors, all closed: on us the doors are closed,—
      We turn back to our dying.

Since we believe not otherwise can kind fires burn;
Nor ever suns smile true on child, or field, or fruit.
For God's invincible spring our love is made afraid;
Therefore, not loath, we lie out here; therefore were born,
      For love of God seems dying.

To-night, His frost will fasten on this mud and us,
Shrivelling many hands, puckering foreheads crisp.
The burying-party, picks and shovels in their shaking grasp,
Pause over half-known faces. All their eyes are ice,
      But nothing happens.

STRANGE MEETING

Words from this poem, and from other poems of Owen's, were set
to music by Benjamin Britten in his *War Requiem,* commissioned by
Coventry Cathedral and first performed there in 1962.

It seemed that out of battle I escaped
Down some profound dull tunnel, long since scooped
Through granites which titanic wars had groined.
Yet also there encumbered sleepers groaned,
Too fast in thought or death to be bestirred.
Then, as I probed them, one sprang up, and stared
With piteous recognition in fixed eyes,
Lifting distressful hands as if to bless.

And by his smile, I knew that sullen hall,
By his dead smile I knew we stood in Hell.
With a thousand pains that vision's face was grained;
Yet no blood reached there from the upper ground,
And no guns thumped, or down the flues made moan.
'Strange friend,' I said, 'here is no cause to mourn.'
'None,' said the other, 'save the undone years,
The hopelessness. Whatever hope is yours,
Was my life also; I went hunting wild
After the wildest beauty in the world,
Which lies not calm in eyes, or braided hair,
But mocks the steady running of the hour,
And if it grieves, grieves richlier than here.
For by my glee might many men have laughed,
And of my weeping something had been left,
Which must die now. I mean the truth untold,
The pity of war, the pity war distilled.
Now men will go content with what we spoiled.
Or, discontent, boil bloody, and be spilled.
They will be swift with swiftness of the tigress,
None will break ranks, though nations trek from progress.
Courage was mine, and I had mystery,
Wisdom was mine, and I had mastery;
To miss the march of this retreating world
Into vain citadels that are not walled.
Then, when much blood had clogged their chariot-wheels
I would go up and wash them from sweet wells,
Even with truths that lie too deep for taint.
I would have poured my spirit without stint
But not through wounds; not on the cess of war.
Foreheads of men have bled where no wounds were.
I am the enemy you killed, my friend.
I knew you in this dark; for so you frowned
Yesterday through me as you jabbed and killed.
I parried; but my hands were loath and cold.
Let us sleep now. . . .'

W. J. Turner was an Australian. The vivid light of Australia and the
fact that you could move from a big city like Melbourne, where his
father was Cathedral organist, into utterly wild bush-country at the
end of the tramway track, gave his poetry an immediate and perhaps
violent impact, very un-English, exciting and quite new. He was a
Romantic person to whom 'mud is none the less mud' and his
Australian background may help to explain many strangenesses in
his verse.

TALKING WITH SOLDIERS

The mind of the people is like mud,
From which arise strange and beautiful things,
But mud is none the less mud,
Though it bear orchids and prophesying Kings,
Dreams, trees, and water's bright babblings.

It has found form and colour and light,
The cold whiteness of the Arctic Pole;
It has called a far-off glow Arcturus,
And some pale weeds, lilies of the valley.

It has imagined Virgil, Helen and Cassandra;
The sack of Troy, and the weeping for Hector—
Rearing stark up 'mid all this beauty
In the thick, dull neck of Ajax.

There is a dark Pine in Lapland,
And the great, figured Horn of the Reindeer
Moving soundlessly across the snow,
Is its twin brother, double-dreamed,
In the mind of a far-off people.

It is strange that a little mud
Should echo with sounds, syllables, and letters,
Should rise up and call a mountain Popocatapetl,
And a green-leafed wood Oleander.

These are the ghosts of invisible things;
There is no Lapland, no Helen and no Hector,
And the Reindeer is a darkening of the brain,
And Oleander is but Oleander.

Mary Magdalena and the vine Lachrymae Christi,
Were like ghosts up the ghost of Vesuvius,
As I sat and drank wine with the soldiers,
As I sat in the Inn on the mountain,
Watching the shadows in my mind.

The mind of the people is like mud:
Where are the imperishable things,
The ghosts that flicker in the brain—
Silent women, orchids, and prophesying Kings,
Dreams, trees, and water's bright babblings?

THE LION

Strange spirit with inky hair,
    Tail tufted stiff in rage,
I saw with sudden stare
    Leap on the printed page.

The stillness of its roar
    From midnight deserts torn
Clove silence to the core
    Like the blare of a great horn.

saw the sudden sky;
    Cities in crumbling sand;
The stars fall wheeling by;
    The lion roaring stand:

The stars fall wheeling by,
    Their silent, silver stain,
Cold on his glittering eye,
    Cold on his carven mane.

The full-orbed Moon shone down,
   The silence was so loud,
From jaws wide-open thrown
    His voice hung like a cloud.

Earth shrank to blackest air,
   That spirit stiff in rage
Into some midnight lair
    Leapt from the printed page.

DEATH AND DESPAIR

Death and despair were his reward,
Walk not over the green sward,
Turn away and mount the stile
And over the hill for many a mile
For into the coffin go night and day
So, over the hill and far away!

What! you linger and still you stay,
Tell me the reason that you gaze?
The worm, the sparrow, the chaffinch play,
Do you likewise, follow their ways;
Loosen your legs, ere stiff in the clay
They lie for a numberless number of days.

Of air and sky I have drunk my fill,
My legs are weary, my body worn.
So many times I have climbed the hill
Have sat out the stars and watched the morn,
My heart is empty, my mind is ill,
I have no appetite left to fill.

What! do you dare to stand and tell:
You breathe the living fragrant air,
Over the next, the very next hill
The sea is rolling, do you not hear?
Do you not hear its gentle voice?
Up and away! rejoice! rejoice!

I have sat so long by the ocean's side;
I have dreamed so long on the ocean's floor;
Sailing by every wind and tide
The sirens' songs have told me more
Than they have told any man before
But my heart with them will not abide:

My heart, my heart it is so sore;
The song of the lark I cannot bear;
The cuckoo I'll not hear again,
Nor the distant rumbling business train;
I have no business here and fain
Would do and suffer nothing more.

Death and despair are your reward,
Walk not over the green sward.
Turn from the living, turn away,
Into the coffin with night and day;
The sparrows chatter, the chaffinch play,
Death and despair are your reward.

D. H. Lawrence (1885-1930)

LAST LESSON OF THE AFTERNOON

It is well worth comparing this poem with others such as Stephen
Spender's *In an Elementary School Classroom,* W. B. Yeats's *Among
Schoolchildren* and John Betjeman's *An Early Incident in the Life of
Ebenezer Jones, Poet;* Thomas Gray's *Ode on a Distant Prospect of Eton
College* (where he was at school) is also worth comparing.

When will the bell ring, and end this weariness?
How long have they tugged the leash, and strained apart,
My pack of unruly hounds! I cannot start
Them again on a quarry of knowledge they hate to hunt,
I can haul them and urge them no more.

No longer now can I endure the brunt
Of the books that lie out on the desks; a full threescore
Of several insults of blotted pages, and scrawl
Of slovenly work that they have offered me.
I am sick, and what on earth is the good of it all?
What good to them or me, I cannot see!

So, shall I take
My last dear fuel of life to heap on my soul
And kindle my will to a flame that shall consume
Their dross of indifference; and take the toll
Of their insults in punishment?—I will not!—

I will not waste my soul and my strength for this.
What do I care for all that they do amiss!
What is the point of this teaching of mine, and of this
Learning of theirs? It all goes down the same abyss.

What does it matter to me, if they can write
A description of a dog, or if they can't?
What is the point? To us both, it is all my aunt!
And yet I'm supposed to care, with all my might.

I do not, and will not; they won't and they don't; and that's all!
I shall keep my strength for myself; they can keep theirs as well.
Why should we beat our heads against the wall
Of each other? I shall sit and wait for the bell.

Frances Cornford (1886-1960

CITY EVENING

This is the hour when night says to the streets:
'I am coming'; and the light is so strange
The heart expects adventure in everything it meets;
Even the past to change.

J. C. Squire (1884-1958)

BALLADE OF SOPORIFIC ABSORPTION

Ho! Ho! Yes! Yes! It's very all well,
    You may drunk I am think, but I tell you I'm not,
I'm as sound as a fiddle and fit as a bell,
    And stable quite ill to see what's what.
    I under *do* stand you surprise a got
When I headed my smear with gooseberry jam:
    And I've swallowed, I grant, a beer of lot—
But I'm not so think as you drunk I am.

Can I liquor my stand? Why, yes, like hell!
    I care not how many a tossed I've pot,
I shall stralk quite weight not yutter an ell,
    My feech will not spalter the least little jot:
    If you knownly had own!—well, I gave him a dot,
And I said to him, 'Sergeant, I'll come like a lamb—
    The floor it seems like a storm in a yacht,
But I'm not so think as you drunk I am.'

For example, to prove it I'll tale you a tell—
    I once knew a fellow called Apricot—
I'm sorry, I just chair over a fell—
    A trifle—this chap, on a very day hot—
    If I hadn't consumed that last whisky of tot!
As I said now, this fellow, called Abraham—
    Ah? one more. Since it's you! Just a do me will spot—
But I'm not so think as you drunk I am!

Envoi

So Prince, you suggest I've bolted my shot!
Well, like what you say, and soul your damn!
    I'm an upple litset by the talk you rot—
But I'm not so think as you drunk I am.

Roy Campbell (1901-1957)

Roy Campbell was born and brought up in South Africa, and his whole thinking and being was based on a continent not European. In religion he was a Catholic, and much of his life he spent in Spain. His poetry, like Byron's, is outside the English tradition. It is always lively, provocative and technically brilliant.

DREAMING SPIRES

Through villages of yelping tykes
With skulls on totem-poles, and wogs
Exclaiming at our motor bikes
With more amazement than their dogs:

Respiring fumes of pure phlogiston
On hardware broncos, half-machine,
With arteries pulsing to the piston
And hearts inducting gasoline:

Buckjumping over ruts and boulders,
The Centaurs of an age of steel
Engrafted all save head and shoulders
Into the horsepower of the wheel—

We roared into the open country,
Scattering vultures, kites, and crows;
All Nature scolding our effrontery
In raucous agitation rose.

Zoology went raving stark
To meet us on the open track—
The whole riff raff of Noah's Ark
With which the wilderness was black.

With kicks and whinnies, bucks and snorts,
Their circuses stamped by:
A herd of wildebeast cavorts,
And somersaults against the sky:

Across the stripes of zebras sailing,
The eyesight rattles like a cane
That's rattled down an area-railing
Until it blurs upon the brain.

The lions flee with standing hackles,
Leaving their feast before they've dined:
Their funeral poultry flaps and cackles
To share the breeze they feel behind.

Both wart- and road-hog vie together,
As they and we, petarding smoke,
Belly to earth and hell for leather,
In fumes of dust and petrol choke.

We catch the madness they have caught,
Stand on the footrests, and guffaw—
Till shadowed by a looming thought
And visited with sudden awe,

We close our throttles, clench the curb,
And hush the rumble of our tyres,
Abashed and fearful to disturb
The City of the Dreaming Spires—

The City of Giraffes!—a People
Who live between the earth and skies,
Each in his lone religious steeple,
Keeping a light-house with his eyes:

Each his own stairway, tower, and stylite,
Ascending on his saintly way
Up rungs of gold into the twilight
And leafy ladders to the day:

Chimneys of silence! at whose summit,
Like storks, the daydreams love to nest;
The Earth, descending like a plummet
Into the oceans of unrest,

They can ignore—whose nearer neighbour
The sun is, with the stars and moon
That on their hides, with learned labour,
Tattooed the hieroglyphic rune.

Muezzins that from airy pylons
Peer out above the golden trees
Where the mimosas fleece the silence
Or slumber on the drone of bees:

Nought of this earth they see but flowers
Quilting a carpet to the sky
To where some pensive crony towers
Or Kilimanjaro takes the eye.

Their baser passions fast on greens
Where, never to intrude or push,
Their bodies live like submarines,
Far down beneath them, in the bush.

Around their head the solar glories,
With their terrestrial sisters fly—
Rollers, and orioles, and lories,
And trogons of the evening sky.

Their bloodstream with a yeasty leaven
Exalts them to the stars above,
As we are raised, though not to heaven,
By drink—or when we fall in love.

By many a dismal crash and wreck
Our dreams are weaned of aviation,
But these have beaten (by a neck!)
The steepest laws of gravitation.

Some animals have all the luck,
Who hurl their breed in nature's throat—
Out of a gumtree by a buck,
Or escalator—by a goat!

When I have worked my ticket, pension,
And whatsoever I can bum,
To colonise the fourth dimension,
With my Beloved, I may come,

And buy a pair of stilts for both,
And hire a periscope for two,
To vegetate in towering sloth
Out here amongst these chosen few . . .

Or so my fancies seemed to sing
To see, across the gulf of years,
The soldiers of a reigning King
Confront those ghostly halberdiers.

But someone kicks his starter back:
Anachronism cocks its ears.
Like Beefeaters who've got the sack
With their own heads upon their spears;

Like Leftwing Poets at the hint
Of work, or danger, or the blitz,
Or when they catch the deadly glint
Of satire, swordplay of the wits,—

Into the dusk of leafy oceans
They fade away with phantom tread;
And changing gears, reversing notions,
The road to Moshi roars ahead.

MASS AT DAWN

I dropped my sail and dried my dripping seines[1]
Where the white quay is chequered by cool planes
In whose great branches, always out of sight,
The nightingales are singing day and night.

---

[1] nets.

Though all was grey beneath the moon's grey beam,
My boat in her new paint shone like a bride,
And silver in my baskets shone the bream:
My arms were tired and I was heavy-eyed,
But when with food and drink, at morning-light,
The children met me at the water-side,
Never was wine so red or bread so white.

W. B. Yeats (1865-1939)

THE SCHOLARS

Yeats uses the Roman love poet Catullus, (whose poetry he could not read in the original Latin) quite deliberately to contrast the way poets work and scholars comment. When Julius Caesar was virtually a dictator, Catullus wrote an epigram just laughing at him and saying: 'I don't care whether you're black or white'. He knew he might be executed, exiled—even praised. Yeats is contrasting two ways of living and thinking; who means most to us—Catullus or the editor of Catullus?

Bald heads forgetful of their sins,
Old, learned, respectable bald heads
Edit and annotate the lines
That young men, tossing on their beds,
Rhymed out in love's despair
To flatter beauty's ignorant ear.

All shuffle there; all cough in ink;
All wear the carpet with their shoes;
All think what other people think;
All know the man their neighbour knows.
Lord, what would they say
Did their Catullus walk that way?

TWO SONGS OF A FOOL

I

A speckled cat and a tame hare
Eat at my hearthstone
And sleep there;
And both look up to me alone
For learning and defence
As I look up to Providence.

I start out of my sleep to think
Some day I may forget
Their food and drink;
Or, the house door left unshut,
The hare may run till it's found
The horn's sweet note and the tooth of the hound.

I bear a burden that might well try
Men that do all by rule,
And what can I
That am a wandering-witted fool
But pray to God that He ease
My great responsibilities?

II

I slept on my three-legged stool by the fire,
The speckled cat slept on my knee;
We never thought to enquire
Where the brown hare might be,
And whether the door were shut.
Who knows how she drank the wind
Stretched up on two legs from the mat,
Before she had settled her mind
To drum with her heel and to leap?
Had I but awakened from sleep
And called her name, she had heard,
It may be, and had not stirred,
That now, it may be, has found
The horn's sweet note and the tooth of the hound.

This poem refers to the Easter Rising of the Irish against the English
in Dublin. The names in the poem are the real names of some of the
leaders in the revolt.

I have met them at close of day
Coming with vivid faces
From counter or desk among grey
Eighteenth-century houses.
I have passed with a nod of the head
Or polite meaningless words,
Or have lingered awhile and said
Polite meaningless words,
And thought before I had done
Of a mocking tale or a gibe
To please a companion
Around the fire at the club,
Being certain that they and I
But lived where motley is worn:
All changed, changed utterly:
A terrible beauty is born.

That woman's days were spent
In ignorant good-will,
Her nights in argument
Until her voice grew shrill.
What voice more sweet than hers
When, young and beautiful,
She rode to harriers?
This man had kept a school
And rode our wingèd horse;
This other his helper and friend
Was coming into his force;
He might have won fame in the end,
So sensitive his nature seemed,
So daring and sweet his thought.

This other man I had dreamed
A drunken, vainglorious lout.
He had done most bitter wrong
To some who are near my heart,
Yet I number him in the song;
He, too, has resigned his part
In the casual comedy;
He, too, has been changed in his turn,
Transformed utterly:
A terrible beauty is born.

Hearts with one purpose alone
Through summer and winter seem
Enchanted to a stone
To trouble the living stream.
The horse that comes from the road,
The rider, the birds that range
From cloud to tumbling cloud,
Minute by minute they change;
A shadow of cloud on the stream
Changes minute by minute;
A horse-hoof slides on the brim,
And a horse plashes within it;
The long-legged moor-hens dive,
And hens to moor-cocks call;
Minute by minute they live:
The stone's in the midst of all.

Too long a sacrifice
Can make a stone of the heart.
O when may it suffice?
That is Heaven's part, our part
To murmur name upon name,
As a mother names her child
When sleep at last has come
On limbs that had run wild.
What is it but nightfall?

No, no, not night but death;
Was it needless death after all?
For England may keep faith
For all that is done and said.
We know their dream; enough
To know they dreamed and are dead;
And what if excess of love
Bewildered them till they died?
I write it out in a verse—
MacDonagh and MacBride
And Connolly and Pearse
Now and in time to be,
Wherever green is worn,
Are changed, changed utterly:
A terrible beauty is born.

September 25, 1916

THE SECOND COMING

One must never forget that W. B. Yeats was an Irishman and that, though this poem came out of the First World War, Yeats was not necessarily involved in that war. In fact, he went on holiday to Normandy in 1917. Not only this, but he had a theory of history, and the cycle from the birth of Christ to 2,000 A.D. (he worked in this pattern) seemed to him to be being fulfilled. The 'twenty centuries of stony sleep' are the two thousand years *before* the birth of Christ; what next?
Spiritus Mundi—'the spirit of the world'—is simply a religious book or idea.

Turning and turning in the widening gyre
The falcon cannot hear the falconer;
Things fall apart; the centre cannot hold;
Mere anarchy is loosed upon the world,
The blood-dimmed tide is loosed, and everywhere
The ceremony of innocence is drowned;
The best lack all conviction, while the worst
Are full of passionate intensity.

Surely some revelation is at hand;
Surely the Second Coming is at hand.
The Second Coming! Hardly are those words out
When a vast image out of *Spiritus Mundi*
Troubles my sight: somewhere in sands of the desert
A shape with lion body and the head of a man,
A gaze blank and pitiless as the sun,
Is moving its slow thighs, while all about it
Reel shadows of the indignant desert birds.
The darkness drops again; but now I know
That twenty centuries of stony sleep
Were vexed to nightmare by a rocking cradle,
And what rough beast its hour come round at last,
Slouches towards Bethlehem to be born?

DEATH

Nor dread nor hope attend
A dying animal;
A man awaits his end
Dreading and hoping all;
Many times he died,
Many times rose again.
A great man in his pride
Confronting murderous men
Casts derision upon
Supersession of breath;
He knows death to the bone—
Man has created death.

Robert Frost (1875-1964)

Robert Frost was an American who lived in the north-east of America, in 'New England'. His first poetry was acclaimed in England by his friend Edward Thomas (see p. 370). Frost always wrote, like Wordsworth, practically, of country and country people he knew; nothing is ever false or made-up for effect.

HYLA BROOK

By June our brook's run out of song and speed.
Sought for much after that, it will be found
Either to have gone groping underground
(And taken with it all the Hyla breed[1]
That shouted in the mist a month ago,
Like ghost of sleigh-bells in a ghost of snow)—
Or flourished and come up in jewel-weed,
Weak foliage that is blown upon and bent
Even against the way its waters went.
Its bed is left a faded paper sheet
Of dead leaves stuck together by the heat—
A brook to none but who remember long.
This as it will be seen is other far
Than with brooks taken otherwhere in song.
We love the things we love for what they are.

'OUT, OUT—'

The buzz-saw snarled and rattled in the yard
And made dust and dropped stove-length sticks of wood,
Sweet-scented stuff when the breeze drew across it.
And from there those that lifted eyes could count
Five mountain ranges one behind the other
Under the sunset far into Vermont.
And the saw snarled and rattled, snarled and rattled,
As it ran light, or had to bear a load.
And nothing happened: day was all but done.
Call it a day, I wish they might have said
To please the boy by giving him the half hour

---

[1] frogs.

That a boy counts so much when saved from work.
His sister stood beside them in her apron
To tell them 'Supper.' At the word, the saw,
As if to prove saws knew what supper meant,
Leaped out at the boy's hand, or seemed to leap—
He must have given the hand. However it was,
Neither refused the meeting. But the hand!
The boy's first outcry was a rueful laugh,
As he swung toward them holding up the hand
Half in appeal, but half as if to keep
The life from spilling. Then the boy saw all—
Since he was old enough to know, big boy
Doing a man's work, though a child at heart—
He saw all spoiled. 'Don't let him cut my hand off—
The doctor, when he comes. Don't let him, sister!'
So. But the hand was gone already.
The doctor put him in the dark of ether.
He lay and puffed his lips out with his breath.
And then—the watcher at his pulse took fright.
No one believed. They listened at his heart.
Little—less—nothing!—and that ended it.
No more to build on there. And they, since they
Were not the one dead, turned to their affairs.

THE BEARER OF EVIL TIDINGS

The bearer of evil tidings,
When he was halfway there,
Remembered that evil tidings
Were a dangerous thing to bear.

So when he came to the parting
Where one road led to the throne
And one went off to the mountains
And into the wild unknown,

He took the one to the mountains.
He ran through the Vale of Cashmere,
He ran through the rhododendrons
Till he came to the land of Pamir.

And there in a precipice valley
A girl of his age he met
Took him home to her bower,
Or he might be running yet.

She taught him her tribe's religion:
How ages and ages since
A princess en route from China
To marry a Persian prince

Had been found with child; and her army
Had come to a troubled halt.
And though a god was the father
And nobody else at fault,

It had seemed discreet to remain there
And neither go on nor back.
So they stayed and declared a village
There in the land of the Yak.

And the child that came of the princess
Established a royal line,
And his mandates were given heed to
Because he was born divine.

And that was why there were people
On one Himalayan shelf;
And the bearer of evil tidings
Decided to stay there himself.

At least he had this in common
With the race he chose to adopt:
They had both of them had their reasons
For stopping where they had stopped.

As for his evil tidings,
Belshazzar's overthrow,
Why hurry to tell Belshazzar
What soon enough he would know?

FIRE AND ICE

Some say the world will end in fire,
Some say in ice.
From what I've tasted of desire
I hold with those who favour fire.
But if it had to perish twice,
I think I know enough of hate
To say that for destruction ice
Is also great
And would suffice.

ON A BIRD SINGING IN ITS SLEEP

A bird half wakened in the lunar noon
Sang half way through its little inborn tune.
Partly because it sang but once all night
And that from no especial bush's height;
Partly because it sang ventriloquist
And had the inspiration to desist
Almost before the prick of hostile ears,
It ventured less in peril than appears.
It could not have come down to us so far
Through the interstices of things ajar
On the long bead chain of repeated birth
To be a bird while we are men on earth
If singing out of sleep and dream that way
Had made it much more easily a prey.

It would be difficult to find a greater contrast to Robert Frost (p. 393) than T. S. Eliot. Eliot was an American who came to England and was finally naturalised as an Englishman. But, coming from 'raw' America, what he truly loved was Europe, and his *Wasteland* is this Europe in ruins after 1918.

An intensely religious man, Eliot came back to the England his forbears had left in the seventeenth century in the *Mayflower*. The whole of his poetry can be understood most clearly in this light: the return of a Puritan to a country three centuries older. The important thing about Eliot is his Christian religious energy and his brilliant ability as a poet.

ANIMULA

'Issues from the hand of God, the simple soul'
To a flat world of changing lights and noise,
To light, dark, dry or damp, chilly or warm;
Moving between the legs of tables and of chairs,
Rising or falling, grasping at kisses and toys,
Advancing boldly, sudden to take alarm,
Retreating to the corner of arm and knee,
Eager to be reassured, taking pleasure
In the fragrant brilliance of the Christmas tree,
Pleasure in the wind, the sunlight and the sea;
Studies the sunlit pattern on the floor
And running stags around a silver tray;
Confounds the actual and the fanciful,
Content with playing-cards and kings and queens,
What the fairies do and what the servants say.
The heavy burden of the growing soul
Perplexes and offends more, day by day;
Week by week, offends and perplexes more
With the imperatives of 'is and seems'
And may and may not, desire and control.
The pain of living and the drug of dreams
Curl up the small soul in the window seat
Behind the *Encyclopaedia Britannica*.
Issues from the hand of time the simple soul
Irresolute and selfish, misshapen, lame,

Unable to fare forward or retreat,
Fearing the warm reality, the offered good,

Denying the importunity of the blood,
Shadow of its own shadows, spectre in its own gloom,
Leaving disordered papers in a dusty room;
Living first in the silence after the viaticum.

Pray for Guiterriez, avid of speed and power,
For Boudin, blown to pieces,
For this one who made a great fortune,
And that one who went his own way.
Pray for Floret, by the boarhound slain between the yew trees,
Pray for us now and at the hour of our birth.

From THE ROCK

The Rock was a pageant play first performed in 1934. Eliot was only part-author, but the choruses were his first attempt at writing in the style which he later developed in *Murder in the Cathedral,* and are well worth reading for themselves. The whole work is misleadingly called a play, for the action which intersperses the choruses is banal and incoherent.

CHORUS:
The Word of the Lord came unto me, saying:
O miserable cities of designing men,
O wretched generation of enlightened men,
Betrayed in the mazes of your ingenuities,
Sold by the proceeds of your proper inventions:
I have given you hands which you turn from worship,
I have given you speech, for endless palaver,
I have given you my Law, and you set up commissions,
I have given you lips, to express friendly sentiments,
I have given you hearts, for reciprocal distrust.
I have given you power of choice, and you only alternate
Between futile speculation and unconsidered action.
Many are engaged in writing books and printing them,

Many desire to see their names in print,
Many read nothing but the race reports.
Much is your reading, but not the Word of God,
Much is your building, but not the House of God.
Will you build me a house of plaster, with corrugated roofing,
To be filled with a litter of Sunday newspapers?

1ST MALE VOICE:

A Cry from the East:
What shall be done to the shore of smoky ships?
Will you leave my people forgetful and forgotten
To idleness, labour, and delirious stupor?
There shall be left the broken chimney,
The peeled hull, a pile of rusty iron,
In a street of scattered brick where the goat climbs,
Where My Word is unspoken.

2ND MALE VOICE:

A Cry from the North, from the West and from the South
Whence thousands travel daily to the timekept City;
Where My Word is unspoken,
In the land of lobelias and tennis flannels
The rabbit shall burrow and the thorn revisit,
The nettle shall flourish on the gravel court,
And the wind shall say: 'Here were decent godless people:
Their only monument the asphalt road
And a thousand lost golf balls.'

CHORUS:

We build in vain unless the Lord build with us.
Can you keep the City that the Lord keeps not with you?
A thousand policemen directing the traffic
Cannot tell you why you come or where you go.
A colony of cavies or a horde of active marmots
Build better than they that build without the Lord.
Shall we lift up our feet among perpetual ruins?
I have loved the beauty of Thy House, the peace of Thy
          Sanctuary,
I have swept the floors and garnished the altars.
Where there is no temple there shall be no homes,

Though you have shelters and institutions,
Precarious lodgings while the rent is paid,
Subsiding basements where the rat breeds
Or sanitary dwellings with numbered doors
Or a house a little better than your neighbour's;
When the Stranger says: 'What is the meaning of this city?
Do you huddle close together because you love each other?'
What will you answer? 'We all dwell together
To make money from each other'? or 'This is a community'?
And the Stranger will depart and return to the desert.
O my soul, be prepared for the coming of the Stranger,
Be prepared for him who knows how to ask questions.

O weariness of men who turn from God
To the grandeur of your mind and the glory of your action,
To arts and inventions and daring enterprises,
To schemes of human greatness thoroughly discredited,
Binding the earth and the water to your service,
Exploiting the seas and developing the mountains,
Dividing the stars into common and preferred,
Engaged in devising the perfect refrigerator,
Engaged in working out a rational morality,
Engaged in printing as many books as possible,
Plotting of happiness and flinging empty bottles,
Turning from your vacancy to fevered enthusiasm
For nation or race or what you call humanity;
Though you forget the way to the Temple,
There is one who remembers the way to your door:
Life you may evade, but Death you shall not.
You shall not deny the Stranger.

Edwin Muir (1887-1959)

THE RIDER VICTORY

The rider Victory reins his horse
Midway across the empty bridge
As if head-tall he had met a wall.
Yet there was nothing there at all,
No bodiless barrier, ghostly ridge
To check the charger in his course
So suddenly, you'd think he'd fall.

Suspended, horse and rider stare,
Leaping on air and legendary.
In front the waiting kingdom lies,
The bridge and all the roads are free;
But halted in implacable air
Rider and horse with stony eyes
Uprear their motionless statuary.

Archibald MacLeish (b. 1892)

YOU, ANDREW MARVELL

And here face down beneath the sun,
And here upon earth's noonward height,
To feel the always coming on,
The always rising of the night.

To feel creep up the curving east
The earthly chill of dusk and slow
Upon those under lands the vast
And ever-climbing shadow grow,

And strange at Ecbatan the trees
Take leaf by leaf the evening, strange,
The flooding dark about their knees,
The mountains over Persia change,

And now at Kermanshah the gate,
Dark, empty, and the withered grass,
And through the twilight now the late
Few travellers in the westward pass,

And Baghdad darken and the bridge
Across the silent river gone,
And through Arabia the edge
Of evening widen and steal on,

And deepen on Palmyra's street
The wheel rut in the ruined stone,
And Lebanon fade out and Crete
High through the clouds and over blown,

And over Sicily the air
Still flashing with the landward gulls,
And loom and slowly disappear
The sails above the shadowy hulls,

And Spain go under and the shore
of Africa, the gilden sand,
And evening vanish and no more
The low pale light across that land,

Nor now the long light on the sea—

And here face downward in the sun
To feel how swift, how secretly,
The shadow of the night comes on. . . .

Robert Graves is a poet of the keenest sensibility and craftsmanship. It is his profound belief that a poet should be dedicated wholly to poetry, and if he has to earn a living should do so in some totally different occupation, like crane-driving or being a navvy. So, since nearly all poets nowadays have to earn a living, Robert Graves believes it to be wholly wrong that most of them are in jobs connected with literature: dons or schoolteachers, BBC script-writers, advertisement copywriters etc. It is a debatable point; after all, what poets do is to write poetry.

WELSH INCIDENT

'But that was nothing to what things came out
From the sea-caves of Criccieth yonder.'
'What were they? Mermaids? dragons? ghosts?'
'Nothing at all of any things like that.'
'What were they, then?'
                     'All sorts of queer things,
Things never seen or heard or written about,
Very strange, un-Welsh, utterly peculiar
Things. Oh, solid enough they seemed to touch,
Had anyone dared it. Marvellous creation,
All various shapes and sizes, and no sizes,
All new, each perfectly unlike his neighbour,
Though all came moving slowly out together.'
'Describe just one of them.'
                 'I am unable.'
'What were their colours?'
                  'Mostly nameless colours,
Colours you'd like to see; but one was puce
Or perhaps more like crimson, but not purplish.
Some had no colour.'
               'Tell me, had they legs?'
'Not a leg nor foot among them that I saw.'
'But did these things come out in any order?
What o'clock was it? What was the day of the week?
Who else was present? How was the weather?'
'I was coming to that. It was half-past three
On Easter Tuesday last. The sun was shining.

The Harlech Silver Band played *Marchog Jesu*
On thirty-seven shimmering instruments,
Collecting for Caernarvon's (Fever) Hospital Fund.
The populations of Pwllheli, Criccieth,
Portmadoc, Borth, Tremadoc, Penrhyndeudraeth,
Were all assembled. Criccieth's mayor addressed them
First in good Welsh and then in fluent English,
Twisting his fingers in his chain of office,
Welcoming the things. They came out on the sand,
Not keeping time to the band, moving seaward
Silently at a snail's pace. But at last
The most odd, indescribable thing of all,
Which hardly one man there could see for wonder,
Did something recognizably a something.'
'Well, what?'
                          'It made a noise.'
                                          'A frightening noise?'
'No, no.'
              'A musical noise? A noise of scuffling?'
'No, but a very loud, respectable noise—
Like groaning to oneself on Sunday morning
In Chapel, close before the second psalm.'
'What did the mayor do?'
                          'I was coming to that'.

'THE GENERAL ELLIOTT'

He fell in victory's fierce pursuit,
        Holed through and through with shot;
A sabre sweep had hacked him deep
        'Twixt neck and shoulder-knot.

The potman cannot well recall,
        The ostler never knew,
Whether that day was Malplaquet,
        The Boyne, or Waterloo.

But there he hangs, a tavern sign,
    With foolish bold regard
For cock and hen and loitering men
    And wagons down the yard.

Raised high above the hayseed world
    He smokes his china pipe;
And now surveys the orchard ways,
    The damsons clustering ripe—

Stares at the churchyard slabs beyond,
    Where country neighbours lie:
Their brief renown set lowly down,
    But his invades the sky.

He grips a tankard of brown ale
    That spills a generous foam:
Often he drinks, they say, and winks
    At drunk men lurching home.

No upstart hero may usurp
    That honoured swinging seat;
His seasons pass with pipe and glass
    Until the tale's complete—

And paint shall keep his buttons bright
    Though all the world's forgot
Whether he died for England's pride
    By battle or by pot.

IN BROKEN IMAGES

He is quick, thinking in clear images;
I am slow, thinking in broken images.

He becomes dull, trusting to his clear images;
I become sharp, mistrusting my broken images.

Trusting his images, he assumes their relevance;
Mistrusting my images, I question their relevance.

Assuming their relevance, he assumes the fact;
Questioning their relevance, I question the fact.

When the fact fails him, he questions his senses;
When the fact fails me, I approve my senses.

He continues quick and dull in his clear images;
I continue slow and sharp in my broken images.

He in a new confusion of his understanding;
I in a new understanding of my confusion.

W. H. Auden (b. 1907)

MUSÉE DES BEAUX ARTS

Here is a poem about painting. The arts are not in water-tight bulk-heads. They sink or swim together. Auden is not alone in instancing or referring to pictures—or to music. In this case he takes a particular picture and makes his comment on it. Few people paint and write equally well; Blake is an exception. But the real point is that no good artist—painter, musician, poet, playwright—exists *alone*; he must know what is going on, and what has gone on before, in other arts.

About suffering they were never wrong,
The Old Masters: how well they understood
Its human position; how it takes place
While someone else is eating or opening a window or just
        walking dully along;
How, when the aged are reverently, passionately waiting
For the miraculous birth, there always must be
Children who did not specially want it to happen, skating
On a pond at the edge of the wood:
They never forgot

That even the dreadful martyrdom must run its course
Anyhow in a corner, some untidy spot
Where the dogs go on with their doggy life and the torturer's
       horse
Scratches its innocent behind on a tree.

In Brueghel's *Icarus,* for instance: how everything turns away
Quite leisurely from the disaster; the ploughman may
Have heard the splash, the forsaken cry,
But for him it was not an important failure; the sun shone
As it had to on the white legs disappearing into the green
Water; and the expensive delicate ship that must have seen
Something amazing, a boy falling out of the sky,
Had somewhere to get to and sailed calmly on.

LAY YOUR SLEEPING HEAD, MY LOVE

Lay your sleeping head, my love,
Human on my faithless arm;
Time and fevers burn away
Individual beauty from
Thoughtful children, and the grave
Proves the child ephemeral:
But in my arms till break of day
Let the living creature lie,
Mortal, guilty, but to me
The entirely beautiful.

Soul and body have no bounds:
To lovers as they lie upon
Her tolerant enchanted slope
In their ordinary swoon,
Grave the vision Venus sends
Of supernatural sympathy,
Universal love and hope;
While an abstract insight wakes
Among the glaciers and the rocks
The hermit's sensual ecstasy.

Certainty, fidelity
On the stroke of midnight pass
Like vibrations of a bell,
And fashionable madmen raise
Their pedantic boring cry:
Every farthing of the cost,
All the dreaded cards foretell,
Shall be paid, but from this night
Not a whisper, not a thought,
Not a kiss nor look be lost.

Beauty, midnight, vision dies:
Let the winds of dawn that blow
Softly round your dreaming head
Such a day of sweetness show
Eye and knocking heart may bless,
Find the mortal world enough;
Noons of dryness see you fed
By the involuntary powers,
Nights of insult let you pass
Watched by every human love.

THE UNKNOWN CITIZEN

TO

JS/07/M/378

This Marble Monument is Erected
by the State

He was found by the Bureau of Statistics to be
One against whom there was no official complaint,
And all the reports on his conduct agree
That, in the modern sense of an old-fashioned word, he was a
saint,

For in everything he did he served the Greater Community.
Except for the War till the day he retired
He worked in a factory and never got fired,
But satisfied his employers, Fudge Motors Inc.
Yet he wasn't a scab or odd in his views,
For his Union reports that he paid his dues,
(Our report on his Union shows it was sound)
And our Social Psychology workers found
That he was popular with his mates and liked a drink.
The Press are convinced that he bought a paper every day
And that his reactions to advertisements were normal in every
        way.
Policies taken out in his name prove that he was fully insured,
And his Health-card shows he was once in hospital but left it
        cured.
Both Producers Research and High-Grade Living declare
He was fully sensible to the advantages of the Instalment Plan
And had everything necessary to the Modern Man,
A gramophone, a radio, a car and a frigidaire.
Our researchers into Public Opinion are content
That he held the proper opinions for the time of year;
When there was peace, he was for peace; when there was war,
        he went.
He was married and added five children to the population,
Which our Eugenist says was the right number for a parent of his
        generation,
And our teachers report that he never interfered with their
        education.
Was he free? Was he happy? The question is absurd:
Had anything been wrong, we should certainly have heard.

Louis MacNeice (b. 1907)

From AUTUMN JOURNAL

This poem expresses perfectly a historical moment: the 'feeling' of
Munich and the British Prime Minister, Chamberlain, flying to see
Hitler in 1938; the angers and disillusions of the 'thirties. Here is
poetry commenting wryly on 'history'. This is what happened—not
only happened but what people *felt* happening.

Conferences, adjournments, ultimatums,
    Flights in the air, castles in the air,
The autopsy of treaties, dynamite under the bridges,
    The end of *laissez faire*.
After the warm days the rain comes pimpling
    The paving stones with white
And with the rain the national conscience, creeping,
    Seeping through the night.
And in the sodden park on Sunday protest
    Meetings assemble not, as so often, now
Merely to advertise some patent panacea
    But simply to avow
The need to hold the ditch; a bare avowal
    That may perhaps imply
Death at the doors in a week but perhaps in the long run
    Exposure of the lie.
Think of a number, double it, treble it, square it,
    And sponge it out
And repeat *ad lib*. and mark the slate with crosses;
    There is no time to doubt
If the puzzle really has an answer. Hitler yells on the wireless,
    The night is damp and still
And I hear dull blows on wood outside my window;
    They are cutting down the trees on Primrose Hill.
The wood is white like the roast flesh of chicken,
    Each tree falling like a closing fan;
No more looking at the view from seats beneath the branches,
    Everything is going to plan;
They want the crest of this hill for anti-aircraft,
    The guns will take the view

And searchlights probe the heavens for bacilli
     With narrow wands of blue.
And the rain came on as I watched the territorials
     Sawing and chopping and pulling on ropes like a team
In a village tug-of-war; and I found my dog had vanished
     And thought 'This is the end of the old régime,'
But found the police had got her at St. John's Wood station
     And fetched her in the rain and went for a cup
Of coffee to an all-night shelter and heard a taxi-driver
     Say 'It turns me up
When I see these soldiers in lorries'—rumble of tumbrils
     Drums in the trees
Breaking the eardrums of the ravished dryads—
     It turns me up; a coffee, please.
And as I go out I see a windscreen-wiper
     In an empty car
Wiping away like mad and I feel astounded
     That things have gone so far.
And I come back here to my flat and wonder whether
     From now on I need take
The trouble to go out choosing stuff for curtains
     As I don't know anyone to make
Curtains quickly. Rather one should quickly
     Stop the cracks for gas or dig a trench
And take one's paltry measures against the coming
     Of the unknown Uebermensch.
But one—meaning I—is bored, am bored, the issue
     Involving principle but bound in fact
To squander principle in panic and self-deception—
     Accessories after the act,
So that all we foresee is rivers in spate sprouting
     With drowning hands
And men like dead frogs floating till the rivers
     Lose themselves in the sands.
And we who have been brought up to think of 'Gallant Belgium'
     As so much blague
Are now preparing again to essay good through evil
     For the sake of Prague;

> And must, we suppose, become uncritical, vindictive,
> And must, in order to beat
> The enemy, model ourselves upon the enemy,
> A howling radio for our paraclete.
> The night continues wet, the axe keeps falling,
> The hill grows bald and bleak
> No longer one of the sights of London but maybe
> We shall have fireworks here by this day week.

MEETING POINT

> Time was away and somewhere else,
> There were two glasses and two chairs
> And two people with the one pulse
> (Somebody stopped the moving stairs):
> Time was away and somewhere else.
>
> And they were neither up nor down,
> The stream's music did not stop
> Flowing through heather, limpid brown,
> Although they sat in a coffee shop
> And they were neither up nor down.
>
> The bell was silent in the air
> Holding its inverted poise—
> Between the clang and clang a flower,
> A brazen calyx of no noise:
> The bell was silent in the air.
>
> The camels crossed the miles of sand
> That stretched around the cups and plates;
> The desert was their own, they planned
> To portion out the stars and dates:
> The camels crossed the miles of sand.

Time was away and somewhere else.
The waiter did not come, the clock
Forgot them and the radio waltz
Came out like water from a rock:
Time was away and somewhere else.

Her fingers flicked away the ash
That bloomed again in tropic trees:
Not caring if the markets crash
When they had forests such as these,
Her fingers flicked away the ash.

God or whatever means the Good
Be praised that time can stop like this,
That what the heart has understood
Can verify in the body's peace
God or whatever means the Good.

Time was away and she was here
And life no longer what it was,
The bell was silent in the air
And all the room a glow because
Time was away and she was here.

C. Day Lewis (b. 1904)

JIG

That winter love spoke and we raised no objection, at
Easter 'twas daisies all light and affectionate,
June sent us crazy for natural selection—not
Four traction-engines could tear us apart.
Autumn then coloured the map of our land,
Oaks shuddered and apples came ripe to the hand,
In the gap of the hills we played happily, happily,
Even the moon couldn't tell us apart.

Grave winter drew near and said, 'This will not do at all—
If you continue, I fear you will rue it all.'
So at the New Year we vowed to eschew it
Although we both knew it would break our heart.
But spring made hay of our good resolutions—
Lovers, you may be as wise as Confucians,
Yet once love betrays you he plays you and plays you
Like fishes for ever, so take it to heart.

WILL IT BE SO AGAIN?

Will it be so again
That the brave, the gifted are lost from view,
And empty, scheming men
Are left in peace their lunatic age to renew?
Will it be so again?

Must it be always so
That the best are chosen to fall and sleep
Like seeds, and we too slow
In claiming the earth they quicken, and the old usurpers reap
What they could not sow?

Will it be so again—
The jungle code and the hypocrite gesture?
A poppy wreath for the slain
And a cut-throat world for the living? that stale imposture
Played on us once again?

Will it be as before—
Peace, with no heart or mind to ensue it,
Guttering down to war
Like a libertine to his grave? We should not be surprised: we
knew it
Happen before.

Shall it be so again?
Call not upon the glorious dead
To be your witnesses then.
The living alone can nail to their promise the ones who said
It shall not be so again.

Stevie Smith

TENUOUS AND PRECARIOUS

Many Latin nouns end in the letters *us* and adjectives in *osus,* which means *full of. Osus* has been shortened in English to *ous* and English adjectives like *tremendous* are derived from Latin. The brilliant *tour de force* in this poem is that Stevie Smith has used her English adjectives both as Latin nouns and with a deal of witty meaning appropriate to each one. Everyone will know what *Finis* means.

Tenuous and Precarious
Were my guardians,
Precarious and Tenuous,
Two Romans.

My father was Hazardous,
Hazardous,
Dear old man.
Three Romans.

There was my brother Spurious,
Spurious Posthumous,
Spurious was spurious, was
Four Romans.

My husband was Perfidious,
He was perfidious,
Five Romans.

Surreptitious, our son,
Was surreptitious. He was
Six Romans.

Our cat Tedious
Still lives,
Count not Tedious
Yet.

My name is Finis,
Finis, Finis,
Six, five, four,
Three, two,
One Roman.
Finis.

John Betjeman (b. 1906)

BRISTOL AND CLIFTON

'Yes, I was only sidesman here when last
You came to Evening Communion.
But now I have retired from the bank
I have more leisure time for church finance
We moved into a somewhat larger house
Than when you knew us in Manilla Road.
This is the window to my lady wife.
You cannot see it now, but in the day
The greens and golds are truly wonderful.'

'How very sad. I do not mean about
The window, but I mean about the death
Of Mrs. Battlecock. When did she die?'

'Two years ago when we had just moved in
To Pembroke Road. I rather fear the stairs
And basement kitchen were too much for her—
Not that, of course, she did the servants' work—
But supervising servants all the day
Meant quite a lot of climbing up and down.'

'How very sad. Poor Mrs. Battlecock.'
' "The glory that men do lives after them,"[1]
And so I gave this window in her name.
It's executed by a Bristol firm;
The lady artist who designed it, made
The figure of the lady on the left
Something like Mrs. Battlecock.'
'How nice.'

       'Yes, was it not? We had
A stained glass window on the stairs at home,
In Pembroke Road. But not so good as this.
This window is the glory of the church
At least I think so—and the unstained oak
Looks very chaste beneath it. When I gave
The oak, that brass inscription on your right
Commemorates the fact, the Dorcas Club
Made these blue kneelers, though we do not kneel:
We leave that to the Roman Catholics.'
'How very nice, indeed. How very nice.'

'Seeing I have some knowledge of finance
Our kind Parochial Church Council made
Me People's Warden, and I'm glad to say
That our collections are still keeping up.
The chancel has been flood-lit, and the stove
Which used to heat the church was obsolete.
So now we've had some radiators fixed
Along the walls and eastward of the aisles;
This last I thought of lest at any time
A Ritualist should be inducted here
And want to put up altars. He would find
The radiators inconvenient.
Our only ritual here is with the Plate;
I think we make it dignified enough.
I take it up myself, and afterwards,
Count the Collection on the vestry safe.'

_____

[1] Shakespeare, of course.

o*

417

'Forgive me, aren't we talking rather loud?
I think I see a woman praying there.'
'Praying? The service is all over now
And here's the verger waiting to turn out
The lights and lock the church up. She cannot
Be Loyal Church of England. Well, good-bye.
Time flies. I must be going. Come again.
There are some pleasant people living here
I know the Inskips very well indeed.'

David Gascoyne (b. 1916)

ECCE HOMO

Compare Herbert's *Sacrifice* (p. 60)—a mystical poem of its age—with this, a political poem of the present age.

Whose is this horrifying face,
This putrid flesh, discoloured, flayed,
Fed on by flies, scorched by the sun?
Whose are these hollow red-filmed eyes
And thorn-spiked head and spear-stuck side?
Behold the Man: He is Man's Son.

Forget the legend, tear the decent veil
That cowardice or interest devised
To make their mortal enemy a friend,
To hide the bitter truth all His wounds tell,
Lest the great scandal be no more disguised:
He is in agony till the world's end,

And we must never sleep during that time!
He is suspended on the cross-tree now
And we are onlookers at the crime,
Callous contemporaries of the slow
Torture of God. Here is the hill
Made ghastly by His spattered blood

Whereon He hangs and suffers still:
See, the centurions wear riding-boots,
Black shirts and badges and peaked caps,
Greet one another with raised-arm salutes;[1]
They have cold eyes, unsmiling lips;
Yet these His brothers know not what they do.

And on his either side hang dead
A labourer and a factory hand,
Or one is maybe a lynched Jew
And one a Negro or a Red,
Coolie or Ethiopian, Irishman,
Spaniard or German democrat.

Behind His lolling head the sky
Glares like a fiery cataract
Red with the murders of two thousand years
Committed in His name and by
Crusaders, Christian warriors
Defending faith and property.

Amid the plain beneath His transfixed hands,
Exuding darkness as indelible
As guilty stains, fanned by funereal
And lurid airs, besieged by drifting sands
And clefted landslides our about-to-be
Bombed and abandoned cities stand.

He who wept for Jerusalem
Now sees His prophecy extend
Across the greatest cities of the world,
A guilty panic reason cannot stem
Rising to raze them all as He foretold;
And He must watch this drama to the end.

---

[1] a reference to Hitler's Nazis.

Though often named, He is unknown
To the dark kingdoms at His feet
Where everything disparages His words,
And each man bears the common guilt alone
And goes blindfolded to his fate,
And fear and greed are sovereign lords.

The turning point of history
Must come. Yet the complacent and the proud
And who exploit and kill, may be denied—
Christ of Revolution and of Poetry—
The resurrection and the life
Wrought by your spirit's blood.

Involved in their own sophistry
The black priest and the upright man
Faced by subversive truth shall be struck dumb,
Christ of Revolution and of Poetry,
While the rejected and condemned become
Agents of the divine.

Not from a monstrance silver-wrought
But from the tree of human pain
Redeem our sterile misery,
Christ of Revolution and of Poetry,
That man's long journey through the night
May not have been in vain.

Sheila Shannon (b. 1913)

BIRTHDAYS AND DEATHDAYS

Within your eyes no clouded dread discloses
    The secret that I fear;
Nor on your lips the taste of death embitters
    Their winter-warm desire.
We keep each other's birthdays but in silence
    Our deathday passes by:
Each year it comes, our deaths one year more near:
    Was it today, perhaps, or yesterday?
Some unexciting day which unremarked
    Went out at midnight?
Or will tomorrow's anniversary
Mark up another year against our score?

Born under certain stars we bear that seed
    Implanted in us;
The inescapable fate which hunted down
    King Oedipus to nothing.
The anatomist knows us, the psychologist
    Explains our dreams.
Yet you and I, love, know we hardly guess
    What thoughts the other has:
And when we look at midnight out to sea
    Or watch those stars
Which roaming on the outer edge of sight
    Know other suns
What differing images pattern your eyes and mine,
    What differing symbols rise:
As Tess and Adam[1] on that night looked up
    And she compared
The stars to apples on a tree, some sound,
    The other rotten,
'And which are we?' asked Adam; Tess replied,
    'A blighted one.'
And knowing that true, she followed until her star

---

[1] Characters in Hardy's *Tess of the D'Urbervilles*.

Led to that summer morning when Angel stood
And watched the black flag break above the tower
   Of Winchester gaol.

Yet still we will not care nor waste our time
   Guessing our day of death;
But celebrate our birthdays when they come
   And celebrate continuance of our breath.

Roy Fuller (b. 1912)

WAR POET

Swift had pains in his head.
Johnson dying in bed
Tapped the dropsy himself.
Blake saw a flea and an elf.
Tennyson could hear the shriek
Of a bat. Pope was a freak.
Emily Dickinson stayed
Indoors for a decade.
Water inflated the belly
Of Hart Crane, and of Shelley.
Coleridge was a dope.
Southwell died on a rope.
Byron had a round white foot.
Smart and Cowper were put
Away. Lawrence was a fidget.
Keats was almost a midget.
Donne, alive in his shroud,
Shakespeare, in the coil of a cloud,
Saw death very well as he
Came crab-wise, dark and massy.

I envy not only their talents
And fertile lack of balance
But the appearance of choice
In their sad and fatal voice.

Henry Reed (b. 1914)

JUDGING DISTANCES

The cynicism of young men being trained by the middle-aged (First
World War veterans) to fight in another kind of war could hardly be
better expressed. This poem is an attack on an attitude towards war.

Not only how far away, but the way that you say it
Is very important. Perhaps you may never get
The knack of judging a distance, but at least you know
How to report on a landscape: the central sector,
The right of arc and that, which we had last Tuesday,
    And at least you know

That maps are of time, not place, so far as the army
Happens to be concerned—the reason being,
Is one which need not delay us. Again, you know
There are three kinds of tree, three only, the fir and the poplar,
And those which have bushy tops to; and lastly
    That things only seem to be things.

A barn is not called a barn, to put it more plainly,
Or a field in the distance, where sheep may be safely grazing.
You must never be over-sure. You must say, when reporting:
At five o'clock in the central sector is a dozen
Of what appear to be animals; whatever you do,
    Don't call the bleeders *sheep*.

I am sure that's quite clear; and suppose, for the sake of example,
The one at the end, asleep, endeavours to tell us
What he sees over there to the west, and how far away,
After first having come to attention. There to the west,
On the fields of summer the sun and the shadows bestow
    Vestments of purple and gold.

The still white dwellings are like a mirage in the heat,
And under the swaying elms a man and a woman
Lie gently together. Which is, perhaps, only to say
That there is a row of houses to the left of arc,
And that under some poplars a pair of what appear to be humans
    Appear to be loving.

Well that, for an answer, is what we might rightly call
Moderately satisfactory only, the reason being,
Is that two things have been omitted, and those are important.
The human beings, now: in what direction are they,
And how far away, would you say? And do not forget
    There may be dead ground in between.

There may be dead ground in between; and I may not have got
The knack of judging a distance; I will only venture
A guess that perhaps between me and the apparent lovers,
(Who, incidentally, appear by now to have finished,)
At seven o'clock from the houses, is roughly a distance
    Of about one year and a half.

Alun Lewis (1915-1944)

SONG

On seeing dead bodies floating off the Cape

This poem refers to the Second World War.

The first month of his absence
I was numb and sick
And where he'd left his promise
Life did not turn or kick.
The seed, the seed of love was sick.

The second month my eyes were sunk
In the darkness of despair,
And my bed was like a grave
And his ghost was lying there.
And my heart was sick with care.

The third month of his going
I thought I heard him say
'Our course deflected slightly
On the thirty-second day—'
The tempest blew his words away

And he was lost among the waves,
His ship rolled helpless in the sea.
The fourth month of his voyage
He shouted grievously
'Beloved, do not think of me.'

The flying fish like kingfishers
Skim the sea's bewildered crests,
The whales blow steaming fountains,
The seagulls have no nests
Where my lover sways and rests.

We never thought to buy and sell
This life that blooms or withers in the leaf,
And I'll not sir, so he sleeps well,
Though cell by cell the coral reef
Builds an eternity of grief.

But oh! the drag and dullness of my Self;
The turning seasons wither in my head;
All this slowness, all this hardness,
The nearness that is waiting in my bed,
The gradual self-effacement of the dead.

Patric Dickinson (b. 1914)

BOMBERS: EVENING

It may help this poem to say that it was written on the evening—a
horrible wild evening—of D-Day (June 6th, 1944). The actual hill
the sun had set behind is Shoulder-of-Mutton Hill, near Steep in
Hampshire. On top of it is a memorial to Edward Thomas (see p. 370),
a fine poet killed in the First World War. It was caused to be erected
by Alun Lewis (see p. 425), another fine poet killed in the Second
World War.

The sun was nearly home
When the clouds broke and the sky
Unveiled its infinite dome
Like the eyelid from an eye.

I watch the bombers come
Beating upon the air
The dolorous slow drum
Of the executioner.

The sun below the hill
Was hidden from my sight;
But these, thou sunlit still,
Put on the mask of night.

And as I watch and count
The fair impassive wings
I see the victims mount
Self-willed their scaffoldings.

And now the sun has set.
Thoughts jostle and peer and call:
The drums have ceased to beat:
The heads must fall, must fall.

O from that dreadful show,
For all its justice, may
We each in secret know
One thought that turns away.

NO NEWS

The house was cold and still,
A world's end, and outside
Persistent rain—a journalist
All hours for a scoop—and I
The telephone dead was alone
All I could do done
To the last dripping word.

I turned from time and place
To the cooling tower of sleep,
Energy drained, nothing
To do but hope for the morrow
To fall more happily
For all whom I loved.

And then a sound: the house
Woke to such life and sang
As never bird of fable.

You came: two of us here
On this bitter planet blessed
By such as you;
Our harmony so rare
The rain, the journalist,
Went away satisfied—
But found no words to say.

John Wain (b. 1925)

A SONG ABOUT MAJOR EATHERLY

This poem and song about Major Eatherly was suggested by a few lines John Wain read in a newspaper describing the contents of a book about Major Claude R. Eatherly, pilot of the aircraft which carried the second bomb to Nagasaki. According to the author, Major Eatherly later suffered 'brief moments of madness'. The doctors diagnosed 'extreme nervous depression', and Eatherly was awarded a pension of $237 a month. 'He seems to have regarded this pension as a premium for murder, as a payment for what had been done to the two Japanese cities, for he never touched the money.' He took to 'petty thievery', and later was taken from Waco Military Hospital to Fort Worth prison.

I
Good news. It seems he loved them after all.
His orders were to fry their bones to ash.
He carried up the bomb and let it fall.
And then his orders were to take the cash.

A hero's pension. But he let it lie.
It was in vain to ask him for the cause.
'Simply that if he touched it he would die.'
He fought his own, and not his country's wars.

His orders told him he was not a man:
An instrument, fine-tempered, clear of stain,
All fears and passions closed up like a fan:
No more volition than his aeroplane.

But now he fought to win his manhood back.
Steep from the sunset of his pain he flew
Against the darkness in that last attack.
It was for love he fought, to make that true.

II
To take life is always to die a little: to stop
any feeling and moving contrivance, however ugly,
unnecessary, or hateful, is to reduce by so much the total
of life there is. And that is to die a little.

To take the life of an enemy is to help him,
a little, towards destroying your own. Indeed, that is why
we hate our enemies: because they force us to kill them.
A murderer hides the dead man in the ground:
but his crime rears up and topples on to the living,
for it is they who now must hunt the murderer,
murder him, and hide him in the ground: it is they
who now feel the touch of death cold in their bones.

Animals hate death. A trapped fox will gnaw
through his own leg: it is so important to live
that he forgives himself the agony,
consenting, for life's sake, to the desperate teeth
grating through bone and pulp, the gasping yelps.

That is the reason the trapper hates the fox.
You think the trapper doesn't hate the fox?
But he does, and the fox can tell how much.
It is not the fox's teeth that grind his bones,
it is the trapper's. It is the trapper, there,
who keeps his head down, gnawing, hour after hour.

And the people the trapper works for, they are there, too,
heads down beside the trap, gnawing away.
Why shouldn't they hate the fox? Their cheeks are smeared
with his rank blood, and on their tongues his bone
being splintered, feels uncomfortably sharp.

So once Major Eatherly hated the Japanese.

III
Hell is a furnace, so the wise men taught.
The punishment for sin is to be broiled.
A glowing coal for every sinful thought.

The heat of God's great furnace ate up sin,
Which whispered up in smoke or fell in ash:
So that each hour a new hour could begin.

So fire was holy, though it tortured souls.
The sinners' anguish never ceased, but still
Their sin was burnt from them by shining coals.

Hell fried the criminal but burnt the crime,
Purged where it punished, healed where it destroyed:
It was a stove that warmed the rooms of time.

No man begrudged the flames their appetite.
All were afraid of fire, yet none rebelled.
The wise men taught that hell was just and right.

'The soul desires its necessary dread:
Only among the thorns can patience weave,
A bower where the mind can make its bed.'

Even the holy saints whose patient jaws
Chewed bitter rind and hands raised up the dead
Were chestnuts roasted at God's furnace doors.

The wise men passed. The clever men appeared.
They ruled that hell be called a pumpkin face.
They robbed the soul of what it justly feared.

Coal after coal the fires of hell went out.
Their heat no longer warmed the rooms of time,
Which glistened now with fluorescent doubt.

The chilly saints were striding up and down
To warm their blood with useful exercise.
They rolled like conkers through the draughty town.

Those emblematic flames sank down to rest,
But metaphysical fire can not go out:
Men ran from devils they had dispossessed,

And felt within their skulls the dancing heat
No longer stored in God's deep boiler-room.
Fire scorched their temples, frost-bite chewed their feet.

That parasitic fire could race and climb
More swiftly than the stately flames of hell.
Its fuel gone, it licked the beams of time.

So time dried out and youngest hearts grew old.
The smoky minutes cracked and broke apart.
The world was roasting but the men were cold.

Now from this pain worse pain was brought to birth,
More hate, more anguish, till at last they cried,
'Release this fire to gnaw the crusty earth:

Make it a flame that obvious to sight
And let us say we kindled it ourselves,
To split the skulls of men and let in light.

Since death is camped among us, wish him joy.
Invite him to our table and our games.
We cannot judge, but we can still destroy.'

And so the curtains of the mind were drawn.
Men conjured hell a first, a second time:
And Major Eatherly took off at dawn.

IV
Suppose a sea-bird,
its wings stuck down with oil, riding the waves
in no direction, under the storm-clouds, helpless,
lifted for an instant by each moving billow
to scan the meaningless horizon, helpless,
helpless, and the storms coming, and its wings dead,
its bird-nature dead: imagine this castaway,
loved, perhaps, by the Creator, and yet abandoned,
mocked by the flashing scales of the fish beneath it,
who leap, twist, dive, as free of the wide sea
as formerly the bird of the wide sky,
now helpless, starving, a prisoner of the surface,
unable to dive or rise: this is your emblem.
Take away the bird, let it be drowned
in the steep black waves of the storm, let it be broken,
against rocks in the morning light, too faint to swim:
take away the bird, but keep the emblem.

It is the emblem of Major Eatherly,
who looked round quickly from the height of each wave,
but saw no land, only the rim of the sky
into which he was not free to rise, or the silver
gleam of the mocking scales of the fish diving
where he was not free to dive.

Men have clung always to emblems,
to tokens of absolution from their sins.
Once it was the scapegoat driven out, bearing
its load of guilt under the empty sky
until its shape was lost, merged in the scrub.
Now we are civilized, there is no wild heath.
Instead of the nimble scapegoat running out
to be lost under the wild and empty sky,

the load of guilt is packed into prison walls,
and men file inward through the heavy doors.

But now that image, too, is obsolete.
The Major entering prison is no scapegoat.
His penitence will not take away our guilt,
nor sort with any consoling ritual:
this is penitence for its own sake, beautiful,
uncomprehending, inconsolable, unforeseen.
He is not in prison for his penitence:
it is no outrage to our law that he wakes
with cries of pity on his parching lips.
We do not punish him for cries or nightmares.
We punish him for stealing things from stores.

O, give his pension to the storekeeper,
Tell him it is the price of all our souls.
But do not trouble to unlock the door
and bring the Major out into the sun.
Leave him: it is all one: perhaps his nightmares
grow cooler in the twilight of the prison.
Leave him; if he is sleeping, come away.
But lay a folded paper by his head,
nothing official or embossed, a page
torn from your notebook, and the words in pencil.
Say nothing of love, or thanks, or penitence:
say only, 'Eatherly, we have your message.'

Dylan Thomas (1914-1953)

IN MY CRAFT OR SULLEN ART

In my craft or sullen art
Exercised in the still night
When only the moon rages
And the lovers lie abed
With all their griefs in their arms,
I labour by singing light
Not for ambition or bread
Or the strut and trade of charms
On the ivory stages
But for the common wages
Of their most secret heart.

Not for the proud man apart
From the raging moon I write
On these spindrift pages
Nor for the towering dead
With their nightingales and psalms
But for the lovers, their arms
Round the griefs of the ages,
Who pay no praise or wages
Nor heed my craft or art.

FERN HILL

Notice here that Dylan Thomas uses the vowel sounds only, for his rhymes, and does not make use of the consonants. The rhyme scheme is: *abcddabcd.*

Now as I was young and easy under the apple boughs
About the lilting house and happy as the grass was green,
    The night above the dingle starry,
        Time let me hail and climb
    Golden in the heydays of his eyes,
And honoured among wagons I was prince of the apple towns
And once below a time I lordly had the trees and leaves
        Trail with daisies and barley
    Down the rivers of the windfall light.

And as I was green and carefree, famous among the barns
About the happy yard and singing as the farm was home,
In the sun that is young once only,
Time let me play and be
Golden in the mercy of his means,
And green and golden I was huntsman and hersdman, the calves
Sang to my horn, the foxes on the hills barked clear and cold,
And the sabbath rang slowly
In the pebbles of the holy streams.

All the sun long it was running, it was lovely, the hay
Fields high as the house, the tunes from the chimneys, it was air
And playing, lovely and watery
And fire green as grass.
And nightly under the simple stars
As I rode to sleep the owls were bearing the farm away,
All the moon long I heard, blessed among stables, the nightjars
Flying with the ricks, and the horses
Flashing into the dark.

And then to awake, and the farm, like a wanderer white
With the dew, come back, the cock on his shoulder; it was all
Shining, it was Adam and maiden,
The sky gathered again
And the sun grew round that very day.
So it must have been after the birth of the simple light
In the first, spinning place, the spellbound horses walking warm
Out of the whinnying green stable
On to the fields of praise.

And honoured among foxes and pheasants by the gay house
Under the new made clouds and happy as the heart was long,
In the sun born over and over,
I ran my heedless ways,
My wishes raced through the house high hay
And nothing I cared, at my sky blue trades, that time allows
In all his tuneful turning so few and such morning songs
Before the children green and golden
Follow him out of grace,

Nothing I cared, in the lamb white days, that time would take me
Up to the swallow thronged loft by the shadow of my hand,
   In the moon that is always rising,
      Nor that riding to sleep
   I should hear him fly with the high fields
And wake to the farm forever fled from the childless land.
Oh as I was young and easy in the mercy of his means,
      Time held me green and dying
   Though I sang in my chains like the sea.

Helen Spalding (b. 1920)

LET US NOW PRAISE PRIME NUMBERS

Let us now praise prime numbers
With our fathers that begat us:
The power, the peculiar glory of prime numbers
Is that nothing begat them,
No ancestors, no factors,
Adams among the multiplied generations.

None can foretell their coming.
Among the ordinal numbers
They do not reserve their seats, arrive unexpected.
Along the line of cardinals
They rise like surprising pontiffs,
Each absolute, inscrutable, self-elected.

In the beginning where chaos
Ends and zero resolves,
They crowd the foreground prodigal as forest,
But middle distance thins them,
Far distance to infinity
Yields them rarely as unreturning comets.

O prime improbable numbers,
Long may formula-hunters
Steam in abstraction, waste to skeleton patience:
Stay non-conformist, nuisance,
Phenomena irreducible
To system, sequence, pattern or explanation.

Philip Larkin (b. 1922)

CHURCH GOING

Larkin and many other young poets of the 'fifties and onwards have
adopted an accent very different from, say, Dylan Thomas's. Their
work is caustic, dead-pan, satirical. There is a deliberate turning-
away from any sort of emotional indulgence, an honesty which
compels them to admit donating an Irish sixpence, when many poets
would simply have left the incident out.

Once I am sure there's nothing going on
I step inside, letting the door thud shut.
Another church: matting, seats, and stone,
And little books; sprawlings of flowers, cut
For Sunday, brownish now; some brass and stuff
Up at the holy end; the small neat organ;
And a tense, musty, unignorable silence,
Brewed God knows how long. Hatless, I take off
My cycle-clips in awkward reverence,

Move forward, run my hand around the font.
From where I stand, the roof looks almost new—
Cleaned, or restored? Someone would know: I don't.
Mounting the lectern, I peruse a few
Hectoring large-scale verses, and pronounce

'Here endeth' much more loudly than I'd meant.
The echoes snigger briefly. Back at the door
I sign the book, donate an Irish sixpence,
Reflect the place was not worth stopping for.

Yet stop I did: in fact I often do,
And always end much at a loss like this,
Wondering what to look for; wondering, too,
When churches fall completely out of use
What we shall turn them into, if we shall keep
A few cathedrals chronically on show,
Their parchment, plate and pyx in locked cases,
And let the rest rent-free to rain and sheep.
Shall we avoid them as unlucky places?

Or, after dark, will dubious women come
To make their children touch a particular stone;
Pick simples for a cancer; or on some
Advised night see walking a dead one?
Power of some sort or other will go on
In games, in riddles, seemingly at random;
But superstition, like belief, must die,
And what remains when disbelief has gone?
Grass, weedy pavement, brambles, buttress, sky,

A shape less recognisable each week,
A purpose more obscure. I wonder who
Will be the last, the very last, to seek
This place for what it was; one of the crew
That tap and jot and know what rood-lofts were?
Some ruin-bibber, randy for antique,
Or Christmas-addict, counting on a whiff
Of gown-and-bands and organ-pipes and myrrh?
Or will he be my representative,

Bored, uninformed, knowing the ghostly silt
Dispersed, yet tending to this cross of ground
Through suburb scrub because it held unspilt

So long and equably what since is found
Only in separation—marriage, and birth,
And death, and thoughts of these—for whom was built
This special shell? For, though I've no idea
What this accoutred frowsty barn is worth,
It pleases me to stand in silence here;

A serious house on serious earth it is,
In whose blent air all our compulsions meet,
Are recognised, and robed as destinies.
And that much never can be obsolete,
Since someone will forever be surprising
A hunger in himself to be more serious,
And gravitating with it to this ground,
Which, he once heard, was proper to grow wise in,
If only that so many dead lie round.

Ted Hughes (b. 1930)

PIKE

Pike, three inches long, perfect
Pike in all parts, green tigering the gold.
Killers from the egg: the malevolent aged grin.
They dance on the surface among the flies.

Or move, stunned by their own grandeur,
Over a bed of emerald, silhouette
Of submarine delicacy and horror.
A hundred feet long in their world.

In ponds, under the heat-struck lily pads—
Gloom of their stillness:
Logged on last year's black leaves, watching upwards.
Or hung in an amber cavern of weeds

The jaws' hooked clamp and fangs
Not to be changed at this date;
A life subdued to its instrument;
The gills kneading quietly, and the pectorals.

Three we kept behind glass,
Jungled in weed: three inches, four,
And four and a half: fed fry to them—
Suddenly there were two. Finally one

With a sag belly and the grin it was born with.
And indeed they spare nobody.
Two, six pounds each, over two feet long,
High and dry and dead in the willow-herb—

One jammed past its gills down the other's gullet:
The outside eye stared: as a vice locks—
The same iron in this eye
Though its film shrank in death.

A pond I fished, fifty yards across,
Whose lilies and muscular tench
Had outlasted every visible stone
Of the monastery that planted them—

Stilled legendary depth:
It was as deep as England. It held
Pike too immense to stir, so immense and old
That past nightfall I dared not cast

But silently cast and fished
With the hair frozen on my head
For what might move, for what eye might move.
The still splashes on the dark pond,

Owls hushing the floating woods
Frail on my ear against the dream
Darkness beneath night's darkness had freed,
That rose slowly towards me, watching.

Peter Redgrove (b. 1932)

GHOSTS

The terrace is said to be haunted.
By whom or what nobody knows; someone
Put away under the vines behind dusty glass
And rusty hinges staining the white-framed door
Like a nosebleed, locked; or a death in the pond
In three feet of water, a courageous breath?
It's haunted anyway, so nobody mends it
And the paving lies loose for the ants to crawl through
Weaving and clutching like animated thorns.
We walk on to it,
Like the bold lovers we are, ten years of marriage,
Tempting the ghosts out with our high spirits,
Footsteps doubled by the silence . . .

. . . and start up like ghosts ourselves
Flawed lank and drawn in the greenhouse glass:
She turns from that, and I sit down,
She tosses the dust with the toe of a shoe,
Sits on the pond's parapet and takes a swift look
At her shaking face in the clogged water,
Weeds in her hair; rises quickly and looks at me.
I shrug, and turn my palms out, begin
To feel the damp in my bones as I lever up
And step towards her with my hints of wrinkles,
Crows-feet and shadows. We leave arm in arm
Not a word said. The terrace is haunted,
Like many places with rough mirrors now,
By estrangement, if the daylight's strong.

P

Paul Roche (b. 1928)

THE PARADOXES OF TIME

i

'Even among the warmblooded the inequalities are obvious.'
Measure the earth's spin as you will:
Time is slow: Time is fast.
A monkey, a sparrow, a sloth
Each has a different time.
The hot pace of a mouse would ruin a man.
A shrew is old at two.
Time is fast.
The hummingbird beats its wings a hundred times
While the iguana lifts an eyelid.
Time is slow: Time is fast.

ii

Forget about Triassic and Jurassic.
See it as a clock unwinding
Its special and peculiar tension.
One hundred and fifty-two years, perhaps two hundred,
Is what the giant tortoise takes
To unwind its spring.
What does it matter: the circuit of the moon?
Time is slow.

iii

A microbe cell divides in two.
Ten in an hour means a thousand in three.
But microbes die as fast as they can multiply—
Or else in twenty-four hours
Twenty-four million million million
Tons outweigh the earth by more than four
Times its mass:
Times are fast.

iv

But slow or fast
Your personal most private being
Is laminated with elastic minutes:
'How many visual images came to your attention'
Within the hour?' 'How many times
Your interest shifted?' How intensely
Did you feel a pleasure or forget a pain?
We have heard of people drowning . . .
Lifetimes flashed in thirty seconds.
Others hypnotized three minutes . . .
Drowning in a sea of weeks.
Time is fast and slow.

v

Say then that living time
Is faster when you live it fast.
For 'life being first and foremost activity and action'
Is measured by the energy expended:
How much happens . . . Oh,
But old age races—childhood's crowded days go
crawling:
(Grannie lucubrated all one night to pen a post-card).
Time is fast when it is slow.

vi

Or should we pit galactic clusters—
Atomic furnaces of stars—
Against 'the mere million years of human evolution?'
News is only just arriving
At two hundred thousand miles a second
Of stars already spent and senile
In the years when we were only fishes.
Time is slow when it is fast.

vii

Is Time troublesome
'Because we have so little and there has been so much'?
A galaxy rotates about its centre
Four times only in a billion years.
Can we really say: 'This is eventful'?
Is eternal waiting even waiting
Where so little happens?
Is there even Time without a waiter?
Is 'Numerus Motus'—numbered motion—
There at all without a man,
Fast or slow?

viii

Fall back on this:
True counting is by content.
How much happens in a minute or how little
Can a million years contain?
Ah! But how equate with any measure Actus Purus—
Maximum activity of all?
Every possibility exploded
In the bursting of a moment.
If God 'is always working,' fastest
Time is time which never ceases:
Eternity is never finished time
(Slow or fast)
That finished perfect *as* it started.

Alan Brownjohn (b. 1931)

WILLIAM EMPSON AT ALDERMASTON

Aldermaston is the Government Research Station which has become
the symbol of nuclear power and its destructive horrors. It is against
its existence that many have protested. The poet William Empson
took part in one such demonstration, the significance of which this
poem explores.

This is our dead sea, once a guidebook heath.
Left and right hands worked busily together
A parliament or two,
And there she stands:

Twelve miles of cooling pipes; concrete and secret
Warrens underground; clean little towers
Clamped with strong ladders; red, brisk vans
Which hurry round

The wide, kerbed avenues with pulsing lights
To signify danger; and all this
Extending still its miles, as seas possessed
Of power or anger

Will—except that here
The tide decrees, with threats in yellow paint,
Its own unquestioned bounds, keeps dogs to catch
Someone who gets

Beyond the fence: it seems that otherwise
We shiver from an unclean nakedness,
And need to clothe our hot emotions cold
With wire, and curs.

But let there be some praise, where that is due:
For paint, of enlivening colours, spent
On all these deathly offices. Where typists sit,
Who do not make the thing,

Or scientists, who do not fire the thing,
Or workers, who obey the scientists,
The rooms are beautiful. And anyone
Who passed by car one day

Not knowing what it was would never guess.
(Perhaps some urgent public undertaking
Set up for health, or water? Or a camp
Where other people went

On holidays?) Such airs of carnival,
With death designed as smiling, to conceal
His proper features—these things justified
Replies in kind:

An absurd fête of life, in one Friday field
For which no pass was needed. The effect:
Two sorts of carnival clashing: on this side
The mud, or grass,

The boots and stoves and caravans; that side,
The trim, discreet pavilions of the State.
And one more contrast marked these gaieties:
This side there seemed

Some thousands, while of death's there wasn't one.
Just the white-braided police returned the stare
Of the boys with haversacks, or the fierce
Empirical gaze

Of the man with the Chinese beard, or the pondering glance
Of the woman with the basket on wheels.
And some thought death's precise executives
Had told or asked

The servants of his will to stay away,
Hinting of jobs they might not like to lose,
And they had houses . . . from whose windows, next,
Many faces looked the way

Of the procession; speaking not a word,
But merely watching. How else, then, explain
If this was not the reason, why their children,
Through all the bands and singing,

All the beards and the guitars, did not come out;
But stood behind held curtains, listlessly,
With tight and puzzled faces, or peered through
Some furtive upstairs sunblind

While it passed? No coloured hat, not one
In all the range of shirts and slogans worn,
Seemed odder than these faces. That deep blankness
Was the real thing strange.

'WE ARE GOING TO SEE THE RABBIT . . .'

We are going to see the rabbit,
We are going to see the rabbit.
Which rabbit, people say?
Which rabbit, ask the children?
Which rabbit?
The only rabbit,
The only rabbit in England,
Sitting behind a barbed-wire fence
Under the floodlights, neon lights,
Sodium lights,
Nibbling grass
On the only patch of grass
In England, in England

(Except the grass by the hoardings
Which doesn't count.)
We are going to see the rabbit
And we must be there on time.

First we shall go by escalator,
Then we shall go by underground,
And then we shall go by motorway
And then by helicopterway,
And the last ten yards we shall have to go
On foot.

And now we are going
All the way to see the rabbit,
We are nearly there,
We are longing to see it,
And so is the crowd
Which is here in thousands
With mounted policemen
And big loudspeakers
And bands and banners,

—And everyone has come a long way.
But soon we shall see it
Sitting and nibbling
The blades of grass
On the only patch of grass
In—but something has gone wrong!
Why is everyone so angry,
Why is everyone jostling
And slanging and complaining?

The rabbit has gone,
Yes, the rabbit has gone.
He has actually burrowed down into the earth
And made himself a warren, under the earth,
Despite all these people.
And what shall we do?
What *can* we do?

It is all a pity, you must be disappointed,
Go home and do something else for to-day,
Go home again, go home for to-day.
For you cannot hear the rabbit, under the earth,
Remarking rather sadly to himself, by himself,
As he rests in his warren under the earth:
'It won't be very long, they are bound to come,
They are bound to come and find me, even here.'

Index of first lines

Index of titles

Index of authors

Acknowledgements

For permission to use copyright material we are indebted to the following authors, literary executors and publishers:

Messrs. George Allen & Unwin, Ltd., for 'Song' from 'Ha Ha Among the Trumpets' by Alun Lewis; Mrs. George Bambridge and Messrs. Macmillan & Co. Ltd. for 'Harp Song of the Dane Women' from *Puck of Pook's Hill* by Rudyard Kipling; Mrs. George Bambridge and Messrs. Methuen & Co. Ltd. for 'McAndrew's Hymn' from *The Seven Seas* by Rudyard Kipling; the author and John Murray Ltd. for 'Bristol and Clifton' from *Collected Poems* by John Betjeman; the author and the Digby Press for 'We are going to see the Rabbit' and 'William Empson at Aldermaston' from *The Railings* by Alan Brownjohn; Burns & Oates Ltd. for 'Summer in England, 1914' from *Selected Poems* by Alice Meynell; The Estate of Roy Campbell for 'Mass at Dawn' from *Adamastor* by Roy Campbell; Jonathan Cape Limited for 'The Sleepers', 'The Two Heavens' and 'To Sparrows Fighting' from *Collected Poems* by W. H. Davies, 'Jig' from *Collected Poems 1954* by C. Day Lewis, 'Will it be so again' from *Word Over All* by C. Day Lewis, and 'Judging Distances' from *A Map of Verona* by Henry Reed; The Clarendon Press, Oxford, for 'The Snow Lies Sprinkled', 'Who has not walked upon the shore', 'One Grief of Thine' and 'Poor Poll' from *Bridge's Poetical Works*, and 'I wake and feel' and 'Inversnaid' by Gerard Manley Hopkins; the Cresset Press for 'City Evening' from *Collected Poems* by Frances Cornford; J. M. Dent & Sons Ltd. and the Literary Executors of Dylan Thomas Estate for 'Fern Hill' and 'In my craft or sullen art' from *Collected Poems* by Dylan Thomas; the Literary Trustees of Walter de la Mare and the Society of Authors as their representative for 'Alone', 'An Abandoned Church', 'Away', 'The Exile', 'Napoleon', 'Voices', 'Oh Why?' and 'The Window' from *Collected Poems by Walter de la Mare* (Faber and Faber); Patric Dickinson for 'Bombers: Evening' from *The World I See*; the author and Messrs. Chatto and Windus for 'No News' from *This Cold Universe* by Patric Dickinson; Gerald Duckworth & Co. Ltd. for 'The Call' from *Collected Poems* by Charlotte Mew; Faber & Faber Ltd. for 'Lay your sleeping head, my love', 'The Unknown Citizen' and 'Musée des Beaux Arts' from *Collected Shorter Poems* by W. H. Auden, 'Dreaming Spires' from *Talking Bronco* by Roy Campbell, 'Chorus III from "The Rock" ' and 'Animula' from *Later Poems 1925-35* by T. S. Eliot, 'Pike' from *Lupercal* by Ted Hughes, 'Meeting Point' and extract from 'Autumn Journal' from *Collected Poems 1925-48* by Louis MacNiece, and for 'The Rider Victory' from *Collected Poems* by Edwin Muir; the author and Andre Deutsch Ltd. for 'War Poet' from *Collected Poems* by Roy Fuller; the author for 'Ecco Homo' by David Gascoyne; Trustees of the Hardy Estate and Macmillan & Co. Ltd., for 'The British Museum', 'The Haunter', 'The Five Students', 'A Beauty's Soliloquy during her Honeymoon' and 'A Thunderstorm in Town' from *Collected Poems of Thomas Hardy*; Holt,